T0319424

PLINY'S ROMAN ECONOMY

THE PRINCETON ECONOMIC HISTORY
OF THE WESTERN WORLD

Joel Mokyr, Series Editor

A list of titles in this series appears in the back of the book.

Pliny's Roman Economy

NATURAL HISTORY, INNOVATION, AND GROWTH

RICHARD P. SALLER

PRINCETON UNIVERSITY PRESS

PRINCETON & OXFORD

Published by Princeton University Press
41 William Street, Princeton, New Jersey 08540
99 Banbury Road, Oxford OX2 6JX

press.princeton.edu

All Rights Reserved

Library of Congress Cataloging-in-Publication Data

Names: Saller, Richard P., author.
Title: Pliny's Roman economy : natural history, innovation, and growth / Richard Saller.
Description: Princeton, New Jersey : Princeton University Press, [2022] | Series: The Princeton economic history of the Western world | Includes bibliographical references and index.
Identifiers: LCCN 2021032212 (print) | LCCN 2021032213 (ebook) | ISBN 9780691229546 (hardback ; alk. paper) | ISBN 9780691229553 (ebook)
Subjects: LCSH: Pliny, the Elder. Naturalis historia. | Economics—Rome—History. | Rome—Economic conditions.
Classification: LCC HB77 .S25 2022 (print) | LCC HB77 (ebook) | DDC 330.09/01—dc23
LC record available at https://lccn.loc.gov/2021032212
LC ebook record available at https://lccn.loc.gov/2021032213British Library Cataloging-in-Publication Data is available

Editorial: Rob Tempio and Matt Rohal
Production Editorial: Sara Lerner
Jacket Design: Chris Ferrante
Production: Erin Suydam
Publicity: Alyssa Sanford and Charlotte Coyne

Jacket art: Pliny the Elder, engraving from André Thevet's *Les vrais portraits et vies des hommes illustres* (Paris, 1584). Image: Chronicle / Alamy Stock Photo

This book has been composed in Arno

10 9 8 7 6 5 4 3 2 1

CONTENTS

v

Conclusion   133

PREFACE

JUDGED BY SIZE, contents, organization, and afterlife, Pliny's *Natural History* is unusual, as is the organization of this book. Let me explain. I hope that it will be read by both classicists and economic historians; to accommodate both audiences all the passages from the *Natural History* are presented in translation in the main text, and the original Latin quotations are provided in an appendix because the vocabulary offers insights into Roman imperial values and culture relating to economic behavior. The translations are based on the Loeb edition with my modifications.

Four of the six chapters are followed by a detailed excursus on a very specific topic to illustrate a point made in the main body of the chapter—for example, the excursus following chapter 2 on Pliny's forty remedies for rabid dog bite scattered across ten books of the *Natural History*. The point of the excursus is to provide supporting details for the main argument of the chapter without unduly interrupting the flow of the text with a long digression. In a sense, this is my effort to solve an organizational challenge in a fashion very different from the *Natural History*, which is "so diffuse and miscellaneous that there is hardly a single long description of any subject that is not at some point interrupted by a digression."[1]

My thanks are due to James Macksoud and Kevin Ennis, who were essential in putting the text into a consistent format with accurate citations and bibliography. And I appreciate Kevin's contribution of an archaeological excursus. I am also grateful for the advice of Joel Mokyr, whose published work has exercised a conceptual influence that is obvious in the following chapters and who provided additional advice to improve the manuscript. My colleague Walter Scheidel generously read the first complete draft and offered valuable suggestions. The anonymous readers for Princeton University Press made a number of recommendations, almost all of which have been incorporated to improve the final version. And finally, I thank my wife, Professor Tanya Luhrmann, whose expert writerly advice improved the prose (though not to her standard).

A portion of chapter 1 and all the graphs were previously published in Damian Pavlyshyn, Iain Johnstone, and Richard Saller, "Lead Pollution and the Roman Economy," *Journal of Roman Archaeology* 33:354–64, 2020.

PLINY'S ROMAN ECONOMY

Introduction

PLINY'S NATURAL *History* with its 20,000 "things worth know-ing" was meant to be a useful repository of ancient Mediterranean knowledge and, consequently, is the obvious text to analyze for Roman imperial attitudes toward discovery and innovation. As such, it can shed light on the question of whether the Roman impe-rial economy experienced *sustainable* growth through the Pax Romana of the first two centuries CE. Archaeological research leaves no doubt that productivity improved and the standard of living was enriched over the millennium from the early Iron Age to the height of the empire.[1] My question is more specific: Did the in-stitutions that Rome forcibly imposed around the Mediterranean— notably, peace, laws, and infrastructure—support *continued* economic growth until external forces such as the Antonine Plague of the later 160s CE brought it to a halt? The lack of statistics for the economy makes this question impossible to answer with empirical certainty, leaving scholars to formulate indirect arguments for growth based on proxy data or models or contemporary economic theory. This book argues that the proxy data are inconclusive and, consequently, that the textual evidence for values and attitudes related to production should be taken into account. Pliny's *Natural History* is the primary text to examine for economic attitudes on account of its wide-ranging subject matter, scope, and avowed pur-pose of "utility" (*utilitas*).

A century ago, the naturalist E. W. Gudger labeled Pliny's *Natu-ral History* "the most popular Natural History ever published."[2] The past three decades have witnessed a steady stream of books and articles about the *Natural History*. Why write another, and in

1

particular, a study of Pliny's economic reasoning and observations? My main argument is prompted by recent works by economic historians of early modern Europe who have made the case for a link between encyclopedias of the eighteenth century and the values and attitudes that together formed a culture of growth and innovation, laying the groundwork for the "Great Enrichment."[3] Diderot and D'Alembert's famous *Encyclopédie* (published 1751–72) aimed to disseminate *useful* knowledge for productive growth and was one of the most visible contributions to what Joel Mokyr has described as a culture that encouraged a feedback loop between scientific discovery, technical breakthroughs, and economic growth.[4] And indeed, the *Encyclopédie*'s geographical circulation has been shown to correlate with the cities experiencing the fastest economic growth.[5]

What insights does the *Natural History* provide regarding Roman values and attitudes about economic production during the Pax Romana and in particular about innovation based on new knowledge? And what does the answer to that question tell us about the potential for *sustained* growth? Pliny's *Natural History* as a vast compendium of useful knowledge was the acknowledged ancestor of the early modern encyclopedias, even if "encyclopedia" had yet to be conceived as a genre.[6] Did Pliny's monumental work intend in the same way to disseminate useful knowledge and to foster technical advances? What observations and reasoning that we today might categorize as "economic" can be found in the work? Over the past thirty years Plinian scholarship has sought to interpret the *Natural History* as a coherent whole by considering various themes: Pliny's view of Nature, Pliny's scientific thought, Pliny's ideology of empire, among others.[7] To my knowledge, there is no comparable effort to probe Pliny's economic views as a whole, his reasoning and assumptions.[8] To be sure, certain passages of the *Natural History* have been repeatedly cited—for example, the cost of trade with India, or the praise of empire, or Seneca's costly purchase of a rehabilitated farm, or the history of Roman coinage.[9] And the *Natural History* is by far the most excerpted work in *Greek and Roman Technology: A Sourcebook*, which suggests that it should be the most promising text to examine for Roman attitudes about the technology that enabled the economy to produce and the innovation that supported growth.[10]

The *Natural History* provides evidence both for the potential of Roman imperialism to expand economic resources and for the limits on technical innovation that might have nurtured sustained growth in productivity. The answer to the question of how Pliny's great book could have affected economic growth matters because the question of just how much the Roman economy was growing during the Pax Romana and when the growth stopped remains unclear. There has been a concerted effort in recent decades to find proxies to measure and explain the growth and decline of the empire's economic performance. Explanations are deduced from the timing of the growth and/or decline. For the most part, the proxies have been used to argue that the Roman economy was growing until the onset of the Antonine Plague in 165 CE. The most well-placed, well-cited, and thoroughly discussed papers and books in the last decade have claimed, on the basis of these proxies, that the Roman economy enjoyed *sustained* growth on account of its institutions, growth that was stopped only by the exogenous shock of the Antonine Plague of the late 160s CE.[11] Chapter 1 will offer a critique of those proxies, arguing that at this point none is reliable enough to justify neglecting our aristocratic authors, with their first-person (if admittedly limited) point of view. I argue that we can learn something important about Roman cultural values affecting the economy from reading the *Natural History* as a whole.

The task of sifting Pliny's economic ideas out of the 37 books of the *Natural History* and then summarizing them has turned out to be more challenging than I anticipated for reasons having to do with the (loose) organization of the work, to be described in chapter 2. Trevor Murphy's phrase "referential dizziness" describes my personal reading experience better than I could have.[12] Chapter 2 will go over the familiar ground of Pliny's purpose, audience, method, and organization and point out both the economic implications and some internal inconsistencies. Though Pliny claimed to be assembling practical "things worth knowing" (*res dignae*) for the use of artisans and farmers, in reality this audience could not have afforded the 37 books and would have had a difficult time locating any practical information they might have wanted if they were literate enough to read it.

Chapter 3 seeks to draw on scholarship describing Pliny's attitude to Mother Nature as influenced by Stoic thought of his day. This attitude formed the basis for Pliny's moral thinking about useful knowledge of Nature, with major implications (at least in Pliny's view) for the economic consequences of empire. Pliny held profoundly ambivalent ideas about the economic benefits and vices of empire. The benefits came almost entirely from what could be described as an argument that anticipated Adam Smith by seventeen centuries to the effect that Rome's expansion opened the way to the discovery of new and varied natural resources from the conquered lands, and Roman rule promoted the exchange of these resources through trade during the Pax Romana. On the other hand, Pliny believed that Roman attitudes and power also promoted the misuse, abuse, and even violation of Nature, most egregiously in mining and quarrying. The language in which Pliny describes the abuse is worth noting, particularly the vocabulary of honor and shame. To Pliny, what we might count as economic growth and improvement of living standards cannot be value free—and at the heart of those moral values is the emotional and spiritual devotion to Mother Nature.

Chapter 4 focuses on Pliny's ideas about invention and innovation, the foundations of sustained growth. It starts from David Hume's observation in 1742 that "it is more easy to account for the rise and progress of commerce in any kingdom, than for that of learning." Pliny generalizes about increases in knowledge in a similar vein, and in addition he attests to inventions and discoveries throughout Greek and Roman history. Chapter 4 examines the inventions reported in the *Natural History*, Pliny's understanding of the process of discovery and its motives in the context of the

Pax Romana. Mokyr describes a "culture of growth" in early modern Europe in which a positive feedback loop between scientific research and practical applications fueled sustained increases in productivity. What light does Pliny shed on an ancient culture of growth as manifested in his list of great inventions and his choice of heroes celebrated in Roman culture? What did Romans assume about the sources for amassing wealth, at least as revealed in the *Natural History*? Overall, Pliny believed that discovery, innovation, and enrichment were the results of accident or divine intervention, not of Romans' intentional research. It is striking that Pliny's list of 136 great innovations at the end of Book 7 includes not a single Roman technical innovation.

Scattered throughout the *Natural History* are economic observations and instances of financial reasoning. They do not add up to a coherent theory, but they do provide insights into Pliny's views about different forms of production and commerce, about labor and agency, about price formation and profitability, about investment and consumption, and about trust and fraud. Some of the views have a heavy moralizing overlay, but others do not and so give us limited evidence of Pliny's economic reasoning. Chapter 5 aims to gather and to analyze the examples of Pliny's economic thinking.

Chapter 6 turns to the question at the heart of this book: Did the *Natural History* aim to foster a culture nurturing increases in useful knowledge for succeeding generations to improve productivity? How did readers of the late antique and medieval eras make use of Pliny's work, which for many centuries was among the most frequently copied, quoted, and excerpted classical texts? The reception of the *Natural History* during this millennium provides insights into the limitations on its practical value. And then in the early modern period, given their shared purpose of "usefulness," what is revealed by a comparison of Pliny's *Natural History* and the eighteenth-century encyclopedias that played a part in the culture of growth during the Great Enrichment?[13] The massive French *Encyclopédie* was modeled on much less noticed English predecessors:

John Harris's *Lexicon Technicum* (1704) and Ephraim Chambers's *Cyclopaedia* (1728). Because these earlier encyclopedias *predated* the beginning of the Industrial Revolution and because they were produced in the country that led the way in the growth of the eighteenth century, they may offer a more interesting comparison. The purpose, tone, organization, and content of these monumental works show similarities with the *Natural History* and also telling contrasts.

My aim is not to demonstrate the obvious point that Pliny came before the beginning of the "Scientific Revolution" and Harris and Chambers came after. Rather, my aim is to use the contrast to sensitize historians to some qualities of the *Natural History* that bear on values and attitudes with consequences for the Roman economy. Whereas Pliny intended his *Natural History* to be a treasure chest to prevent the loss of ancient wisdom, Harris and Chambers intended their encyclopedias to serve as up-to-date springboards for future discoveries that were not even thought possible—that is, the *Natural History* was backward-looking, in contrast to Harris's and Chambers's forward-looking optimism. The fundamental values underlying the culture of growth to be found in the *Lexicon Technicum* and *Cyclopaedia* are largely absent in Pliny's monumental work. The effects of this difference of attitude on the imperial economy cannot be quantified but should be taken into account in explaining why, despite its extraordinary duration and size, the Pax Romana generated few major technical breakthroughs, *as Pliny himself lamented.* The fact of Pliny's lament is important and needs to be stressed because the modern-day historian's observation of a scarcity of major technical breakthroughs is sometimes criticized as teleological or a modern anachronism, *but it is in fact Pliny's own insight.* And in the absence of continuing breakthroughs, economists would not expect *sustained* growth.

One last disclaimer: Aude Doody's *Pliny's Encyclopedia: The Reception of the Natural History* makes the appropriate point that it would be anachronistic to blame Pliny for not meeting the standards of modern science.[14] I agree. My aim here is not to *blame*

Pliny or the Romans for failure to develop modern science and a modern economy but to *understand* Pliny's purpose and methods through comparison with early modern encyclopedias, and then to explore the consequences of those differences for the performance of the Roman economy.

1

Proxies for Economic Performance in the Roman Empire

KEITH HOPKINS in a seminal article, "Taxes and Trade in the Roman Empire (200 BC–AD 400)," presented a structural argument for modest growth in the Roman economy, corroborated by proxies implying an increase in "general prosperity." His proxies— the chronological distribution of shipwrecks and the quantity of coinage—were substitutes for the lack of aggregate statistics for the Roman imperial economy. Over the past four decades these proxies and others have been proposed and critiqued, and despite the criticisms the search for viable proxies to measure the success of the Roman economy has continued. This chapter will summarize the past debate and point to weaknesses in some of the very recent proposals for proxies in support of the more general argument of this book that none of the proxies is reliable enough to justify neglect of literary sources such as Pliny's *Natural History*.[1]

Why have Roman economic historians persisted in trying to identify proxies as indices of aggregate performance despite the criticisms that repeatedly followed? The motives of different historians no doubt vary, but at the heart of the matter is the fundamental question of whether the Roman Empire was benign or oppressive and why it ultimately failed. Was Gibbon right in his famous assertion that "if a man were asked to fix the period in the history of the world, during which the condition of the human race was most happy and prosperous, he would, without hesitation," point to the years 96 CE to 180 CE.[2] Roman conquests were undoubtedly brutal, but did Roman rule also, in the long run, make inhabitants of the empire "safer" and "richer"?[3] And if so, how much safer and richer? The level of prosperity of the empire has a bearing on our evaluation of the approaches of New Institutional Economics. Can we demonstrate with proxies that Roman peace, infrastructure, and law had the net effect of continually improving productivity and enriching the population? Or on the other hand, can proxies demonstrate that oppressive Roman institutions eventually put a drag on the economy, as some prominent modern economists have claimed?[4] The current optimistic view is that the Pax Romana nurtured *sustained* growth until the external shock of the Antonine Plague (165 CE) sent that growth trend into reverse. An alternative view is that in the absence of substantial technical breakthroughs to increase per capita productivity the empire could not achieve *sustained* growth for endogenous reasons. The conclusion of this chapter is that despite the increasing sophistication of the arguments for proxies for growth, the most recent efforts do not hold up to close scrutiny and so do not demonstrate sustained growth up to the Antonine Plague.

Hopkins's original article, later revised and updated, presented graphs of dated shipwrecks and minted coins in circulation. The graph of shipwrecks peaked sharply in the last two centuries before the common era, declined somewhat in the next two centuries, and then a steep decline set in. The graph of silver coins in circulation, like that of shipwrecks, displayed a steep rise in the second century BCE.[5] Hopkins was acutely aware of the limitations of the evidence and his interpretation, acknowledging that "all these arguments, and the evidence from which they are derived, are partial, but they draw strength from their inter-relationship."[6]

In the 1990s a set of articles by Hong and colleagues adduced data from environmental science to demonstrate a rise in mining

activity. Their measurements of lead pollution frozen in the Greenland ice core showed that anthropogenic lead pollution rose well
above natural background levels during the classical period, reach-
ing a peak around the turn of the era. The pollution, it was argued,
came primarily from silver mining in Spain in which lead was vapor-
ized in the process of cupellation to refine the ore. The conclusions
were based on fourteen sections from the ice core distributed across
approximately six hundred years of the Roman Republic and
Empire.[7] Hopkins later incorporated these findings as an additional proxy for economic performance: "These scientific estimates
of ancient pollution and total production give us an unprecedented
vision of economic growth and inefficiency in classical antiquity."[8]
The data series from Hong and colleagues with fourteen measurements was not sufficiently fine-grained to provide more precise
dates for the decline of mining and smelting. Refinement of the
data was to come two decades later (see p. 15).

In a much-cited article of 2005, François de Callataÿ summarized the argument from the proxies in the following conclusion:

> The convergence of these graphs [showing atmospheric lead
> pollution, atmospheric copper pollution, and shipwrecks] clar-
> ifies an increased activity during the last centuries B.C. and the
> first three centuries A.D. Of the three, the wrecks is the most
> spectacular with its peak in the period 200 B.C.–A.D. 200. . . .
> Within the margin of a century it is also the one spoken of by J.
> Andreau when he defined the period of greater prosperity of
> economic life as being that which runs "du IIe siècle av. J.-C. au
> premier siècle de l'Empire" [from the second century BCE to
> the first century of the empire]. While lacking the clarity and
> precision of that of the wrecks, the charts for lead and copper
> move in the same direction: they are characterized by signifi-
> cant variations from one measurement to another, which leads
> us to hope that one day we might possess several complete sets
> of data spread out over nearly three millennia. For the present,
> it is wise to resist the temptation to tie such-and-such a high

value obtained for such-and-such a year with any known or supposed historical events.[9]

De Callataÿ's caution was wise, and his hope for more refined data was soon to be satisfied.

About the same time, Willem Jongman and others pointed to another proxy, based on research by Nobelist Robert Fogel and Dora Costa, who identified stature as an index of human health and well-being.[10] In recent centuries populations have grown taller generation by generation as they have grown wealthier, the duration of life has been extended, diets have improved, and many diseases have been brought under control. Jongman in 2007 concluded that "Gibbon was right" based on a study of femur bones excavated by archaeologists: "the rise [in the length of femur bones] is spectacular—the first and early second century peak equates European stature in the early twentieth century. Decline clearly set in in the late second century A.D., to be followed by a recovery later in the third century, and ultimate collapse with the fall of the Western Empire."[11] Whereas the previous studies did not try to tie the proxies to a political history narrative, Jongman's reference to Gibbon placed the turning point in general prosperity in the late Antonine era with consequences for explanations of exogenous as opposed to endogenous causes. A decade later Jongman reversed his conclusion about the trends in stature and health and offered a different explanation (see p. 19–21).

In 2009, Walter Scheidel and Andrew Wilson engaged in a debate that sharpened the focus on the issues and articulated detailed criticisms of previously suggested proxies. Whereas Hopkins and de Callataÿ had deliberately assigned the timeline of growth and decline in terms too vague to distinguish exogenous from endogenous causes, Scheidel drew attention to the consequences for quite different explanations: "In the most basic terms, we must ask whether Roman economic growth was terminated by endogenous or exogenous factors. Was economic development the result of a limited and unrepeatable improvement in productivity that was gradually offset by population growth . . . , or was productivity growth theoretically sustainable in the long run but in practice curtailed by shocks to the system such as political or military crises?"[12] Of course, the other possible external shock was the Antonine Plague. Scheidel highlighted the weaknesses of each of the proxies as a barometer of productivity growth: the trend in number of shipwrecks was influenced by multiple biases; lead pollution as a measure of silver production need not be related to economic performance as shown by the comparison with early modern Spain; trends in animal bones could reflect changes in taste rather than levels of meat consumption. For these and other reasons,[13] the historian should be wary of taking any of these proxies as a reflection of economic performance, but if one does take them seriously, then the appropriate method is to analyze rate of change, not simply to identify the peaks: "Although overall levels of economic performance are by no means irrelevant, from an economic perspective the latter question [rate of change] is of even greater importance." And "in so far as it is legitimate to put much weight on these observations . . . , they would seem to suggest that economic expansion stalled sometime around the turn of the era," not the later second century in the aftermath of the plague.[14] That is, the enrichment was a product of conquest and the consolidation of the empire and was not sustainable.

Scheidel then presented a model to show that, based on various plausible assumptions about population growth and imperial expenditures, even a modest, *sustained* growth rate over a period as long as the Pax Romana makes it hard to understand the strain on imperial finances in the late second and third centuries: "this matrix makes it hard to posit intensive growth of closer to 0.2% than to 0.1% (or indeed even 0%) per year, let alone a higher rate."[15] The article acknowledges increases in the richness of the archaeological record during the centuries of Roman rule but again suggests caution about inferring growth in productivity based on the comparison with early modern Europe when increasing inequality, rather than increasing productivity, produced a lavish material heritage.[16] With due circumspection, Scheidel concluded that the hypothesis of a one-off increase in prosperity resulting from the consolidation of Roman rule was more likely than one of sustained growth abruptly halted by the Antonine Plague.

Wilson's careful response to Scheidel, based on his archaeological expertise, served to underline the uncertainties about several of the proxies (shipwrecks, animal-bone data, and lead pollution).[17] As a result, Wilson suggested that even Scheidel's conditional hypothesis based on taking the proxies seriously should be rejected and that "we are still a long way off the construction of sufficient robust proxies to generate an argument from convergence, though we are making progress."[18] He then proposed other proxies: dated building inscriptions and honorific inscriptions, on the grounds that "the overall spending pattern [on public buildings] may well bear a meaningful relationship to overall economic performance."[19] It seems to me that both of these indicators are vulnerable to the same doubts as others—that is, they were subject to cultural influences as well as economic capacity. In his important article "The Epigraphic Habit in the Roman Empire," Ramsay MacMullen pointed to the "cultural significance" of erecting inscriptions and warned against the assumption "that the body of all inscriptions against which attestation is measured does not itself rise or fall—a false assumption. So administrative, economic, social, and religious history needs to be rewritten."[20] Apart from changing cultural preferences, increasing inequality of wealth could have influenced the trend.[21] In addition, the claim that "large sums" were spent on the public buildings needs to be put in context: J. W. Hanson's inventory registers an increase in urban monuments from 1,803 to 3,928 over the four centuries from 100 BCE to 300 CE, or an average of about five per year; R. Duncan-Jones's price lists put the median construction cost of buildings in Italy at 300,000 HS and 43,500 HS in the African provinces—a small fraction of total production, even if the number of monuments and the costs are greatly understated.[22] In his 2009 article, Wilson concluded that it is immensely difficult to formulate models that allow an unambiguous choice between hypotheses of one-off and sustained growth.[23] But a decade later he offered a more decisive conclusion in favor of sustained growth based on Greenland lead pollution measurements (see p. 15).

Since the constructive exchange between Scheidel and Wilson, others have revived the cases for various proxies with larger data sets and more sophisticated analyses, and they have been met with familiar as well as new criticisms. In addition, suggestions for new proxies have been introduced.

Urbanization has commonly been regarded as an indicator of economic development.[24] In 2016, J. W. Hanson published *An Urban Geography of the Roman World, 100 BC to AD 300*, a massive survey of cities in the Roman Empire. His conclusion was that there were fewer than the 2,000 conventionally mentioned in literary sources, but the 1,388 were larger than usually thought. The increase in number of cities "was most marked in the 1st century BC, before levelling off throughout the 1st, 2nd, and 3rd centuries AD. . . . The increase in sites was most marked in Italy, Asia Minor, the Levant, North Africa, the Balkans, Gaul and Germany, and Spain in the 1st century BC, followed by Asia Minor, the Levant, North Africa, the Balkans, and Britain in the 1st century AD, North Africa and the Balkans in the 2nd century AD, and the Levant in the 3rd century AD."[25] Based on his assessment of the sizes of occupation of the 1,388 sites, Hanson put the total urban population of the empire at 10–12 million—somewhat higher than other estimates.[26]

The ambition of Hanson's inventory showed what is required to generalize about urbanization across the empire as a whole, and it also has invited scrutiny. In the introduction to *Regional Urban Systems in the Roman World, 150 BCE–250 CE*, Luuk de Ligt and John Bintliff started from a methodological caveat: "Some readers may be surprised to discover that none of the papers contained in this volume uses estimates of the sizes of built-up areas as a basis for inferences about population levels. The main reason for this is that in the absence of secure evidence relating to the size of domestic quarters, the average number of houses per hectare, average building height and the average number of rooms per domestic unit, it is impossible to estimate the approximate number of people who might have lived in a certain city at a certain moment of its existence."[27] Based on a close examination of some of the cities in Hanson's database, they concluded that his estimates exaggerated their population.[28] De Ligt and Bintliff's nuanced overview was that much of the growth and prosperity of cities was coastal and that there were "a large number of region-specific scenarios."[29] This complex variation is a major obstacle to making aggregate estimates of trends in the growth of cities over time for the whole empire.

The critical response to every new proposal of a proxy for trends in aggregate economic performance and well-being has not dimmed the hope that science will offer more precision. Recently, the arguments based on Greenland lead pollution and bone lengths have been advanced again with much more extensive data; in addition, a new conceptualization of performance, the Economic Complexity Index, has been presented.[30]

The most noticed and cited has been the study of lead pollution in the Greenland icecap, drawing the attention of major international news outlets.[31] The previous studies had been limited in their historical conclusions by the lack of precise chronological resolution in the data. The study published in *Proceedings of the National Academy of Sciences* (*PNAS*) in 2018 by McConnell, Wilson, and colleagues provided measurements of lead pollution over millennia with stunning resolution of plus or minus two years. This precision permitted them to connect the production of lead flux and hence (on their argument) of the economy to a specific exogenous shock: "Our results indicate *sustained* economic growth during the first two centuries of the Roman empire, terminated by the second-century Antonine Plague."[32]

The article does not offer an explicit statistical analysis of the data to support the historical conclusions, and the graphs are sufficiently noisy to make it difficult to discern trends with the eye alone (see Figure 1). An article I jointly authored with two Stanford statisticians (Pavlyshyn, Johnstone, and Saller 2020)

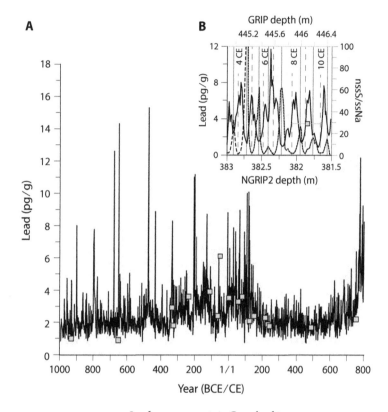

FIG. 1. Lead measurements in Greenland ice.

reanalyzed the data of the *PNAS* article with two aims: (1) to offer a clearer picture of the trends in lead pollution during the Roman era, and (2) to frame those trends within some not-so-obvious cautions about inferences from the data. The measurement of lead pollution by year in the *PNAS* article was taken as given.

Our statistical analysis showed that the historical narrative in the article was broadly correct for the late Republican and for the post-plague (after 165 CE) periods but did *not* show *sustained* growth during the Pax Romana, the 151 years from the end of Augustus's reign to the Antonine Plague (14–165 CE). Furthermore, the lead pollution levels for the Pax Romana were only slightly higher than the levels of the second century BCE before 104 BCE This analysis led to one of two possible conclusions: either arctic lead pollution measurements are (still) not a reliable proxy for economic performance, or aggregate economic production *modestly declined* through the century and a half between the end of Augustus's rule and the Antonine Plague.

Two statistical methods of analysis were presented to describe the trend in Greenland lead pollution during the early empire. The first used a log-transformation of the observations and then sought to fit a linear model to them for the years 14 BCE–165 CE. Figure 2 presents the results showing a decline in non-background lead flux through the Pax Romana by 24.6 percent. (The decline appears less steep because of the logarithmic scale.) The decline after 165 CE is more dramatic, as Figure 3 shows.

The second method illustrated in Figure 4 was change-point detection, a standard statistical method that avoids the observer arbitrarily selecting dates. This analysis automatically picked out 104 BCE, 14 BCE, 145 CE, 174 CE, and 244 CE as historical moments of change. Several points are worth noticing: non-background lead flux decreased during the instability of the late Republican civil wars, and then increased again with the Augustan peace but only to a level similar to the second century BCE. A decline is again noticeable in the two decades *before* the Antonine Plague, followed by even sharper decreases in the late second century and third century CE.[33]

Our conclusion: "The Pax Romana shows a consistently higher atmospheric lead content than the late Republican era, but the non-background lead content seems to have *declined* during the 150 years after the reign of Augustus and *certainly did not continually grow*. Moreover, the average non-background lead flux was not substantially higher during this period than during the period 201–104 BCE—not what would be expected if the Pax Romana had been a period of continuing growth."[34]

In addition, the unavoidable sources of uncertainty need to be understood. For example, the non-background, manmade lead

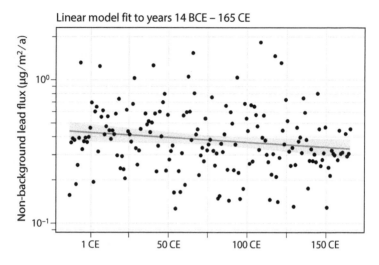

FIG. 2. Log non-background lead flux during the Pax Romana.

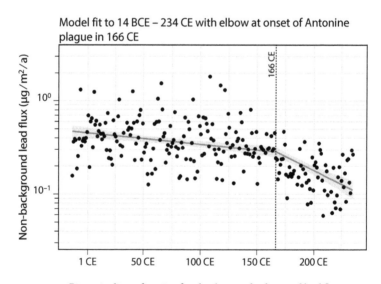

FIG. 3. Piecewise linear function fitted to log non-background lead flux.

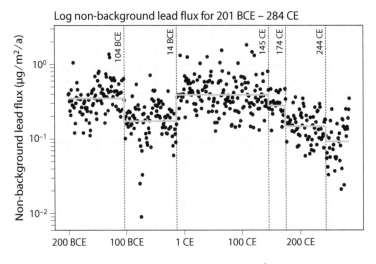

FIG. 4. Constant-mean change-point fit.

flux is calculated by subtracting the naturally occurring lead flux from the measured flux. The level of naturally occurring flux was influenced by atmospheric circulation, which the authors assumed to be similar to that from 1920 to 1999. The study also posits a single source of the manmade pollution, the Spanish silver mines. But we know that lead mining was stepped up in Britain after the Roman conquest in 43 CE, and the proximity of Britain to Greenland means that British sources will be proportionally more heavily represented. The implication is that in order to calculate the emissions of the Spanish mining producing silver, the (unknown) British contribution to the lead flux would need to be subtracted. In the end, our analysis led us to doubt that "there is enough information in the data to draw confident conclusions about long-term, general trends in performance of the Roman economy."[35]

Championing the "rapid progress made in scientific archaeology," Willem Jongman together with collaborators returned to the data of bones and published a more exhaustive study of stature over the centuries of Roman rule, which revised the conclusions of his earlier publications.[36] On the basis of approximately ten thousand femur measurements, Jongman and his colleagues concluded that the stature of the population of the empire declined in the final centuries of the Republic and reached a nadir in the half century 50–100 CE; stature then increased over the next four and a half centuries (figure 4 in their article). Their conclusion was that the population grew richer during the Pax Romana but also less healthy.[37] The sample size is large and the analysis sophisticated. The authors break down the sample into four regions: western Mediterranean, the east, the southeastern provinces, and the northwestern provinces. Table 3 in the article shows the number of bones from each province by region, and figure 3 graphs the counts over the fifty-year time periods. Recognizing that femur size does not have a fixed relationship to total height, the authors present trends over time as "mean factor scores."

Although Jongman and his colleagues acknowledge the uneven distribution of bones by region over time, they apparently do no weighting to compensate for the very large shifts in regional representation over the centuries. Why does this matter? The east region in most periods has the lowest mean factor score and the northwestern provinces always have the highest scores (figure 6 in the article). At the lowest point of the composite mean factor score for 50–100 CE the east represents about one-third of the very small empire-wide total and the northwestern provinces another third. When the composite mean factor score begins to shoot up in the fourth century CE, the east's representation shrinks by an order of magnitude from ~33 to 1–4 percent, while the proportion from the northwest provinces rises from ~33 to ~70 percent in 300 CE.[38] My proportions are somewhat rough because the database broken down by period, region, and sex is not presented. But it seems clear that a good part of the increase after 100 CE in the graph for stature (figure 4 in the article) is a composition effect as the number of femurs from the shorter east declined to single digits per period and the number from the taller northwest increased more than an order of magnitude.

Jongman and colleagues may have been anticipating this criticism when they suggested that the trendlines in mean factor scores disaggregated by region move in the same direction, with the exception of the east. It is not clear to me how precise this generalization is meant to be, but by my count in the millennium 500 BCE–500 CE the mean factor scores of males in the three regions other than the east move in different directions in about twice as many periods as those in which the three trendlines move in the same direction. Furthermore, no two regions hit their nadir in the same period: the low point for the western Mediterranean males is 0 [*sic*]–50 CE; for the east 350–300 BCE; for the southeast provinces 50–0 [*sic*] BCE; and for the northwestern provinces 250–300 CE (figure 3 in the article).[39]

One other criticism: though the article makes the claim that the decrease in stature during the peak of the Principate was caused by urbanization—a plausible hypothesis—there is no breakdown of the data between urban and rural finds. If the causal argument is right, and if skeletal finds are not distributed in proportion to urban and rural habitation, there is another potentially significant compositional distortion of unknown proportions. Overall, it strikes me that despite the sample size and sophistication we are still a long way from a convincing demonstration of trends in stature for the empire as a whole. A glance at table 3 in the article showing numbers of bones by province reveals just how unrepresentative the geographical distribution is: 3,760 of the ~10,000 bone measurements come from just two provinces, Britain and Raetia, which together comprised less than 5 percent of the empire's population. Analyses of specific areas can provide reasonably firm conclusions about trends,[40] but until huge strides are made toward a more even distribution of excavated bones by time and region, generalizations about well-being for the empire as a whole will be beyond reach.

In a 2018 essay, "Ancient Cliometrics and Archaeological Proxy-Data: Between the Devil and the Deep Blue Sea," Koenraad Verboven offered an incisive and compelling case that there are too many unknowns, and therefore too many required assumptions, to calculate a gross domestic product (GDP) for the Roman Empire. Hopkins's famous attempt in 1980 estimated only a minimum required for subsistence based on an educated guess for the population of the empire. After reviewing Hopkins's method and those of his successors, Verboven concluded:

> Important for our purposes is that they are all based on empirically flimsy evidence. Cliometrics in ancient economic history, so far, has been almost entirely deductive—dealing with quantitative factoids, rather than quantitative data. Based on theoretical models and comparative evidence assumptions have been formulated regarding the interconnectedness of chosen parameters. Then, as many as possible of the quantitative data preserved in textual sources are fit in or explained away. While the concept of subsistence minimum provides a clear baseline in terms of "wheat equivalent" the rest of the fabric is based on "controlled conjecture": a combination of educated guesses and comparative evidence to provide plausibility ranges and prop up assumptions.[41]

Instead of a futile focus on the trend of GDP, Verboven suggested other approaches to deploy quantitative archaeological data to document trends in economic performance: "At this moment four promising fields can be distinguished: (a) anthropometrics to measure biological standards of living, (b) rank-size and network analyses to compare the structural features of urban systems, (c) energetics of architecture and fuel consumption to measure levels of ability to capture and control energy, and (d) product diversity and ubiquity as a proxy for the collective productive knowhow and knowledge embedded in societal networks."[42] I have already commented on some obstacles to a, b, and c, and Verboven acknowledges that we are well short of the samples needed to draw conclusions for the empire as a whole.

As a means to measure (d) Verboven introduces the concept of the Economic Complexity Index from modern economics: "In order to measure and explain real economic development rather than shifts in appropriation we need indicators that measure development, rather than growth. This is the objective of the 'Economic Complexity Index' devised by César Hidalgo and Ricardo Hausmann. It measures the complexity of products and countries as a proxy for the 'complexity of the set of capabilities available in a country.' These sets of capabilities are 'chunks of productive knowledge,' some modularized on the level of individuals, others grouped into organizations and networks. The degree of economic complexity is an indicator for a society's ability 'to hold and use a larger amount of productive knowledge.'"[43] This concept in some respects is an elaboration of Jane Jacobs's fundamental tenet of economic development in her *The Economy of Cities*: "economies that do not add new kinds of goods and services, but continue to repeat old work, do not expand much nor do they, by definition, develop."[44] Jacobs's insight was that the incrementalism of simply producing the same things in more efficient ways will eventually run into a ceiling.

Verboven argues that, unlike proxies for GDP, it is possible to devise a method to quantify material remains in an Economic Complexity Index (ECI):

> The economic complexity index . . . should be appealing to archaeologists and historians, because contrary to most other indicators its focus is not on size of production or trade but on diversity. The index is based on network models and combines two parameters: diversity—the number of items a country produces—and ubiquity—the number of countries a particular item is produced in. By combining textual and archaeological data it should be possible to map the diversity and the ubiquity of ancient production and how this changed through time. The metrics resulting from such an exercise could then be used as a proxy for the level of productive knowledge and knowhow in ancient societies.[45]

This is an intriguing suggestion for a path out of the dead end of debates over "significant" growth, or not, in the Roman economy, but Verboven does not pursue the practical problems of quantification of the archaeological record. The fundamental challenges are worth detailed exposition and illustration in the following excursus because some of them will arise in any effort to quantify material remains to measure economic development. Given my lack of experience in archaeology, I asked my colleague Kevin Ennis to consider how the ECI might be implemented based on his experience of excavations at the Sicilian site of Morgantina.

Conclusion

This chapter has been designed to show that the hopes that the precision of the hard sciences, whether archaeological, biological, or environmental, will provide solid proxies for datable trends in Roman economic performance have been continually frustrated. This is not only because we need more data; the reasons for the repeated frustration are intrinsic. The empire was vast and varied with many unknowns.[46] One of the most basic—and one that has received too little attention—was identified by Paul Erdkamp: in order for the proxies to provide evidence for the "significance" of trends in economic performance, we would need to know the baseline from which the growth or decline of any quantifiable data occurred in order to estimate the impact on aggregate production.[47] He also pointed out that, despite claims that the trends in the proxies moved in the same direction over time, "there is no clear trend break in economic performance that is valid for the entire Roman world, even though some of the proxy data used over the past decades may give this impression."[48] Furthermore, "many proxies for the ancient world offer insufficient resolution to link them to short-term societal events."[49] The Greenland lead flux measurements offered hope that the resolution could be sharpened with the result that the Antonine Plague could be identified as the specific external shock that halted growth and set off the decline in economic performance, but a careful statistical analysis has shown that again the conclusion does not stand up to scrutiny.

I do not doubt that the accumulation of evidence from archaeology and the natural sciences will deepen our understanding of
local and regional developments, but it is not clear to me that in
the foreseeable future a method will be devised for aggregating the
evidence to establish the quantitative improvement (or not) in
average living standard for all inhabitants of the empire, not only
those of the Bay of Naples but also, for example, the (unknown
number of) rural slaves and Egyptian apprentices.[50] If proxies are
unlikely to become reliable enough to provide a secure quantitative understanding of the dynamics of the Roman economy, then
(it is my contention) attention to literary texts to understand cultural attitudes affecting the economy is worthwhile.[51] In this regard,
one of the most underexplored texts is Pliny's *Natural History*.

An Excursus from Morgantina: An Archaeologist's Assessment of the Economic Complexity Index (ECI) by Kevin Ennis

At first glance, the ECI is a particularly attractive option for replac-
ing GDP in the study of the ancient economy because, unlike
GDP, it is a measure of diversity of material objects and could in
principle be measured with archaeological data.[52] Moreover, high
economic complexity scores are correlated with GDP for contemporary economies.[53] Therefore, if an ECI could be calculated
for different periods and regions of antiquity, then theoretically it
would be possible to quantify economic performance through
material remains and bring to a close the thorny debate among
archaeologists and historians concerning whether there was significant growth under the Roman Empire.

This excursus takes up the recent suggestion that archaeologists
should calculate ECI scores for various periods of antiquity and
elucidates the theoretical and methodological issues that would
arise in doing so. The issues highlighted in this excursus are not
only pertinent to calculating ECI scores, however, but are applicable

more broadly to any attempt to deploy archaeological data as proxies to quantify economic development. In particular, two important and interrelated sets of issues are explored. On the one hand
is a set of issues associated with translating the ECI from its
original twenty-first-century global capitalist context to the ancient world. On the other hand are the methodological issues
that hinder any attempt at calculating an aggregate ECI from
archaeological field reports. Both sets of issues ultimately suggest that it will be infeasible to calculate an ECI for the foreseeable future, although the concepts that underly the ECI (complexity, diversity, ubiquity) might still be useful as *qualitative*
heuristic devices.

The ECI is intended as a proxy for the complexity of any given
economy. Complexity refers to the complete store of knowledge
(explicit) and know-how (tacit) embedded in a society that en-
ables economically productive activities.[54] Hidalgo and Hausmann, the creators of the ECI, calculate complexity scores for each
country using publicly available, standardized data on exports,
curated by individual governments and the United Nations. Their
calculations combine measures of diversity (i.e., the number of
discrete products) exported by a country and ubiquity (i.e., relative
prevalence or scarcity of any singular product) of those exports.[55]
Hidalgo and Hausmann argue that this proxy is particularly meaningful because ECI scores have been shown empirically to be pre-
dictive of both current economic development and future growth
possibilities.[56]

Whether this empirical correlation between the ECI and GDP
should be interpreted as causal is a matter for debate. Hidalgo and
Hausmann do not address the question of whether complexity
scores and GDP are both the result of other unmentioned historical factors. In fact, in their *Atlas of Economic Complexity*, the authors provide no discussion of the history of industrialization and
colonization in the eighteenth through twenty-first century and
do not assess how these histories might have influenced which
countries find themselves at the top and bottom of the index.[57]

A full assessment of this argument, however, is well beyond the scope of this excursus.

Even if this causal relationship could be established, it is still up for debate whether this connection would be relevant in ancient contexts. Hidalgo and Hausmann demonstrated the correlation between complexity and growth using export data from 128 countries during the period from 1964 to 2008.[58] These are data from a post–Industrial Revolution world, where the nation-state is the dominant form of political organization, globalization has completely reshaped all production, and capitalism has spread into every aspect of the human experience. In such a context, manufacturing and information technology have far outstripped the agricultural sector in terms of economic importance.[59] The significance of technological change for economic growth in the modern context is not in doubt. For the Roman world, on the other hand, if one views technological improvements such as the water mill, water-lifting devices, and *opus caementicium* as having a limited impact on aggregate productivity in a predominantly agrarian economy, then such a proxy for the store of knowledge and knowhow of the Roman world would not be particularly useful.[60] As such, the ECI cannot circumvent the debates about Roman productivity, because its use requires an acceptance of the a priori assumptions about the Roman economy that are at the center of the debate.

There are further obstacles in translating this proxy from a twenty-first-century context to the Roman world. In the twenty-first century the nation-state serves as the discrete unit for analysis.[61] No similarly obvious unit of analysis exists for the ancient world. An ECI for the entirety of the Roman world is not a possibility since the proxy is inherently a relational measure. To calculate ubiquity scores, it is necessary to have contemporary units that form a comparative frame.[62] As such, provinces might seem the most natural choice, but recently some have questioned whether the province is truly a useful unit for archaeological comparison.[63] Even if we could agree on the boundaries of culturally or ecologically coherent regions as the basis for comparison, there is good reason to think that calculating comparable ECIs would be challenging. Interregional comparative work is difficult and relatively rare, in part, as Greg Woolf has argued, because of variations in recording practices in different national traditions of archaeology.[64] Without standardized transnational reporting practices the calculation of an aggregate ECI for the whole Roman Empire will be impossible.

As a result, a different promising avenue for utilizing the ECI might be to compare different periods within a single region in terms of economic complexity or to compare different sites within a given region. Nonetheless, even such a study would have to contend with the issue of typology. What counts as a discrete category of product? Hidalgo and Hausmann never actually address that question in their own work, because they can rely on published data sets, produced by governmental agencies and the UN, which have their own interests and biases.[65] The issue of defining categories of products for export is even more fraught when dealing with archaeological data.[66] From an economic complexity perspective, the decision regarding what should be considered a separate product should be made based on whether one thinks that the difference between two products represents a real difference in the total store of knowledge and know-how, and whether that knowledge and know-how could enable the creation of new products in the future. Such a decision requires highly speculative thinking and is likely to yield different results depending on who is creating the typology.

The case of Morgantina, an extremely well-excavated site in inland Sicily, can illustrate the issue more concretely. Suppose we try to compare the complexity of archaic Morgantina with that of the Late Hellenistic and Republican periods. This is simple enough qualitatively. Even a passing glance at the finds from these two periods stored in the local museum would reveal that there is a greater range of products (diversity) in Late Hellenistic and Republican contexts and that these products are more dissimilar to products created in earlier periods than those from the archaic (ubiquity). A quantitative assessment, however, would be exceedingly difficult. Using Hidalgo and Hausmann's method, we should start by inventorying the exports of each period and calculating diversity and ubiquity scores. But exports are difficult to track in the archaeological record since the location where an artifact is deposited generally represents the end point in that artifact's life history. Without a full inventory of all sites that have Morgantina exports, a sense of the full range of goods that were being exported everywhere in the region during each period, and a means of associating every import with its origin point in Morgantina, this is impossible.

As such, we would need to pivot to consider the full range of objects produced at Morgantina during this period that are present on the site itself. Comparing the major publication on the archaic pottery to that of the Hellenistic and Republican periods raises a series of challenges. First, the primary publication for the archaic pottery mostly focuses on the tombs, while the Hellenistic and Republican pottery publication utilizes the full range of contexts at Morgantina.[67] Second, the Hellenistic and Republican publication provides a detailed study using x-ray florescence to demonstrate which fabric types were local and which were imported.[68] No such study was conducted for the archaic remains and, therefore, the author of the archaic volume is entirely dependent on preexisting typologies to identify locally produced pottery.[69] As a result, the level of certainty with which specific pottery shapes can be assigned as local or imported is drastically different between these two publications. Finally, the nomenclature used for pottery in each of these publications is different, and it is clear that the different authors are using different criteria to determine what is a unique form.[70] How subtly should we differentiate between different pottery shapes? Are the ubiquitous *olpai* found during the archaic period a discrete product? Or are they all just one of many jugs? All these concerns highlight the difficulty of standardizing data from different publications even at a single site.

Three other problems from an archaeological perspective can be briefly noted here: differential preservation, excavation practice, and sampling strategies. First, even if one could establish a method for deciding on types, only certain types of objects are preserved in the archaeological record. Aside from certain special taphonomic circumstances, the products of the leatherworking and woodworking industries, just to name two important examples, are essentially absent in most parts of the Roman Empire. The issue is even more difficult when one considers agricultural production. Furthermore, preservation conditions can differ vastly even within a single region. Second, different excavations have different practices in terms of what is considered a find, what is kept after excavation, and what is published in final reports. Site reports often do not even explicitly lay out the criteria on which such decisions are made. Third, sampling strategies are always at play at every archaeological site. These strategies can vary widely between sites and different sampling strategies can result in the creation of vastly different sorts of assemblages. As such, it is hard to imagine how one could ever reach the level of resolution necessary for a quantified product complexity index based on archaeological data.

Finally, even if all of the above issues were overcome, how would it ever be possible to calculate ubiquity, defined as the number of countries that make a product? Calculating it requires having a closed data set because in order to claim that an object is only produced in a restricted set of countries, one must know that other countries do not produce it at a particular point in time.[71] If this is not the case, even if a list of products could be ascertained for any given province or region, the list is incapable of providing insight into the capabilities and technical know-how of that region because one cannot know whether all these products are simple and produced everywhere or are complicated and only made in that specific region.[72] It is worth noting with regard to ubiquity that there are only a few manufactured items for which the elder Pliny notes that particular cities had a special reputation (see chapter 5).[73]

Despite the major obstacles to aggregate quantification, the logic behind the ECI can still provide productive new avenues for research for historians and archaeologists. Although we are already accustomed to thinking about diversity of archaeological assemblages through the lens of typology, the concept of ubiquity, as defined by Hidalgo and Hausmann, has not yet been used to full effect for studying Roman material culture. This will only be possible, however, if the work is qualitative and done at the regional level for the time being. The foregoing analysis has highlighted two distinct but interrelated problems with quantification using archaeological data. The process is beset, on the one side, by the possibility of projecting a proxy with internal relations specific to contemporary capitalism inappropriately onto the past and, on the other side, by the issue of comparability between archaeological sites, specifically as it relates to the concepts of typology, preservation, excavation practice, and sampling. Nonetheless, the theoretical and methodological concerns expressed here should not be taken as a rejection of quantification writ large. Indeed, quantification has an important place in the field of economic history, if only it continues to subject its proxies to close scrutiny for anachronism and shows a greater sensitivity to the limits of archaeological interpretation.

2

Pliny's Purpose, Audience, and Method

THE TITLE of this book, *Pliny's Roman Economy: Natural History, Innovation, and Growth*, represents an acknowledgment that the imperial economy was perceived and experienced very differently by the millions of inhabitants of the empire, depending on whether they were female or male, citizen or slave, wealthy or poor, urban or rural, Italian, Egyptian, or British. Consequently, to draw inferences from the *Natural History* about Pliny's understanding of economic behavior we need to situate him and to describe his purpose, audience, methods, and organization.[1]

Recent scholarship on the Roman economy has emphasized the distortions that can come from reliance on literary texts by aristocratic authors such as Cicero.[2] Pliny was a wealthy estate owner from northern Italy and was a member of the equestrian order, serving in some of the highest offices granted to that order. His full career in public offices in the provinces and in Italy is not securely known, but it certainly took him to several provinces in the Western Empire and culminated with the Prefecture of the imperial fleet at Misenum on the Bay of Naples, where he died during the eruption of Vesuvius in 79 CE.[3]

Pliny wrote the *Natural History* in the 70s CE in the aftermath of the excesses of Nero's reign. In *The Corrupting Sea*, Peregrine Horden and Nicholas Purcell associate him with an aristocratic

culture, which at least overtly looked down on crafts.[4] Sir Ronald
Syme suggested a somewhat different stress in his article about
Pliny: "More diligent perhaps and exacting than senators and con-
suls were the knights in the imperial service; and the financial du-
ties of a procurator might stimulate precision and the spirit of
enquiry."[5] There is some truth to both of these characterizations
in my judgment. On Syme's view, Pliny is a more interesting witness to economic behavior, and it is surely true that the quality of
the *Natural History* argues for his view: it was not meant to be (and
is certainly not) a literary masterpiece on Pliny's own admission.[6]
On the other hand, as we shall see, Pliny does not treat the "crowd"
(*turba*) of artisans and farmers with respect, a marked contrast
with the early modern encyclopedists.[7]

Pliny's nephew and heir, the younger Pliny, describes his uncle's
remarkable work habits in a well-known letter to Baebius Macer
(Ep. 3.5). The *Natural History* was the last and longest of a series of
strikingly diverse works, ranging from javelin-throwing on
horseback to biography to history to grammar. The sheer magnitude of the achievement of the *Natural History* is captured in the
elder Pliny's boast that it is a compilation of 20,000 "things worth
knowing," *res dignae*, drawn from 2,000 works, on subjects encompassing the whole cosmos. The nephew's letter describes the daily
routine that made this feat possible: after taking care of official
business, uncle Pliny returned home and devoted every spare min-
ute to his scholarly work on little sleep. His method of compiling
was to have a slave read to him while he took notes, not stopping
even while dining. To illustrate this relentless, obsessive, rapid-fire
method, the younger Pliny tells the (artfully constructed) anecdote of a friendly bystander who reprimanded the slave-reader for
mispronouncing a word and told him to go back and repeat it cor-
rectly; Pliny in turn scolded the friend on the grounds that "we lost
more than ten lines on account of your intervention" (Ep. 3.5.12).[8]
Much of the recent scholarship has argued that the *Natural History*
should be interpreted as a coherent literary whole; others have
read the work as an "exasperating" mix.[9] I will address this issue in

more detail (see p. 41), but my view is that this rapid and relentless mode of compilation accounts for the sometimes loose organization and the often wandering lists of "facts" described below, as illustrated in the excursus on cures for rabid dog bite (see p. 44–47). In any case, literary interpretation of the work need not preclude the use of the text to explore Pliny's economic thought.

Purpose

The *Natural History* obviously was not intended to be a work of economic history.[10] The dedicatory letter to the future emperor, Titus Flavius Vespasianus, suggests its purpose in a playfully self-deprecating fashion.[11] Pliny intends the *Natural History* to serve the end of *utilitas*, "usefulness," rather than *gratia*, "pleasure" (N.H. pr.16)—vocabulary he repeats when in Book 28.2 he launches into a list of medicines derived from animals regardless of how repulsive they may be (e.g., a draft of the blood of gladiators or camel brain as a remedies for epilepsy [N.H. 28.4, 91], the urine of pre-pubescent children as an antidote for asp venom [N.H. 28.65], or the dung of a she-goat in honey-wine for urinary disorders [N.H. 28.213]). The aim of "usefulness" required the inclusion of boring material (*sterilis materia*) and of a vocabulary including "rustic, foreign, even barbarian" words (N.H. pr.13). In an elite culture that valued rhetorical style and a refined choice of words this was strong admission. The "utility" of the monumental work lay in its serving as a repository for ancient knowledge, which was in danger of being forgotten and lost forever. To this end Pliny lays claim not to originality but to a comprehensiveness that no other author, Greek or Roman, had achieved (N.H. pr.17; also 37.205).[12]

Modern works on the *Natural History* have variously assessed the seriousness of Pliny's pursuit of "usefulness." Having described the work as "astonishingly uneven," K. D. White concluded that "Pliny's encyclopedia deserves the serious attention of all students of classical science and technology; in spite of its obvious shortcomings, it is much more than an assemblage of curious information to amuse the idle antiquarian or dilettante."[13] Mary Beagon's influential *Roman Nature: The Thought of Pliny the Elder* sees the work as one aimed at "practical philanthropy."[14] Valérie Naas's interpretation emphasizes Pliny's "selection of the extraordinary and the moral and ideological perspective" (*sélection de l'extraordinaire et la perspective morale et idéologique*), rather than any mundane utility of the *Natural History*.[15] For Trevor Murphy "the table of contents [Book 1, the *Summarium*] is a *nod* in the direction of utility, compensating for Pliny's playfully drifting aesthetic," but apart from the books on agriculture the *Natural History* is not really motivated by the goal of "how-to."[16] Most recently, Tamara Lewit assembled the archaeological evidence for the local variability in the evolution of olive and grape presses, overly schematized by Pliny, and concluded that the *Natural History* was not really intended for direct users.[17] Eugenia Lao likewise labeled the supposed technical instruction "didactic fiction."[18] More generally, Serafina Cuomo argued that none of the surviving treatises of the early empire (e.g., Vitruvius, Frontinus) provided the information necessary for practitioners.[19] John Healy's thorough *Pliny the Elder on Science and Technology* summarized the *Natural History* as a combination of "applied science" and "fantasy," and concluded that the *Natural History* is most useful for our own knowledge of the history of ancient science.[20] Taking the 37 books as a whole, I find it hard to believe that Pliny devoted years of sleep deprivation to write 400,000 words on 20,000 "things worth knowing" (*res dignae*) out of a playful aesthetic. I take at face value his assertion that his purpose was usefulness (*utilitas*) rather than pleasure (*gratia*). He frequently uses some form of *utilis*, especially in the books on agriculture, and in a straightforward pragmatic sense—for example, in the best uses of manure (N.H.17.53–54). And yet in pursuit of a boastfully monumental achievement he had not given realistic thought to how his work could actually be used (see p. 42). Chapter 6 will take a selective look at how the *Natural History* was used, and not used, by subsequent generations.[21]

Audience

One reason I am not inclined to interpret the *Natural History* as an intricately organized work of literary art is the inconsistencies, one of the most glaring of which is Pliny's view of his target audience. Pliny's dedication (N.H. pr.6) points to the inconsistencies: on the one hand, the *Natural History* is a huge work dedicated to Titus, but the emperor is not expected to have the leisure to wade through it; moreover, it is written in an inelegant style but dedicated to the global arbiter of literary taste (Titus) on the pretense that it will be consulted by the *vulgus*, by the "herd of farmers and artisans" (*agricolarum, opificum turbae*). Denigrating references to the working "herd" are scattered throughout the books. *Opifices*, "craftsmen," are characterized as an *indocta turba*, "an ignorant crowd" (N.H. 33.90), and the craft of dyeing is given short shrift on the explicit ground that it is not one of the "liberal arts" (*liberales artes*; N.H. 22.4). In his discussion of the value of astronomy to identify the appropriate season to sow (N.H. 18.206) Pliny laments that it is hard to share knowledge of the divine heaven with "rustic ignorance" (*imperitiae rusticae*).[22] And yet the *agrestes* are acknowledged to be the people with the practical knowledge, for example, to distinguish poisonous mushrooms from the edible (N.H. 22.94); they are the ones with on-the-ground knowledge of medicinal plants but without the literacy needed to communicate it (N.H. 25.16, similarly 24.5).

Here again, contemporary scholars differ in their assessments of the readership of the *Natural History*. On the optimistic side, Kevin Greene suggests that Pliny's magnum opus disseminated technical know-how widely and would have been found in the office of every provincial governor.[23] Schneider concludes that Pliny's compilation disseminated technical knowledge but did not serve as a springboard for further innovation.[24] On the other side, Goodyear in an ungenerous but realistic spirit wrote that the work was for "unlearned amateurs"; Isager regarded Pliny's stated aim of writing for peasants and artisans as unrealistic; and based on

Pliny's oversimplification of the evolution of presses Lewit inferred that he reached only a "tiny" readership.[25]

In the absence of direct evidence of dissemination and impact among actual practitioners, I am more inclined to the latter views, given the difficulty of use and the cost. Pliny's *Natural History* was a work of just over 400,000 words—huge in a society where copies had to be made one by one by scribal hand. My rough estimate using the relative prices from Diocletian's Edict for scribal work by line and artisans' wages is that to copy a set of the 37 books would have cost about nine months' pay for an artisan.[26] It seems to me that Pliny senses the implausibility of his stated aim to provide "utility" to practitioners but does not come to terms with the gap between his learned work and the illiterate or barely literate workers.[27] In chapter 6, I will contrast the reach and impact of the *Natural History* with eighteenth-century encyclopedias—a time when the printing press reduced the relative cost of Ephraim Chambers's *Cyclopaedia* by an order of magnitude despite the fact that it was five times as large.[28]

Method

With his 20,000 "things worth knowing," Pliny stood at the summit of the Roman tradition of compilers of past knowledge.[29] His 37 books in a single work dwarfed the more numerous and varied works of his principal predecessor and main source, Marcus Terentius Varro, who over a long life (116–27 BCE) published an astounding oeuvre of more than 490 books.[30] Pliny boasts that he has mined 2,000 books by 100 authorities, but he may have understated the breadth of his reading. By one count 453 authorities appear, but it is uncertain how many of these he himself read since at times he was compiling from compilations.[31] How did Pliny evaluate what was "worthy," *digna*? Presumably, in order to meet his goal of utility the things should be true, but in the midst of a list of remedies for babies' afflictions he slips in a general comment that "certain details can scarcely be included as serious items, but I must not omit them, since they have been put on record" (N.H. 30.137).

In other words, inclusiveness overrode truth as a criterion. Yet Pliny does not routinely call out those items not to be taken seriously and leaves it to the reader to discriminate. Furthermore, to be useful the 20,000 *res* should be organized in a fashion that would make them findable in the massive work on 37 scrolls.[32]

The very description of 20,000 "things worth knowing" (*res dignae*) implies an epistemology that knowledge comprised *discrete* items rather than *propositional* knowledge—that is, *systems* of knowledge organized on the basis of *principles*.[33] This is evident in Book 11, which is devoted to insects—a topic that fascinates Pliny because of their small size. In the absence of microscopes many of the essential features of insects were not observable by the naked eye.[34] After surveying some of the uncertainties, Pliny asserts that he will stick to the "observable features of things" (*naturas rerum manifestas*) and not speculate about the "causes" (*causas*; N.H. 11.8). The (false) account in Book 37.60 of the discovery of goat's blood to crack diamonds ends with the assertion that *ratio*, "reason, order, system," is not to be sought in any part of Nature.[35] The consequence of this approach is that the *Natural History* does not attempt to offer frameworks systematically to understand the facts based on underlying causes. Accordingly, the achievement of each of the following 36 books is represented in the *Summarium* as a simple, undifferentiated count of hundreds of "items and findings and observations" (*res et historiae et observationes*) in that book.[36]

This epistemology had profound implications for the value of the welter of facts. William Stahl pointedly concluded that Pliny and other "Roman intellectuals of the classical period failed to appreciate the systematic character of scientific disciplines."[37] The result was Pliny's "inability to comprehend Greek science or to distinguish between absurd anecdote and sober theory, between ungrounded opinion and brilliant original thinking."[38] The *Natural History* offers many illustrations of Stahl's characterization. For instance, the account of cloudbursts and sudden whirlwinds, "dreaded by sailors," ends with the suggestion of a "tenuous remedy" of pouring out vinegar as the whirlwind advances (N.H. 2.132). Among the most curious illustrations of absurd, unsystematic "facts" are the forty remedies for rabid dog bites, scattered across ten books, including a draft of "a decoction of the dung of badger, cuckoo, and swallow" (N.H. 28.156).[39]

What were Pliny's methods of validation of his "facts," if not their logical fit in systems of knowledge? G.E.R. Lloyd (1984) draws the distinction in scientific method between the empirical and the experimental, and comments that Greek scientists such as Theophrastus engaged in the former but not the latter. For the most part Pliny engaged in neither because it was not his purpose. At times he exhibited the capacity to be critical, for example in his treatment of astrology or the efficacy of incantations as cures.[40] And he relentlessly ranted against the frauds of the Magi and Greek doctors, though that was inspired more by ethnic bias than by philosophical principle or empiricism.[41] In the sphere of herbal medicine Pliny laments the fact that it is easier to listen to words in a lecture hall than to go into the wilds in search of plants (N.H. 26.11).[42] Occasionally empirical claims of autopsy validate the facts. Lloyd notes, however, that the claims are usually associated with "marvels" (*mirabilia*) and do not constitute "sustained or systematic researches into more mundane problems."[43] Pliny's efforts to move beyond compiling previous observations to make his own contributions are relatively rare and dubious. So Olaf Pederson's assessment of the explanation for the shining and hiding of the planets (N.H. 2.62): "Unfortunately, one has to admit that [Pliny's] own attempt to improve [on his predecessors] is not at all successful."[44]

In a vague statement of method regarding "foreign and even outlandish customs" Pliny indicates that he has sought out nearly consensual judgments and done diligent research (N.H. 28.2). Since we usually do not have his sources for specific "facts," it is impossible to verify Pliny's claim of near consensus and diligence. His most common means of validation was appeal to past authority, based on his reverence for the ancients and on the assumption that it was difficult to imbue new facts with "authority" (*auctoritas*).[45] As Liba Chaia Taub observes, he had a special reverence for archaic Greek poets writing seven hundred years earlier and "considered Hesiod (whom he regarded as the Father of Agriculture) to be as valid an authority on celestial matters as specialist [Hellenistic] astronomers."[46] For authority to validate agricultural knowledge Pliny cites the two-centuries-old writings of the elder Cato sixty-four times and the *De Re Rustica* of his own contemporary Columella only eight times.[47] In Book 18 the justification for turning to the elder Cato for "gems of wisdom" (*oracula*) is that they have been proven useful by experience (N.H. 18.25). But at times the criterion of antiquity of the source must have come into conflict with another (scientifically irrelevant) principle of preferring "our heavyweights" (*nostri graviores*)—that is, Romans—over the Greeks (N.H. pr.24).[48]

There are occasional exceptions to the principle of "the older the better." Pliny paid handsome tribute to Antonius Castor as the "foremost authority" (*summa auctoritas*) of his age in botanical knowledge and recorded that he visited his garden (N.H. 25.9). In his account of the vast interior of Asia, Pliny does "not deny that my description of it will differ in many points from that of the ancients [*veteres*], as I have devoted much care and attention to ascertaining thoroughly the recent events in that region from Domitius Corbulo and the kings sent from there as suppliants or kings' children sent as hostages" (N.H. 6.23). A similar explanation is given for correcting accounts of the "elders" (*prisci*) about Taprobane (modern-day Sri Lanka; N.H. 6.84). These amount to a clear signaling of exceptions to the general rule that authority was to be found in the elders.

Pliny's herculean effort, sleep-deprived and in haste, to survey two thousand books may explain some other weaknesses. Despite his professed reverence for the ancients Pliny could be sloppy in reporting their findings, as Lloyd remarks with reference to Pliny's use of Theophrastus.[49] Moreover, the work includes some unexplained basic contradictions, such as Cato's advice not to buy a run-down farm on the cheap and Remmius Palaemon's famous success at doing just that (see chapter 5). Pliny seems to alternate between celebrating the possibilities of commerce and decrying the demoralizing consequences.[50]

Organization

How to organize a compilation of more than 20,000 things worth knowing must have been no small challenge, and the solution cannot have been obvious. It was a challenge faced sixteen centuries later: Richard Yeo's *Encyclopedic Visions* (2001) documents at length the competing options for organization tried by Pliny's successors in the early eighteenth century. For example, the author can arrange the material in numerous short subjects listed in alphabetical order with cross-references to direct the reader to related subjects. Alternatively, the organization can take the form of much longer thematic or disciplinary treatments privileging the coherence of systems of knowledge. (The last printed edition of the *Encyclopedia Britannica* did both.)[51]

At a high level Pliny's arrangement of the 37 books was sensible: the cosmos in Book 2, the geography of the Roman Empire and its neighbors in Books 3–6, animals including humans in Books 7–11, plants especially for agriculture in Books 12–19, remedies derived from plants in Books 20–27, remedies from animals in Books 28–32, minerals and gems in Books 33–37.[52] The challenge, as Pliny was aware, was spotting the useful "facts" in a book including many hundreds or even thousands of items, which were not ordered in any intuitively obvious way;[53] so he composed his *Summarium* in Book 1 as a guide for readers. For each of the following 36 books the *Summarium* lists in several (modern) paragraphs the "things" to be found, ending with a count of the "items and findings and observations" (*res et historiae et observationes*) in the book and then the authorities used. Pliny recognized that the *Natural History*'s usefulness would depend on the efficacy of the *Summarium*. How useful was it, really?

Aude Doody's "Finding Facts in Pliny's Encyclopedia" has provided a detailed and insightful analysis of the *Summarium*, based on the premise that the *Natural History* might be read in one of two ways: either as short excerpts of a particular "thing" or as a whole work from beginning to end.[54] She points out that in the many manuscripts and printed editions the *Summarium* is presented visually in different ways and that the chapter numbers within the 36 books were not in the original.[55] The latter fact surely made the process of tracking down the useful *res* within a book laborious, but that would not have been the end of the difficulties.

Books 20–32 give many hundreds of medical remedies each, but there are only a few, exceptional cases in which the *Summarium* matches the remedy to a specific malady; for the most part, the *Summarium* is just a bare list of remedies, offering no guidance whatsoever to what the *medicinae* allegedly cure.[56] For example, the *Summarium* for Book 23 on *medicinae* derived from cultivated trees starts with the following: "from vines 20 [remedies]; vine-leaves 7; tendrils 7; juice of unripe grape 14; wild vine 21" and so on. It is unclear to me how Pliny imagined the utility of this list in locating the right *medicina* for a particular ailment. How would one know that, among the fourteen ailments, the juice of the unripe grape "cures sores in a moist part of the body, such as the mouth, tonsils or genitals. . . . [and] is also good for dysentery, spitting of blood, and quinsy" (N.H. 23.7)? Katerina Oikonomopoulou also points out that the summary is not always accurate and rightly concludes that it was "designed to impress, rather than to serve as an actual practical aid."[57]

Conclusion

The ubiquity of excerpts from the *Natural History* in Humphrey, Oleson, and Sherwood's *Greek and Roman Technology: A Sourcebook* (first edition)—by my count, 217 passages altogether—warrants consideration of its utility for economic production in the Roman world. Indeed, the phenomenon of excerpting the useful bits from Pliny's unwieldy whole goes back to antiquity with the third-century Solinus's *Collectanea* and the anonymous fourth-century compilation of a compilation of a compilation, *Medicina Plinii* (see chapter 6). In assessing the impact of Pliny's vast assortment of "things worth knowing," it is important not to lose the tone and context in the process of excerpting. We should not, with the hindsight of contemporary science, choose those "facts" that seem to us today to be valid or plausible.[58] The "tiny" readership of "unlearned amateurs" would not have filtered the "facts" in the same way. An unimportant but amusing illustration of the modern filtering I have in mind can be found in the *Sourcebook*:[59] it excerpts Pliny's down-to-earth advice about when to harvest timber from Book 16.184–92 and 195, omitting the intervening chapters 193–94 containing Cato's recommendation to "never touch timber except when the moon is on the change," Varro's analogous (important) recommendation to get a haircut only at the full moon to avoid baldness, and Tiberius's adherence to this advice for his own haircuts. The deletion for the sake of space in the *Sourcebook* is entirely understandable, but such selective quotation and omission of the absurd may give an exaggerated impression of the value of Pliny's usefulness. As French observed with regard to the more than 900 medical cures, "it would need the eye of faith and a huge amount of work to try to work out which, if any, could have been effective. The possibilities for confusion were endless."[60]

Pliny's avowed goal of "usefulness" (*utilitas*) may very well have been sincere, but it was at least partially unrealistic for the readership he claims to be aiming to improve. How the "crowd" (*turba*) of illiterate "farmers" (*agrestes*) and uneducated "artisans" (*opifices*) would have gained access is unclear at best. And if they gained access, how they would have found the useful "facts" for their own purposes without great effort is also unclear. And finally, if they found the relevant "facts," on what principles they would have sorted the valid from the useless or harmful is equally uncertain.

The *Natural History* contains some recent knowledge acquired by Pliny's own observation or compiled from Julio-Claudian authors. But his reverence for ancient authority meant that the preponderance of sources was older, much older.[61] By my count of datable authorities, more than half came from eras more than two hundred years before publication of the *Natural History*; as Pliny acknowledged, he wrote in a culture that was reluctant to grant "authority" (*auctoritas*) to new things. Sometimes, I think, ancient historians grow insensitive to the time scales we work with—in this case, the notion that useful knowledge was more likely to be found in *centuries*-old texts. The contrast with the excitement of new discoveries to be found in the early modern encyclopedias is striking and will be explored in chapter 6.[62]

Excursus: Pliny on Remedies for Rabies

This excursus is meant to offer a specific illustration to think about Pliny's purpose, audience, method, and organization. Rabies in the *Natural History* might seem an odd topic for an excursus, but it was a preoccupation of Pliny and gives a flavor of the work that is needed to supplement the scholarship advocating its coherence.[63] As far as I can see, the main monographs and collections of the past generation devoted to the elder Pliny do not mention the subject.[64] On the other hand, histories of rabies regularly mention Pliny in unflattering terms.[65] Anyone who has not read the *Natural History* from beginning to end, and has read only the commonly quoted passages, might not be aware of the random quirkiness of the work.[66]

The first of Pliny's mentions of rabies comes in Book 2 on the cosmos and astronomy, prompted by the "fact" that dogs are more susceptible to contracting rabies at the rising of the Lesser Dogstar (N.H. 2.107). The next mention, found in Book 8 on animals, gives a precautionary measure for a dog after it has been bitten: mix dung, preferably chicken droppings, in its food, or if the disease has already started, hellebore. For humans, the only cure, *cynorrhodon*, was recently discovered by a divine sign (*oraculum*).

And "Columella states that if a dog's tail is docked by being bitten off and the end joint amputated 40 days after birth, the spinal marrow having been removed the tail does not grow again and the dog is not liable to rabies" (N.H. 8.153). In Book 25 Pliny gives a brief account of the *oraculum*, to be discussed in chapter 4 on his conception of methods of discovery (N.H. 25.17, 125).

King Mithridates was infamous for his intricate knowledge of poisons and remedies. After Pompey finally dispatched him, the king's commentary written in his own hand included among many other cures one for rabid dog bite: "the kernels of walnuts chewed by a fasting person and applied to the bite of a mad dog are said to be a sovereign remedy" (N.H. 23.149).[67] Another herbal treatment was alysson, so named "because it protects persons bitten by a dog from rabies if they take it in vinegar and wear it as an amulet" (N.H. 24.95).

Though he is repelled by the use of human parts as remedies, in Book 28 Pliny reports (without endorsing) that the doctor "Antaeus made pills from the skull of a hanged man to cure the bites of a mad dog" (N.H 28.7). Later in the same book, more remedies: "Each person's own urine, if it be proper for me to say so, does him the most good, if a dog-bite is immediately bathed in it, if it is applied on a sponge or wool to the quills of an urchin that are sticking in the flesh, or if ash kneaded with it is used to treat the bite of a mad dog, or a serpent's bite" (N.H 28.67). Rabies is among the numerous afflictions cured by menstrual blood, if used in the right way: "Lais and Salpe hold that the bite of a mad dog, tertians, and quartans [fevers] are cured by menstrual fluid on wool from a black ram enclosed in a silver bracelet" (N.H. 28.82). "All are agreed that, if water or drink is dreaded after a dog-bite, if only a cloth contaminated [with menstrual blood] be placed beneath the cup, that fear disappears at once, since of course that sympathy, as the Greeks call it, has an all-powerful effect, for I have said that dogs begin to go mad on tasting that blood" (N.H. 28.84).[68] Hyena parts were believed to have curative powers: "to eat the flesh [of hyena] neutralizes the bites of a rabid dog, the liver being the most efficacious" (N.H. 28.104). And another, animal-based prophylactic to protect dogs: "The [human] mother of a boy gives milk by a taste of which they deny dogs will become rabid" (N.H. 28.75).

The inventory of remedies is more than doubled in the most extensive list in Book 29:

> If a person has been bitten by a rabid dog, protection from hydrophobia is given by an application to the wounds of ash from the burnt head of a dog.[69] Now all reduction to ash . . . should be carried out in the following way: a new earthen vessel is covered with clay and so put in a furnace. The same method is also good when the ash is to be taken in drink. Some have prescribed as a cure eating a dog's head. Others too have used as an amulet a worm from a dead dog, or placed in a cloth under a cup the sexual fluid from a bitch, or have rubbed into the wound the ash from the hair under the tail of the rabid dog itself. . . . Under the tongue of a rabid dog is a slimy saliva, which given in drink prevents hydrophobia, but much the most useful remedy is the liver of the dog that bit in his madness to be eaten raw, if that can be done, if it cannot, cooked in any way, or a broth must be made from the boiled flesh. There is a little worm on the tongue of dogs which the Greeks call *lytta* (madness), and if this is taken away when they are puppies they neither go mad nor lose their appetite. It is also carried three times round the fire and given to those bitten by a rabid dog to prevent their going mad. The brains of poultry are an antidote, but to swallow them gives protection for only a year. They say that it is also efficacious to apply to the wound a cock's comb pounded up, or goose grease with honey. The flesh of dogs that have gone mad is also preserved in salt to be used for the same purposes given in food. Puppies too of the same sex as the bitten patient are immediately drowned and their livers swallowed raw . . . [plus 7 additional exotic remedies]. (N.H. 29.98)

In later books the range of cures is extended to include the sediment from the manufacture of garum (N.H. 31.96) and cauterization with iron (N.H. 34.151).

From this assemblage of 40 remedies scattered across ten books several observations come to mind. The obvious one is "the cures that Pliny mentions belong much more to the magical than the medical tradition."[70] Some of the recommendations are based on sympathetic magic; others are not based on any apparent logic; and certainly the efficacy of none of them can have been subjected to systematic observation. Pliny's purpose was not to disseminate only verifiable facts. The second, less obvious point relates to audience: all but one of these remedies are (mercifully) not to be found associated with rabies in the *Summarium*; a Roman in search of a cure for the bite of a rabid dog would have had to read all 37 books to find all 40 remedies.[71] Did Pliny really believe that someone in need of a cure would read the whole of the *Natural History*? (One cannot help but wonder whether it would have been possible to do so before succumbing to the disease.) Pliny's method was a helter-skelter collection of all reports of cures for rabid dog bite without sorting out apparent contradictions: he reports dog-rose as the "only cure," *unicum remedium*, in Book 8.152 but then lists an additional 39 cures in other books. As for organization, it is hard to discern any principle that would help a reader in need locate most of the remedies. The contrast with the early modern English encyclopedias is discussed in chapter 6.[72]

3

Parens Natura and Smithian Growth

HUMANS' STANDARD of living depends fundamentally on our relationship with Nature as a source for energy and for material resources animate and inanimate. It follows that improvement in the standard of living depends in part on a society's attitudes toward Nature—whether it is a resource for unbounded exploitation or is bounded by the sacred.[1] Like many of his aristocratic contemporaries, Pliny was strongly influenced by a Stoic milieu that regarded Nature as divine, a belief that is evident in the concluding religious invocation of his massive work:

> *Salve, parens rerum omnium Natura, teque nobis Quiritium solis celebratam esse numeris omnibus tuis fave.* (N.H. 37.205)

> Hail Natura, Mother of all things, show favor that you have been celebrated in all your manifestations by me alone of Romans.

John Sellars explained the difference between the Stoics' relation to Nature and the traditional Christian attitude:

> The Stoic God is very much in Nature. It is very easy for us to think of God as an external creator of Nature, an external force that shapes Nature. But for the Stoics God simply is Nature.

Whereas the late ancient Church Fathers and early modern Christian readers of Stoicism were often keen to stress the difference between God and Nature in the light of Christian teaching (and so stress the distinction between the two principles), numerous ancient sources note that the Stoics were happy to identify God with Nature, even if that claim might sometimes be qualified to say that God is the active force within Nature. For the Stoics, the cosmos is a living being (Diogenes Laertius 7.142).[2]

This Stoic principle of divine Nature (*Parens Natura*) motivates and pervades the *Natural History*, as Andrew Wallace-Hadrill and Mary Beagon have delineated in detail.[3] As a parent, Natura created the world for Man's benefit—"the wonderful generosity of Nature" (*mira benignitas Naturae*; N.H. 16.64, 7.1).[4] "Pliny is a crusader, with a passionate mission: by showing how nature is designed for man, to persuade man how properly to make use of his natural environment."[5] Furthermore, the Roman ethic of gift exchange required that Man demonstrate his gratitude in return for the "wonderful generosity" by acquiring knowledge of the natural world and showing appropriate respect; conversely, ignorance of Nature is among the "crimes of an ungrateful spirit" (*crimina ingrati animi*; N.H. 2.159).[6] Pliny expects to win approval for offering the very most comprehensive account of Nature, and as we shall see, he has fairly specific ideas about the appropriate and inappropriate exploitation of Nature with direct consequences for how humans engage in economic production.

In Pliny's evolutionary view, Man in his primitive state as a part of Nature enjoyed the unadulterated "greatest gift" (*summum munus*) of Nature provided by the trees and forests, which offered him food and shelter. In addition, the divine Parent created animals, "implanting also healthful medicines in their vitals"—a wondrous thought (N.H. 27.146). In Pliny's day, man's productive capabilities have developed to the point that he can now seek marble from mountains, clothing from China, pearls from the Red Sea, and emeralds from deep in the earth (N.H. 12.2). It is possible for Pliny to compose an unprecedentedly comprehensive inventory of Nature's "things worth knowing" because Rome's unprecedented conquests opened the way to the discovery of new plants, animals, and minerals. Following in the wake of the identification of this vast multitude of natural resources and their uses, the Pax Romana facilitated their exchange across the seas. The underlying principle here resembles that of Adam Smith 1,700 years later— that is, certain parts of the empire had a comparative advantage in producing certain resources, and trade of those resources could improve the standard of living on all sides.

Pliny famously made this point at the beginning of Book 14: "Who does not think that now life has been improved by an interconnected world through the greatness [maiestas] of the Roman empire, by the commerce of goods and by the bond of joyous peace, and that everything, even those which had before been hidden, have been made available in widespread use." Book 27.2 expanded on the theme, celebrating the assorted plants coming from the corners of the empire, from Scythia to Mount Atlas, from Britain to Ethiopia: "plants carried to and fro throughout the whole world for mankind's well-being [salus humana], enabled by the greatness of the Pax Romana."[7] Contemporary archaeologists excavating in the ancient Mediterranean have uncovered large quantities of material remains to support Pliny's broad generalization about the benefits of trade under Roman rule.[8]

Trade was only one of the benefits. More broadly, in Pliny's exuberant judgment Italy deserves praise because it "brought together empires and tamed the customs and drew together different and uncouth tongues of so many peoples by a community of language, and gave civilization to Man, and in short became the fatherland of all peoples in the whole world" (N.H. 3.39).

While in Pliny's view the whole empire benefited from trade under the Pax Romana, the conquering city of Rome was the privileged hub and taste-maker. His brief review of cheeses from the provinces begins: "at Rome where the goods of all peoples are judged at first-hand, from the provinces the cheese from the district of Nimes is most outstanding, then cheeses from the villages of La Lozere and Gevaudan" (N.H. 11.240). After noting the qualities of other provincial cheeses, the list concludes with another of his 20,000 "things worth knowing": "it is handed down [*tradunt*] that Zoroaster lived in the desert for 20 years on cheese treated so that it was not affected by age" (N.H. 11.242).

Unlike cheese, most of the 20,000 "items" in the *Natural History* are naturally occurring products, not manmade and not manufactured. Pliny devotes the largest share of his attention to plants (Books 12–27), and especially plants for medicinal use (Books 20–27).[9] Midway through these sixteen books, Book 22.1 opens with a paean to Natura's lavish herbal generosity:

> Nature and our earth might have filled the measure of our wonder at them in anyone who reviews even the preceding book only, with all Nature's gifts in it, and all the kinds of plants created for the uses [*utilitatibus*] and pleasures [*voluptatibus*] of mankind. But how many more kinds remain, and how much more wonderful they are in their discovery! For of the plants mentioned already the greater number, owing to their excellence as food, perfume or ornament, have led to repeated experiments; of the rest it is their efficacy that proves that nothing is created by Nature without some more hidden reason [*occultiore causa*] than those just mentioned.

Here Pliny draws an opposition between the useful and the pleasurable that structures much of his outlook. To find the not yet discovered, the *occultior*, man needs to search everywhere because "not even the woods and the wilder face of Nature are without medicines, for there is no place where that sacred parent did not distribute remedies for the healing of mankind, so that even the very desert provides remedies" (N.H. 24.1).

The "renown of plants" (*claritas herborum*) is mostly due to the work of the ancients, who left nothing untried and who kept nothing secret. In contrast, Pliny laments that his contemporaries try to keep their herbal lore secret and so "to cheat life of others' benefits" (N.H. 25.1). As laudable as the ancients were in this respect, the highest praise goes to the gods for the munificence of Nature itself (N.H. 27.1).[10]

As remarkable as Nature's herbal medicines were, Pliny's credulity did have limits (N.H. 25.14ff.): reports by Xanthus and by Juba of drugs that brought men back to life "lack credence" (*fide carent*) but nevertheless fill us with admiration and compel us to admit that they contain "much truth" (*multum veri*). It is unclear to me what Pliny intends the reader to conclude from this confusing statement. In addition, man has only scratched the surface because most of the powers of plants are still unknown, and some of those known to the illiterate peasantry cannot be disseminated in writing because the peasantry is illiterate. The next chapter will offer a more detailed consideration of Pliny's concept of how useful knowledge is accumulated; here suffice it to say (1) that man's role is regarded as secondary to sacred Nature's; (2) that man's secondary role was largely filled by the ancients; (3) that the wisdom of the ancients consisted, for the most part, of knowledge of plants and other natural resources rather than craft skills; and (4) that in Pliny's view the circulation of knowledge was inhibited in his day by the greed of the professionals and by the illiteracy of peasants with hands-on experience.

On the surface it appears that Pliny anticipated the Smithian view of modern economics that trade could improve the standard of living for all those involved. But the Stoic premises of the bountifulness of divine Nature had a different implication as well: the bounty should not be tinkered with because the goal was not to improve Nature's gifts but to live in accord with Nature. As Wallace-Hadrill summarized Pliny's position, "any sort of compound is regarded by Pliny as unnatural and luxurious. The products of Nature are absolute and perfect in themselves. . . . It is human fraud and misplaced ingenuity that invented the workshops where compounds are made."[11] For example, the parent and "divine maker of things" (*divina rerum artifex*) did not make the wax salves; they were products of Man's ingenuity, his workshops motivated by greed (*avaritia*); Nature's works are "perfect"; concoctions serve luxury, not "well-being" (*salus*; N.H. 22.117–18). The most outrageous concoctions came from the Bithynian court of Mithridates: one antidote was "composed of 54 ingredients, no two having the same weight, and some as little as one-sixtieth of a denarius" (N.H. 29.24). As Mary Beagon suggested, in this respect Pliny voiced "a general feeling in the ancient world that it was permissible to understand but not to control Nature."[12]

In thinking through the economic implications of this philosophical foundation it is worth remembering R. J. Forbes's distinction between discovery and constructed artifacts in his classic study of ancient technology and engineering: "We often tend to forget the subtle distinction between discovery and invention. Man discovered only what already existed in Nature. . . . He did not change the form of these discoveries but took them as he found them, adapting them to his purposes in various ways. . . . But as soon as man used these objects or created something different from the materials of Nature, he had made something that had not existed before. Herein lies the difference between discovery and invention."[13] The Latin words *inventio* and *inventum* in the *Natural History* efface the distinction, but clearly Pliny was primarily interested in discovery; to the extent that he was suspicious of contrived artifacts to harness or to improve sacred Nature, his attitude would have been a disincentive to many forms of technical innovation. As we shall see in chapter 6, this attitude is in sharp contrast to his early modern successors in the encyclopedic tradition.

The *Natural History* exudes moral disapproval of what Pliny considered violations of or insults to Nature. One may see irony in the fact that where contemporary archaeologists and historians see technical sophistication in Roman mining, Pliny felt moral outrage at this transgression motivated by greed for precious metals.[14] It was acceptable to take what Nature openly offered on the surface but damned as a violation of Mother Nature to mine or quarry what was below the surface.[15] Pliny drew a curious distinction between all the manifold benefits Nature provided for Man elsewhere and the inviolate mountains not meant for Man's use.[16]

It is worth noting the charged language of Pliny's value-laden judgments. In disgust he reports the story that "the triumvir Antony used gold vessels to meet all his foul needs—a crime that shamed [*pudet*] even Cleopatra. . . . Antony alone by an insult [*contumelia*] to Nature lent cheapness to gold" (N.H. 33.50).[17] Pliny expressed strong moral condemnation of Marcus Lepidus (cos. 78 BCE) for similarly dishonoring a treasure of Nature: Lepidus used a block of Numidian marble as a door threshold in his house, described as a "very base use" (*vilissimus usus*; N.H. 36.49). These passages illustrate how the divinity of Nature pervades all its fabric to the point that a disgusting or demeaning use of an inanimate metal or stone could be interpreted as an unspeakable "insult" or a degrading use in a culture that deeply felt matters of honor and shame.[18]

Pliny's treatment of iron, a primary resource of Nature, rests on a moral binary contrasting its utility with its potential for harm:

> It serves as the best and worst tool of life, inasmuch as with it we plough the ground, plant trees, trim the trees that prop our vines, force the vines to renew their youth yearly by ridding them of decrepit growth; with it we build houses and quarry rocks, and we employ it for all other useful purposes, but we likewise use it for wars and slaughter and brigandage, and not only in hand-to-hand encounters but as a winged missile, now projected from catapults, now hurled by the arm, and now actually equipped with feathery wings, which I deem the most criminal artifice of man's genius, inasmuch as to enable death to reach human beings more quickly we have taught iron how to fly and have given it wings. Therefore, the blame [*culpa*] is not assigned to Nature. (N.H. 34.138)

The notion of iron flying through the air to kill is, in Pliny's view, a perverse inversion of the natural order that placed iron underground.[19] Having made his moral point, he adds a little practical information about iron, but only a little, and even less of his information would have been of use in practical applications. Hubert Zehnacker rightly points out the contrast between the extensive attention given by Pliny to precious metals and the cursory attention to iron, despite the latter's far greater importance in technical applications.[20]

Just as iron could be used for criminal purposes, so too poisonous herbs; and just as blame for the evil uses of iron should be assigned to humans and not to Nature, so too the blame for poisons belongs to humans (N.H. 18.2). Even poisonous honey was provided by Nature for humans' moral improvement—to make him "more cautious and less greedy" (N.H. 21.78). Pliny's moral rhetoric is well known: his lesson here is that humans should be restrained and decorous in the gifts they take from Nature.

The condemnation of luxury is perhaps the most consistent theme throughout the *Natural History*. Mary Beagon and Andrew Wallace-Hadrill have explored Pliny's ideas in detail; let me summarize here and offer just a few illustrations.[21] Pliny regards the urge to find novel luxuries to be the motive that is "the most efficacious and greatest force" (*efficacissima vis atque maxima*; N.H. 5.12) and is nearly universal in human nature, felt well beyond the borders of the Roman world: "yet Taprobane [Sri Lanka] even, isolated as it is by Nature from the rest of the world, is not exempt from our vices. Gold and silver are held in esteem even there. They have a marble which resembles tortoise-shell in appearance; this, as well as their pearls and precious stones, is highly valued; all our luxuries in fact, those even of the most exquisite nature, are there carried to the very highest pitch. They asserted that their wealth is much greater than ours, but admitted that we know better than they how to obtain real enjoyment from opulence" (N.H. 6.89).[22] Pliny seems to have had an obsession with pearls, alluded to in this passage: "no greater inroads have been made upon our morals, and no more rapid advances have been made by luxury, than those effected through the medium of shell-fish" (N.H. 9.104).

The condemnation of luxury has several dimensions. One is that audacious luxury is simply not in accord with Nature on account of its adulteration of pure natural elements to improve on Nature. So Pliny takes a particularly dim view of unguents and pigments: "luxury, delighted to have conquered Nature with unguents, also has challenged flowers which are esteemed for their color" (N.H. 21.45; see also 13.1).[23] Another famously unnatural combination, though more an adjacency than a mixture, was the luxury of serving oysters from the sea on snow from the mountains (N.H. 32.64). One taste for luxury had a detrimental impact on Nature that is familiar today. Pliny reports that the demand for ivory depleted the population of African elephants with large tusks (N.H. 8.7–8).[24]

A second dimension is that luxury was a violation of Nature in its sheer wasteful excess, regardless of whether the materials themselves were intrinsically exotic or ordinary and acceptable. Perfumes were the worst wastes because "they lose their scent at once, and die in the very hour when they are used" (N.H. 13.20). Although pottery in itself was not objectionable, Vitellius's gargantuan ceramic serving platter costing one million sesterces was unnatural.[25] Here are just a few colorful examples of unnatural excess scattered across the *Natural History* for condemnation. Aviaries in themselves are unnatural insofar as they confine birds, which Nature created to be free in the sky, and an outrageously crude and disgusting example of the abuse of birds for unnatural excess was attributed to the tragic actor Clodius Aesop. He served a casserole valued at 100,000 sesterces made up of songbirds and talking birds priced at 6,000 sesterces apiece; his motive was "no other pleasure [*suavitas*] than the desire to indulge in a sort of cannibalism in eating these birds, and not even showing any respect for that lavish fortune of his, even though won by his voice" (N.H. 10.141–42).

Aesop's excess luxury presumably took place in private; a public, equally macabre display of excess took place in the arena. Pliny expresses disapproval of expensive pigments in general and finds the use of these pigments especially perverse when decorating the

carts on which gladiators were transported to the arena. His conclusion, heavy with irony, was "we like gladiators going into the
fray to ride in splendor to the scene of their death or at least
slaughter [*caedes*]" (N.H. 35.49). Arenas drew more eyes for display of luxury than any other venue and so were the location for
luxurious display. One of Nero's extravagantly costly displays of
pointless excess was the use of rare amber to decorate the arms,
the funeral biers, all the equipment, and the nets protecting the
audience from the wild beasts (N.H. 37.45).

As Wallace-Hadrill has pointed out, another dimension of
Pliny's objection to luxury was its use for ostentatious display of
wealth and social inequality in contrast to the simpler and more
natural society of early Rome.[26] Pliny lamented that in his day
there were grades in quality of even ordinary foods based on class:
one kind of bread for the "rich" (*proceres*) and another for the
"common people" (*volgi*); the wealthy drank vintages of wine
older than they were (N.H. 19.53–55); and even water came in different forms for the wealthy and for the plebs. The most monumental examples of "stupid ostentation" (*stulta ostentatio*) were
the pyramids of the Egyptian pharaohs, monuments to their vanity (N.H. 36.75). The pyramids were permanent additions to the
landscape in contrast to one of Rome's most extravagant asser-
tions of status, M. Scaurus's temporary theater, for which he imported 360 monolithic columns and marble walls in 58 BCE as the
Republic was disintegrating. Pliny observes that the theater was
used for only a month or so, after which Scaurus took away the
decorative elements for his own Tusculan villa (N.H. 36.5, 36.50,
36.114–15). Pliny claims that this wild extravagance exceeded even
the "insanity" of Caligula and Nero and did more than anything
else to destroy the "morality" of the Roman people (N.H. 36.113).[27]
At least there was some poetic justice in the fact that Scaurus's
"angry slaves" burned down the villa, incurring a loss of 30,000,000
sesterces (N.H. 36.115).

The blame for extravagant luxury in the view of Pliny and other
Roman authors lay with the Greeks, who had the double misfortune

to suffer Roman conquest and then to be blamed for the corruption of the morals of their Roman conquerors. To that end, Pliny chronicled the import of various Greek luxuries with dates, items, and conquering commander: "It was this victory of Pompey over Mithridates that made fashion veer to pearls and gemstones. The victories of Lucius Scipio and Cnaeus Manlius had done the same for chased silver, garments of cloth of gold, and dining couches inlaid with bronze; and that of Mummius for Corinthian bronzes and fine paintings" (N.H. 37.12).[28]

Pliny's historical framework is one of deep ambivalence: an optimism that the Pax Romana has improved life for inhabitants of the empire through exchange and a pessimism that a primary urge for unproductive luxuries imported from the east has led to a decline in mores and a violation of Mother Nature. This ambivalence is most clearly expressed in Pliny's question at the beginning of Book 7: is Nature a *Parens* or a *Noverca*, a "step-mother"?[29]

> [In the animal kingdom] the first place will rightly be assigned to man, for whose sake great Nature seems to have created all other things—though she asks a cruel price for all her generous gifts, making it hardly possible to judge whether she has been a kind parent to man or a harsh stepmother. (N.H. 7.1)

In this chapter I have tried to describe Pliny's Stoic views of the economic implications of the Romans' relationship with Mother Nature, both positive and negative. His deference to Nature had the consequence that he regarded it as arrogant and improper for Man to attempt to know too much. He uses the adjective "impudent" (*improbus*) to describe Hipparchus's effort to inventory the stars in order to know which were born and which died (N.H. 2.95) and Eratosthenes's calculation of the circumference of the earth.[30]

Pliny's avowed aim was to compile a monumental list of "things worth knowing" about Nature in order to live in harmony with divine Nature. For him, an increase in useful knowledge was to be achieved by Roman acquisition of new territories with new and different natural resources. As Trevor Murphy put it, "If the natural phenomena of the world were the *Natural History*'s subject, it was ... the military, political, and commercial power of Rome that made the world available as material for the book."[31] But of course this scenario of the accumulation of additional discoveries was limited as Rome reached the outer bounds of imperial acquisition, just as the accumulation of additional booty was restricted as the prospects of new conquests diminished. There were still hidden resources to be discovered on land in India, Ethiopia, and Scythia, but in one sphere at least Pliny rather astonishingly thought that the Romans had exhausted all the discoveries to be made: while there were still terrestrial animals and birds to be discovered, all aquatic plants and animals were known—exactly 144 species in number (N.H. 32.142–43).

Pliny's concept of the addition of useful knowledge through discovery implied finite limits, which had been reached in the case of aquatic creatures. Here Forbes's distinction between discoveries and constructed artifacts is important insofar as the latter category has no limits imposed by Nature. As we shall see in the next chapter, Pliny has only a little to say about the latter.

4

Innovation and Economic Growth in the *Natural History*

SUSTAINED ECONOMIC growth requires innovation, which, if it is to continue indefinitely, requires a flow of additions to the stock of useful knowledge. Yet, as David Hume observed just before the beginning of the Industrial Revolution in *Of the Rise and Progress of the Arts and Sciences* (1742), "it is more easy to account for the rise and progress of commerce in any kingdom, than for that of learning; and a state, which should apply itself to the encouragement of the one, would be more assured of success, than one which should cultivate the other. Avarice, or the desire of gain, is an universal passion, which operates at all times, in all places, and upon all persons: But curiosity, or the love of knowledge, has a very limited influence, and requires youth, leisure, education, genius, and example, to make it govern any person."[1]

In the preceding chapter we explored Pliny's ideas about how the grandeur (*maiestas*) of the Roman Empire promoted "the rise and progress of commerce," which enriched (at least some segments of) the peoples under Roman rule.[2] This chapter focuses on Pliny's attitudes toward "new things" (*res novae*): his reports of inventions and inventors, his conception of how new discoveries were made, his reflections on what systemic factors nurtured and inhibited the addition of useful knowledge, and the implications of his 20,000 "things worth knowing" for a "culture of growth" in the Roman world. His ideas in some sense anticipated the quotation from Hume, and he lamented the degenerate values of his age that failed to nurture "the love of knowledge."

Joel Mokyr has been a leading proponent of the crucial role of culture in the early modern developments that set the stage for "the Great Enrichment" of the nineteenth century. In his view the institutional framework was important, but "the puzzle is that better markets, more cooperative behavior, and more efficient allocations simply do not in themselves account for modern economic growth. What is far harder to explain is the growth of technological creativity and innovation in Europe."[3] "Modern economic growth or 'the Great Enrichment' depended on a set of radical changes in beliefs, values, and preferences—a set I will refer to as 'culture.' . . . The fundamental belief that the human lot can be continuously improved by bettering our understanding of natural phenomena and regularities and the application of the understanding to production has been the cultural breakthrough that made what came after possible."[4] "And while most technological progress and productivity growth are very much the result of the slow and gradual accumulation of small changes . . . such small changes—or microinventions . . . —tend to run into diminishing returns after a while. What is needed is the injection of new ideas."[5] Smithian growth can be understood in terms of interactions between humans. Technological growth in terms of humans' beliefs and attitudes toward understanding natural regularities and exploiting them.[6] Given that Pliny's subject matter is Nature, and given that he catalogues major inventions and inventors, his *Natural History* would seem to be the obvious text in which to seek insights into Roman imperial culture regarding attitudes and practices generating innovation.

Following a geographical inventory of the Roman Empire in Books 3–6, Pliny turns to the animal kingdom in Books 7–11, beginning in Book 7 with humans as the center of Nature's creation.[7] Book 7 concludes with a lengthy list of inventions or discoveries (*inventa*) along with the men and women who discovered them

(N.H. 7.191–215)—a sort of inventors Hall of Fame.[8] By my count, it includes 166 inventions (excluding doublets and imports) by 136 inventors (including peoples such as the Egyptians and excluding alternatives for the same invention).

Some of the items would appear in a contemporary ranking of humanity's greatest discoveries and technical breakthroughs. For example, Pliny includes discoveries that we would identify with the Neolithic Revolution: the cultivation of grain, the domestication of oxen and horses, the cultivation of vines and trees. Pliny notes the revolutions in metal-working that archaeologists and prehistorians use to mark the Chalcolithic Age, the Bronze Age, and the Iron Age. Other inventions that formed the basis of the main sectors of ancient, non-agricultural production include pottery and the potter's wheel, the technologies of textile production, mining, construction, carpentry, and navigation. Pliny understands the fundamental importance of the invention of alphabetic writing and notes the sciences of astronomy and medicine. Altogether, Pliny clearly has an appreciation of the basic technologies that contributed to the standard of living in the Romans' advanced agricultural economy.

Pliny's range of inventions or discoveries extends well beyond our category of "technology" to the arts, to forms of social, political, and economic organization, to customs and symbols, and then to some items that can only be described as bizarre to the modern mind. Among artistic discoveries Pliny includes musical instruments such as the pipe, flute, and lyre, as well as forms of artistic performance such as singing while playing the harp. The social, political, and economic institutions on the list are an eclectic mix: exchange, trade, towns, slavery, treaties, tyranny, popular government, kingship, weights and measures. The list of customs and symbols is even more eclectic: the diadem, diluting wine with water, the practices of divination from victims and from birds, funeral games, wrestling, and ball-throwing. And then there are some truly weird (to my eye) novelties such as dancing in armor and daily shaving.[9]

What does this account of things invented or discovered reveal about how Pliny understood technical advances and economic production?[10] While identifying the fundamental technologies of prior ages, Pliny's conception of discovery is much broader, not limited to the technical and extending to the trivial. He does not think of *inventa* primarily in the way that Francis Bacon conceived of the accumulation of useful knowledge in the early seventeenth century.[11] Furthermore, in Pliny's inventory the very breadth of the discoveries makes the absences noteworthy: apart from astronomy there are no discoveries from physical sciences, which in the modern era have been essential for technical advances.

The chronological and ethnic distribution of the inventors is also revealing. Of the 136 inventors it is striking that 112 (82 percent) date from the prehistoric eras with at least 60 of those from the world of Greek myth; another 9 were from the Greek archaic age, 5 from classical Greece, 7 from the Hellenistic kingdoms, and *none* of the technical inventions from imperial Rome (I do not count daily shaving as a technical invention).[12] The Hellenistic inventions on this list are predominantly the oversized warships of tens, twelves, thirties, and forties—the larger ones an advertisement of royal status more than fighting efficiency.[13] Overall, it is striking that most, and certainly the most important technical advances on the list, were attributed to mythical heroes and gods.[14] The implication is that Pliny did not view the crucial steps in the history of technology as a progression based on human research and application, as Francis Bacon did.

The ethnic/geographical distribution of inventors was, not surprisingly, heavily concentrated in the Greek world, mythical or historical: some nine-tenths were Greek individuals or peoples. Among the remaining tenth Egyptians, Phoenicians, and peoples of Asia Minor predominate. Given the overwhelmingly male bias of classical culture, it is no surprise that the inventors are almost exclusively male, with the exceptions of Ceres, Arachne, and the Amazon Penthesilea, inventor of the battle-ax. As we shall see, Pliny records other, later inventions elsewhere in the *Natural*

History, but they are not the fundamental breakthroughs registered in the Hall of Fame in Book 7 where the Romans are conspicuous by their absence.[15]

The largest concentration of inventions after Book 7 comes, appropriately, in the books devoted to agriculture, the largest sector of the economy and the subject of a series of earlier agricultural treatises; these books are generally the ones with practical applications for improved productivity.[16] For cereal cultivation and processing Pliny notes the wheeled plow invented in Raetia (N.H. 18.172), the famous Gallic harvester (N.H. 18.296), and an Italian whetstone that could be used to sharpen scythes with water rather than oil (N.H. 18.261). The list of ways to grind grain includes the water mill, but Pliny also claims that most of Italy still uses a "bare pestle" (N.H. 18.97) and spelt is pounded by a pestle powered by "convicts in chains" (*pilo vinctorum poenali*; N.H. 18.112). In the realm of arboriculture Pliny has an interest in innovative grafting techniques: the art of grafting was a "chance discovery" (*casus*) by an anonymous farmer (N.H. 17.101) and long ago reached its "peak achievement" (*columen*; N.H. 15.57).[17] But improvements have recently been made with the employment of the Gallic augur (N.H. 17.116) and Columella's invention of a new method of grafting an olive branch to a fig tree (N.H. 17.137–38). The advice for picking and processing olives for oil includes a "new invention" for crushing (N.H. 15.5). Pliny offers a good deal of advice about viticulture and how to make it profitable (see chapter 5).[18] In addition to identifying wine regions and varietals, he describes a "new invention" for planting vine shoots (N.H. 17.162) and the Greek invention of the screw press (N.H. 18.317).[19] In general, despite his veneration of Cato, Pliny wishes to document "how much life has progressed" beyond the "few varieties" of grapes mentioned in the *De agricultura* 230 years before (N.H. 14.44–45).

Unlike the catalogue of inventions in Book 7, these scattered reports of agricultural *inventa* included some that were recent and by real humans. Their geographical origins from Gaul to Greece point to the advantages of dissemination through cultural exchange. But only the water mill amounts to a major break-through, and to it only eight words are devoted.[20] It is striking that Pliny pays much less attention to this non-organic source of energy than to Fulvius Lipinnus's invention for fattening snails (N.H. 9.173–74) or Columella's method of grafting an olive branch to a fig tree and his method for growing cucumbers year-round (N.H. 19.68).[21]

Perhaps the most noteworthy and useful development by the Romans came in the non-agricultural sector: the use of pozzolana to make *opus caementicium*.[22] Pliny attributes this "invention" (*commentum*) to *terra*, "Earth": "for who could sufficiently marvel at the fact that the most inferior portion of earth's substance, which is in consequence designated dust, on the hills of Pozzuoli, encounters the waves of the sea and as soon as it is submerged turns into a single mass of stone that withstands the attacks of the waves and becomes stronger every day, especially if it is mixed with broken quarry-stone from Cumae?" (N.H. 35.166). I have quoted Pliny's account of the discovery of pozzolana in full because it was probably the most consequential Roman technical development for the economy—a wonder to be credited to *terra* rather than to mankind or any specific inventor—and yet it still warrants fewer words than Columella's cucumber.

Among the other fundamentally useful inventions is the manu-facture of paper, *charta*, from papyrus on which cultural life (*humanitas vitae*), or certainly the memory of it, is based (N.H. 13.68).[23] Pliny gives one of his most extended accounts to explain how papyrus was made into a medium for writing (N.H. 13.68–83). Curiously, he cites Varro for the claim that this invention was the result of Alexander the Great's conquest of Egypt and foundation of Alexandria—a date that is wildly wrong by some three millennia (and a reminder that archaeology as a discipline is a modern invention). This error would seem to be a result of Pliny's bias toward attributing *inventa* to the Greeks.

For the invention of glass Pliny related a story (*fama*), the credibility of which he does not endorse but for which he offers no

alternative. Once a ship put in at Sidon; the merchants in prepara-
tion for cooking used lumps of *nitrum* from their cargo to support
the cooking pots; when the heated soda mixed with the sand on the
beach, a new liquid was formed—the unintended origin of glass. In
a familiar moralizing refrain Pliny adds that with the usual ingenuity
men started introducing other additives (N.H. 13.191–92).[24]

The uses of flax to make fabrics provoke deep ambivalence in
Pliny. On the positive side, after remarking on the violence of the
sea, he asks "by what greater ingenuity of men has nature been
aided than by sails and oars?" (N.H. 32.1). And yet earlier in Book
19 the invention of the flax sail is pointedly condemned: "no curse
[*exsecratio*] is sufficient for the inventor of [the flax sail]. . . . Who
was not content that man should die on land?" (N.H. 19.6).[25] Invention carries risks, which are exaggerated by Pliny's moral rhetoric.

Pliny devotes much attention to firsts in the fine and decorative
arts.[26] Artists are honored by inclusion in Book 7's inventors' Hall
of Fame and are also named in later books. For example, Pheidias
is called out as the first to have made embossed sculptures (N.H.
34.54). Carvilius Pollio developed the technique of cutting tortoise shells to decorate bedsteads and cabinets—"a man of prodigious and clever talent for the utensils of luxury" (*luxuriae instrumenta*; N.H. 9.39). Pasiteles was the first to make mirrors of silver
to improve the reflecting quality (N.H. 33.130). Other firsts are
recorded without the names of the inventors: the novelty of placing honorary statues on arches (N.H. 34.27) and the Claudian and
Neronian novelties of painting marble and accenting marble sur-
faces with different colored marbles (N.H. 35.3).[27] The latter practice is attributed with typical acerbic irony to luxury's wish to
improve on Nature's gift of the mountains to ensure that as much
value as possible will perish in fires. Two general points are worth
observing about the *inventa* in the arts. In contrast to the more
mundane urban crafts, the fine and luxury decorative arts bring
honor to the individual artist, making him or her deserving of recognition by name. Second, Pliny's accounts of artists in the *Natural History* beyond the list in Book 7 are mostly found in Books

33–36 on metals, pigments, and stones. Pliny finds the creation of aesthetic works out of these natural materials more estimable than the creation of ordinary goods through the improvement of productive technology.

Along with fundamental discoveries of the distant past and artistic firsts the *Natural History* includes inventions in culinary and other assorted luxuries. With foods as with other products Pliny's position is "simple is most useful" (*utilissimus simplex*; N.H. 11.282), and he laments that nothing is neglected for the sake of "man's stomach" (*hominis ventri*); consequently, flavors are mixed, imported from India, Egypt, Crete, Cyrene, every land, and some are even "poisons" (*veneficia*; N.H. 15.105). Some of the gourmet inventions would find a place on contemporary menus—for example, foie gras, whose inventor is uncertain. But Pliny knows who invented the grilling of the soles of geese feet: Messalinus Cotta (N.H. 10.52). The master inventor in the realm of culinary luxury was of course Apicius, "who thought it especially desirable for mullets to be killed in a sauce made of their own companions, garum" (N.H. 9.66).[28] The Delians get credit for the discovery of how to fatten hens (N.H. 10.139). Of course, it was the Romans who raised pisciculture to a very sophisticated art: Sergius Orata invented the oyster pond (N.H. 9.168); Fulvius Lippinus invented the snail pond and a recipe for fattening snails with reduced new wine and spelt; and (according to Varro) the "glory" of the art of fattening snails achieved the magnitude of a single snail shell large enough to hold 80 quadrantes, about 11 liters (N.H. 9.173–74). One can sympathize with Pliny's irony in highlighting the Romans' *gloria* in culinary advances.[29]

Reports of other sorts of luxurious inventions are spread across the other books. The Persians are said to have invented unguents, the most evanescent of luxuries (N.H. 13.3). Pausias of Sicyon in collaboration with Glycera wins credit for being the first to mix flowers of different colors in garlands (N.H. 21.4). Of more notable impact was the invention by Pamphile of Cos of the process for making silk, the "glory" of which was to make women appear naked while dressed in clothing.[30] Similarly, Pliny sees moral perversity in the invention of veneers—a luxury that originated in the effort to disguise cheaper woods with more expensive, but then evolved in Neronian times to application of a veneer of tortoise shell painted to look like wood (N.H. 16.232–33). And then there was the monumental insanity "invented" by Curio in 52 BC, the pair of revolving theaters, a product of his ingenuity (N.H. 36.116–17).

This broad, but by no means exhaustive, list of inventions/discoveries in the *Natural History* can serve as a basis for analyzing Pliny's conception of the process of *inventio*. One can imagine a spectrum of possibilities from (1) accidental discovery to (2) deliberate observation to (3) systematic observation to (4) experimentation designed as a test of theory to (5) a planned feedback loop from experimentally validated theory to application.[31] As we shall see in chapter 6, the early modern encyclopedists, John Harris and Ephraim Chambers, viewed their compilations as platforms for future invention. Did Pliny's conception of *inventio* conceive of the *Natural History* in a similar way? Was this the "usefulness" (*utilitas*) that he professed to be his goal?

Pliny asserts that the two principal sources of discovery are the gifts of divine Nature (the gods) and chance (*casus*), both of which conceive of humans as passive beneficiaries of good fortune.[32] Recall that the discovery of pozzolana to make *opus caementicium* was a gift of Nature. The uses of plants for medicinal purposes that take up so much of the *Natural History* are collectively characterized as "the enormous and mysterious work of divinity" (*opus ingens occultumque divinitatis*; N.H. 19.189). How did Pliny reconcile this idea with his "admiration for men of old"? "The greater the number of plants waiting to be described, the more one is led to revere the careful research of the ancients and their kindness in passing on the results. Without a doubt even the bounteousness of Nature herself might seem to have been surpassed by them in this way *if the discoveries had been the result of human endeavor*. But as it is, it is clear that this bounteousness has been the work of the gods, even when the actual discoverer was a man" (N.H. 27.1–2). How this might happen is illustrated by the "discovery" of one cure for rabid dog bite that is attributed to an *oraculum*: "Recently the mother of a man serving in the praetorian guard saw in a dream how she sent to her son to be taken in drink the root of the wild rose, called *cynorrhodon*, which by its appearance had attracted her the day before in a shrubbery" (N.H. 25.17). In other cases, animals reveal remedies to humans, and "anyone who believes that these discoveries could, by chance, have been made by a man, he shows himself to be ungrateful [*ingrate*] for the gods' gifts [*munera deorum*]" (N.H. 27.6).

Prefacing his story about the discovery of how to graft vines with the comment that chance (*casus*) is more often the teacher than Nature, Pliny tells of the careful farmer who in building a fence put a base of ivy wood beneath the fence post and discovered that the ivy came to grow from the post (N.H. 17.101). Of a more trivial nature, it was by mistake that a craftsman discovered (*invenisse*) the process of dyeing cloth a second time with Tyrian purple, thus layering one luxury on another (N.H. 9.140).[33] It is not clear that Pliny's views about the gods and chance being the sources of discovery/invention are consistent and coherent, but it is clear that he does not emphasize individual human initiative as a primary source.

For Pliny the most amazing discovery was that goat's blood could crack diamonds, the hardest of substances. He asks, "To whose *inventio* or by what chance (*casu*) was this discovered? What inference could have led anyone to use the foulest of creatures for testing a thing of immense cost. Such an *inventio* belongs to the divine spirits (*numina*) as well as every such gift (*munus*). Nor is reason (*ratio*) to be sought in any part of nature; rather, will (*voluntas*)" (N.H. 37.60).[34] This statement coheres with the *Natural History*'s compilation of more than 20,000 discrete "facts" and has fundamentally important implications for Pliny's notion of how technical progress happens. For if there is no *ratio* or systematic knowledge to understand the natural world, no regularities, only mysteries revealed by chance, it is not possible to design programs of research to manipulate it. The best one can do—and what Pliny aims to do—is to catalogue past chance discoveries to avoid losing them. Given the abundant generosity of Nature, there remain more plants to happen upon because Nature creates nothing "without some more obscure cause" (*sine aliqua occultiore causa*; N.H. 22.1).[35]

Pliny recognizes the value of personal observation, autopsy, but the sheer scope of his work made it impossible for him personally to observe most of his "things worth knowing." G.E.R. Lloyd has pointed out that his claims of autopsy are usually connected with marvels (*mirabilia*) and do not suggest "sustained or systematic researches into more mundane problems."[36] And it goes without saying that he did not take the next step of a program of controlled experimentation—something that not even the leading Greek scientists such as Theophrastus undertook.[37]

Pliny commented on the scarcity of investigation and discovery in his day and offered a systemic explanation that anticipated modern-day economic historians.[38] Taco Terpstra, for example, has recently argued that technical innovation stalled in the Roman Empire because in contrast to the competition between Hellenistic kingdoms that spurred royal financial support for scientists and engineers, the emperors of the Pax Romana did not feel the heat of competition with nearby kingdoms. Nor did Roman emperors provide the kind of patronage for scientists and engineers that Chinese emperors did.[39] As Stahl noted with regard to the earlier Hellenistic era, "not until modern times was research to experience such bountiful support from government funds."[40]

In Books 2 and 14 Pliny pointed to the lack of competition under the Pax Romana as a cause for a lack of interest in "investigation" (*inquisitio*). Noting the number of Greek authors making meteorological observations, Pliny writes:

> this makes me wonder all the more that, although when the world was at variance, and split up into kingdoms, that is, sundered limb from limb, so many people devoted themselves to

these abstruse researches, especially when wars surrounded them and hosts were untrustworthy, and also when rumors of pirates, the foes of all mankind, terrified intending travelers— so that now-a-days a person may learn some facts from the notebooks of people who have never been there more truly than from the knowledge of natives—yet now in these glad times of peace under an emperor who so delights in literature [*literae*] and knowledge [*artes*], no addition whatever is being made to knowledge by means of original research [*nova inqui-sitio*], and in fact even the discoveries of our predecessors are not being thoroughly studied. The rewards were not greater when the ample successes were spread out over many students, and in fact the majority of these made the discoveries in question with no other reward at all save the consciousness of ben-efiting posterity. Age has overtaken the character of mankind, not their profits, and now that every sea has been opened up and every coast offers a hospitable landing, an immense multi-tude goes on voyages—but their object is profit [*lucrum*], not knowledge [*scientia*]; and in their blind focus on avarice they do not reflect that *scientia* is safer. (N.H. 2.117–18)[41]

Pliny's claim here that nothing at all is added by new investiga-tion is hyperbole, contradicted elsewhere in the *Natural History*, but it contains an important element of truth. Terpstra and Scheidel, along with a number of early modern historians, have underlined the energizing effects of a fragmented state system in the late Middle Ages and early modern period that required com-petition for survival.[42] One of the most explicit manifestations of this competition was the emergence in the late seventeenth century of a genre of works on political economy (e.g., William Petty's *Political Arithmetick*) to measure national economic resources and to increase them against competitor states—something for which there was no Roman parallel.[43]

Pliny returns in Book 14 to the theme of decline in the additions to the stock of knowledge and loss of ancient discoveries.

There is one thing I cannot sufficiently wonder—that of some trees the very memory has perished, and even the names recorded by authors have passed out of knowledge. For who would not admit that now that intercommunication has been established throughout the world by the grandeur [*maiestas*] of the Roman Empire, life has been advanced by the interchange of commodities and by partnership in the blessings of peace, and that even things that had previously lain concealed have all now been established in general use? Still, it must be asserted, we do not find people acquainted with much that has been handed down by the writers of former days: so much more productive was the research of the ancients [*prisci*], or else so much more successful was their industry, when a thousand years ago at the dawn of literature Hesiod began putting forth rules for agriculture, and not a few writers followed him in this concern [*cura*]—which has been a source of more toil to us, inasmuch as nowadays it is necessary to investigate not only subsequent discoveries but also those that had already been made by the men of old, because general slackness has decreed an utter destruction of records. And for this fault who can discover other causes than the general movement of affairs in the world? The fact is that other customs have come into vogue, and the minds of men are occupied about other matters: the only forms of knowledge [*artes*] that are cultivated are those of avarice. Previously a nation's sovereignty was self-contained, and consequently the people's genius was also circumscribed; and so a certain barrenness of fortune made it necessary to exercise the gifts of the mind, and innumerable kings received the honor of the *artes*, and put these riches in the front place when displaying their resources, believing that through these they could prolong their immortality. This was the reason why the rewards of life and also its achievements were then so abundant. But later generations have been positively handicapped by the expansion of the world and by our multiplicity of resources. (N.H. 14.2–4)[44]

I want to highlight several points in this passage. As elsewhere, Pliny recognizes the value of empire in enabling trade, hence Smithian growth through comparative advantage. Here he notes that the accumulation of knowledge makes it more and more challenging to preserve the knowledge of the ancients like Hesiod and to add new discoveries (a theme echoed by the early modern encyclopedists, as we shall see). That structural reason, however, is only part of Pliny's explanation. He also looks to the better past of smaller kingdoms when rulers were honored for their sponsorship of new knowledge and blames the current decline on the moral failing of greed, which pushes men in other directions for enrichment (see p. 53).[45]

The theme of decline of investigation and discovery was part of a more general tale of decline with the result that Vespasian found himself dealing with "a tired state of affairs" (*fessis rebus*; N.H. 2.18). Of course, the narrative of decline was as old as Greco-Roman civilization, but in this case there may be some coarse-grained empirical evidence to corroborate it. Paul Keyser and Georgia Irby-Massie's *Encyclopedia of Ancient Natural Scientists: The Greek Tradition and Its Many Heirs* (2008) assembles a convenient database of 1,014 scientists, making it possible to examine their chronological distribution over more than a millennium of ancient Mediterranean civilization. The distribution of the entries is depicted in a graph entitled "Number of scientists (with 'narrow' date-ranges) per generation."[46] Supporting Pliny's claim, it shows a peak in the competitive Hellenistic era of the late fourth century BCE, another lower peak in the second quarter of the first century CE, and a decline in the later first and the second centuries CE. The authors hypothesize that "the decline [dating from the Hadrianic period] seems due to the centralization of political power under Hadrian and abolition of semi-autonomous polities throughout the Mediterranean world, with the consequent loss of a context within which science would flourish."[47] But in fact the peak, celebrated by Pliny, was reached centuries before Hadrian.

If one looks more closely at the distribution by century of only the mathematicians and engineers ("mechanics"), excluding the physicians whom Pliny thought to be frauds, the picture can be clearly seen in Figure 5: the number per century during the Hellenistic era was more than 35, in contrast to the first century CE with only 12.[48] One might wonder whether the observable scarcity in the later first and second centuries CE could be due to the fact that Pliny was no longer available as a source for reporting names, but that cannot be the explanation for two reasons. First, the decline in numbers starts long before Pliny wrote and cannot be attributed to the absence of Pliny as a source; second, an examination of Keyser and Irby-Massie's database shows that Byzantine authors, not Pliny, were the predominant sources of the names in the inventory before and after Pliny's day and could have reported Roman imperial figures after Pliny's death, had they existed.

It appears that Pliny had reason to bemoan the decline of investigation (*inquisitio*), which was an essential ingredient in the culture of growth in early modern Europe. The reason to make this point is that it is often said that it is anachronistic to compare early modern growth with the more anemic performance of the Roman imperial economy,[49] but it is not an anachronism or teleological insofar as Pliny made a similar observation about lack of research and enrichment based on technical advances.

Any assessment of a "culture of growth," to use Mokyr's phrase, is bound to be descriptive rather than quantitative. What indicators can be found in the *Natural History*? Who were the cultural heroes to inspire the next generation? What did Pliny consider to be the motivating sources of enrichment? Were those sources primarily rent-seeking or productive in a feedback loop from propositional knowledge to application? More generally, did Pliny have an optimistic, progressive view?

A search for seventeenth-century cultural heroes to be emulated turns up obvious figures from the field of science: as a result of his achievements in mathematics and physics Isaac Newton became venerated in his own lifetime as "the incomparable

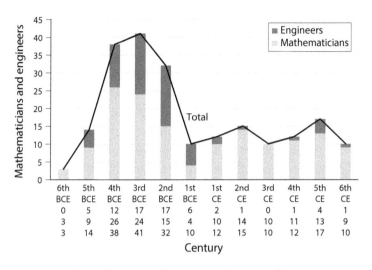

	6th BCE	5th BCE	4th BCE	3rd BCE	2nd BCE	1st BCE	1st CE	2nd CE	3rd CE	4th CE	5th CE	6th CE
	0	5	12	17	6	2	1	0	1	1	4	1
	3	9	26	24	15	4	10	14	10	11	13	9
	3	14	38	41	32	10	12	15	10	12	17	10

Century

FIG. 5. Attested ancient mathematicians and engineers by century.

Mr. Newton."[50] Who were the celebrities worthy of adulation and emulation in the *Natural History*, those who in Valérie Naas's phrase were "men beyond the ordinary"?[51] Mary Beagon observes that the most highly respected Roman figures in Pliny's view came from the realm of politics and warfare.[52] The elder Cato's authority receives praise, and as the best farmer (*optimus agricola*) he is regarded as a source of gems of wisdom (*oracula*) in agricultural matters (N.H. 14.44). Though his wisdom was two centuries old, he was cited far more often than recent agronomists. Pliny singles out Scipio Nasica for having been selected by the Senate as the best man (*optimus vir*; N.H. 7.120).[53] The dictator Caesar's greatness was assessed ambivalently: on the one hand, he was the "very most outstanding in vigor of mind" (*animi vigore praestantissimum*); on the other hand, his killing of 1,192,000 victims in battle was "an insult to the human race."[54]

The men who "shone" in the "knowledge of the various arts" (*variarum artium scientia*) include Berosus (third century BCE) in astronomy; Apollodorus in philology; Hippocrates (fifth to fourth century BCE), Cleombrotus, Critobulus, and Asclepiades (second to first century BCE) in medicine; Archimedes (third century BCE) in geometry and mechanics; Chersiphron (sixth century BCE), Philo (third century BCE), and Ctesibius (third century BCE) in engineering; Dinochares in surveying; and in the visual arts Apelles and others (N.H. 7.123–25). As in the list of inventors later in Book 7, these stars in *scientia* were Greek, not Roman, and from the distant past.[55] Even in the realm of military technical advances no Roman inventor appears (N.H. 7.200–202).[56]

The institution of chattel slavery meant that the Romans put a monetary value on human talent or capital. Pliny takes note of the highest-priced slaves and their skills in Book 7: in the past it was Daphnis, the *grammaticus*, and in his own time an actor and a eunuch (N.H. 7.128–29). The implied historical narrative is one of degeneration from an age that valued literary knowledge to one that valued entertainment and exotic sexuality. Prices for slaves as reported by Pliny do not reflect a high premium placed on technical knowledge.

The exception to the relatively modest value placed on technical knowledge were doctors, who in the Julio-Claudian age were among the most visible celebrities and commanded huge salaries from the emperors and other wealthy aristocrats. Pliny deplores the fact that "no actor, no driver of a three-horse chariot, was attended by greater crowds than Crinas of Massilia as he walked abroad in public, when he united medicine with another art, being rather careful and god-fearing [*cautior religiosiorque*], and regulated the diet of patients by the motions of the stars according to the almanacs of the astronomers, keeping watch for the proper times, and outstripped Thessalus in authority. Recently he left ten million [sesterces as an inheritance]" (N.H. 29.9). For Pliny those overpaid doctors were the faux-heroes who deserved the elder Cato's scathing warning to his son to avoid (N.H. 29.14), and he blamed them above all for the "decline of morals" (*lues morum*) of his day, validating Cato as a prophet (*vates*; N.H. 29.27).

Altogether, Pliny's lists of cultural heroes include no one comparable to "the incomparable Mr. Newton"—that is, no recent

Roman scientist. Moreover, Pliny complained that his own effort at preserving treasured knowledge from the past was not respected; indeed it was ridiculed. "Who could not with justice censure modern ways? The cost of living has been increased by luxuries and extravagance; never has there been more zest for life or less care taken of it. . . . Moreover, most people actually ridicule [*inrisui*] me for carrying on research in these matters, and I am accused of busying myself with trifles [*frivoli operis*]" (N.H. 22.14–15).[57] It is true that the younger Pliny reported that his uncle was offered 400,000 HS for his notebooks, but in spite of this the elder Pliny describes his contemporary culture as one without much respect for contributing to useful knowledge and emulating great scientists.

Altogether, Pliny thought of the dominant culture of individual and state enrichment primarily in terms of trade, rent-seeking, and predation, rather than in terms of innovation and capital investment in manufacturing. Pliny's ideas about real growth from trade were described in chapter 3.[58] The concept of rent-seeking encompasses behaviors that attempt to increase one's own wealth at the expense of another's without creating new wealth. A clear example would be legacy-hunting, which Pliny and other Roman moralists claimed to be rampant and the most lucrative pursuit (*captatio in quaestu fertilissimo*; N.H. 14.5).[59] The ultra-wealthy imperial freedmen listed in Book 33.134–38 must have made their fortunes through rent-seeking in their administrative and advisory roles, as did the imperial slave Drusillanus, who served dinner on a one-ton set of silver platters (N.H. 33.145). Pliny saw in human nature an urge for honors and greed for riches to be achieved through wars and slaughter for land, and the Romans were the quintessential predators (N.H. 2.174).[60] Pliny devoted attention to fame acquired through the greatest works of art in different genres; as Isager points out, they were the works of Greek artists that came to Rome as booty, much of which was displayed in triumphs.[61] Recounting Pompey's extravagant triumph of 61 BCE, Pliny concluded "austerity was defeated and more truly luxury triumphed" (*severitate victa et veriore luxuriae triumpho*; N.H. 37.14). Pliny also noted the columns and obelisks brought to Rome and displayed as symbols of victory (N.H. 36.44–45).[62] Overall, to the extent that Pliny expresses a "culture of growth," it is largely growth through conquest, rent-seeking, and trade.

Conclusion

In an essay on innovation in the Roman world Miko Flohr laid out the case for a "culture of innovation" based on texts such as Pliny's *Natural History* and material evidence for a more comfortable standard of living. In addition to the increasing use of the water mill, Flohr highlights the invention of *opus caementicium* for construction, molded pottery production, improved mining techniques enabling the manufacture of more metal products, and glass-blowing. The last of these originated in the eastern Mediterranean in the first century BCE and was widely disseminated to become the "key innovation in the material culture of the Roman Empire." The increased mining of lead allowed for its much wider use in pipes, cauldrons, and other artefacts. The availability of concrete, together with the arch and standardization of building materials, made possible the infrastructure and monumental appearance of Roman cities. While I recognize the increases in material culture summarized by Flohr, it does not seem to me that a comprehensive reading of Pliny's *Natural History* provides evidence of a "culture of innovation." Flohr points to Pliny's list of great inventions and neglects to observe that not one of the technical innovations in that list is Roman, nor does he note that Pliny saw lack of competition as the cause of a decline of investigation.[63]

A comprehensive reading shows that the *Natural History* anticipated Hume's principal points in this chapter's opening quotation. Pliny believed that greed was a primary human motivation incentivizing trade and that learning old things and discovering new were sadly lacking in his day. He was in all likelihood right in that assessment: there were incremental technical improvements but very few major breakthroughs, given the size, duration, and sophistication of the Roman Empire.[64] Whereas the eighteenth-century encyclopedists were enthusiastic about the prospects for progress, Pliny expressed mixed views. On the one hand, he thought the peoples under Roman rule were better-off for the benefits from Rome, their "second sun"; on the other hand, he believed that the moral decline brought back to Rome from foreign conquests had infected many domains of knowledge and skill. "Sloth has destroyed the arts" (*artes desidia perdidit*; N.H. 35.5); painting is a "dying art" (*moriens ars*; N.H. 35.19); the best artists in silver working lived long ago.[65] The very idea of technical progress was doubtful: as Isager put it, "in [Pliny's] opinion Man long ago went outside this framework [of knowledge of Nature] in his determination to satisfy egoistic need (*luxuria, avaritia*). In this context technological progress becomes pejorative and indefensible, for it fails to serve any human consideration."[66] Pliny observed a decline even in human stature: "it is almost observable that the whole race of mortals is becoming smaller by the day with offspring rarely taller than their fathers" (N.H. 7.73).[67] It seems that in the most literal sense the *Natural History* does not convey a "culture of growth." It is probably futile to try to assemble all of Pliny's scattered comments about progress and decline into a logical, coherent whole, but his aim to preserve ancient knowledge from loss is consistent with his concern about decline. The contrast with his successors in the encyclopedic tradition will be obvious in chapter 6.

Excursus: Aulus Gellius on Pliny and the Culture of Authoritative Knowledge

Aulus Gellius (c. 125–after 180) was "the earliest and most important instance of the reception of Pliny the Elder," providing testimony to the place of the *Natural History* in the imperial culture of authoritative knowledge and prestige in the three or four generations after Pliny's death. Gellius's *Attic Nights* is a good source for identifying the profiles of the cultural heroes of the Pax Romana, because Gellius's "cultural, historical and literary knowledge is always accompanied by some commentary or value judgment on it."[68] Leofranc Holford-Strevens suggests that Gellius's narratives not be read as a literal recounting of events but for their verisimilitude in representing the symposium culture of the High Empire.[69] Gellius's vignettes depicting encounters of learned men display the values that motivated the mastery of certain kinds of knowledge and invite comparison with the salons and societies of seventeenth- and eighteenth-century Europe that were integral to the circulation of knowledge in the Republic of Letters and to Joel Mokyr's "culture of growth." What learned men garner Gellius's superlatives? What is the nature of the scholarly exchanges in the vignettes? What are the cultural values expressed in the narratives, and with what vocabulary?

As the earliest surviving commentator on the *Natural History*, Gellius expresses a distinct ambivalence in his assessment of Pliny. He is described as "a man endowed with great authority in his time on account of his talent and standing" and as the "most learned man of his age."[70] On the other hand, Gellius reports that Pliny includes tales (*fabulae*) that are beyond belief and failed to identify a false argument.[71] Leofranc Holford-Strevens and Joseph Howley see Gellius positioning himself as a critical reader in contrast to Pliny, "the industrious but uncritical compiler" who includes "excessive *mirabilia* [marvels]."[72]

Gellius is less ambiguous in his assessments of other men of learning. From a past era M. Terentius Varro stands out as the most learned, followed by P. Nigidius.[73] Among the foremost cultural heroes of his own day is Favorinus, the sophist and polymath, whose multifarious expositions extended to the virtues of breast-feeding.[74] Holford-Strevens characterized Gellius's depiction of Favorinus as "the best of company, the delight of his friends and followers whom he led as if tethered to his tongue."[75] Other oratorical stars highlighted in the *Attic Nights* include Herodes Atticus for his authority, articulateness, and elegance (*gravitas, copia, elegantia*) and in an earlier generation Cicero and Hortensius for their outstanding brilliance (*clarior*).[76]

Among the specific categories of highly esteemed experts the grammarians appear most often in the *Attic Nights*. While many *grammatici* are denigrated in the vignettes, others are held up for praise. Above all, Sulpicius Apollinaris, Gellius's teacher, is recognized for his "outstanding knowledge of literature."[77] Valerius Probus is praised in similar words;[78] Sinnius Capito and L. Aelius Stilo are described as "most learned" (*doctissimus*).[79] More interesting is the language with which Gellius describes Terentius Scaurus, who is a most celebrated *grammaticus* (*nobilissimus*), and Julius Hyginus, who conversely is "by god not the least celebrated *grammaticus*" (*non hercle ignobilis*).[80] The attribution of honor stands in sharp contrast to the low regard that Gellius has for most *grammatici*.

Gellius also highlights philosophers, rhetors, historians, poets, jurists, and doctors for laudatory assessments using words such as "most eloquent" (*facundissimus*), "celebrated" (*celebratus*), "wisest" (*sapientissimus*), "foremost" (*princeps*), "most famous" (*inclutissimus*), "distinguished" (*inlustris*), and "most thoughtful" (*prudentissimus*). Book 17.21 presents a chronology of distinguished men (*inlustres viri*) from the founding of Rome to the Second Punic War. That list is heavy on political and literary figures with only slight attention to scientists. All in all, Gellius's cultural heroes are mainly distinguished for their literary learning and verbal skills.

Gellius portrays dramatic verbal encounters and interactions among these learned men. Many of the episodes are congenial dinner parties or symposia; others are chance meetings.[81] Gellius narrates the interactions as agonistic with the honor of the participants at stake. Robert Kaster neatly summarized the antagonistic encounters:

In anecdote after anecdote Gellius shows that whatever their claims or pretensions, most grammarians were nonetheless neither scholars nor gentlemen. Their main claims to cultural

standing—their control of the language, and especially their
rules—are repeatedly deflated, and their intellectual failure is
usually combined with ethical lapse and social catastrophe. The
grammarian who misguidedly trusts in his skill and arrogantly
claims center stage is reduced to "blushing and sweating" before his betters. . . . Yet such vignettes tell only part of the story.
They report easy victories over faceless grammarians, but they
do not convey the importance that Gellius attributed to grammar itself. That was a serious business for Gellius, as he demonstrates not only in his insistent attacks on the grammarians . . .
but also in the high proportion of chapters that are devoted to
grammatical questions. . . . Accordingly, heroes must be sum-
moned up to show how it should be done and to put the villains
to rout; and the hero himself can be a grammarian, provided he
is the right sort—a good grammarian, like Gellius's teacher,
Sulpicius Apollinaris.[82]

The touches of affect in the narrative heighten the drama of
victory and defeat in the pursuit of status. For example, in a vignette
centered on the meaning of *praeterpropter* ("more or less") at
Fronto's house a well-known grammarian is asked the meaning of
the word; he replies that it is "hardly worthy of the honor of investigation" since it is a "plebeian" word used by "workmen" (*opifices*).
In a raised voice Fronto challenges the grammarian by pointing
out that the word was used by Cato, Varro, and Ennius; the company of learned men laugh at the grammarian, who, red-faced,
retreats in humiliation.[83] The cultural hero, Fronto, establishes his
superiority by his intimate knowledge of elite Latin literature (not
by an assertion of the irrelevance of the social standing of the user).
"*Auctoritas* [authority in matters of Latinity] is the highest principle
in Gellius's eye, neither *ratio* nor *consuetudo* can take its place."[84]

The characters in these stories act out the values of honor and
humiliation in a hierarchical society in which ignorance is shameful and rustic. Gellius's stated purpose in writing the *Attic Nights*
was to save men from "a base and rustic ignorance of things and

words," from dishonor in a world in which erudition is honorable" (*honestae*) and lack of "cultural literacy" is "dishonorable" (*indecorum*).[85] This is a world divided between those who speak "properly" (*integre*) and those who speak in the language of the plebeian herd (*in plebe vulgaria*); a world in which the misuse of the word *penus* ("household stores") is not just wrong but "base" (*turpe*) and associated with the slave market.[86]

These performances of values reinforcing the social hierarchy are in several respects the antithesis of those of the scientific societies of the seventeenth and eighteenth centuries. The preface of the *Attic Nights* asserts that the purpose of the work is to lead the reader to "serious consideration of the useful arts" (*utilium artium contemplationem*).[87] The usefulness lies in establishing a social identity superior to the craftsmen and farmers, whose language is vulgar and shameful—that is, performances articulating separation from the working world. The expert knowledge that yields victory in these agonistic exchanges is textual. Whereas Pliny did not sort out the contradictions in his views that, on the one hand, he was compiling "things worth knowing" for rustics (*agrestes*) and craftsmen (*opifices*) and, on the other, these workers were illiterate and vulnerable to foolishness, Gellius was consistent in his contempt for the working class. Chapter 6 will show just how much the values embodied in the cultural heroes changed by the age of the early English encyclopedists.

5

Pliny's Economic Observations and Reasoning

THE QUESTION of the presence or absence of "economic rationality" in the ancient world has provoked an ongoing debate over the past century. Did the Greeks and Romans develop sophisticated systems of analysis to make decisions in order to maximize efficiency and return on investments measured in strictly monetary terms? What tools of analysis were at their disposal to make those judgments? The debate has not reached a conclusion because, as so often in ancient economic history, the evidence is fragmentary, and there is no agreement on the conceptualization of the problem. In a major contribution Dominic Rathbone examined the extensive accounts from the Heroninus estate in Roman Egypt, but even with all this documentation the historian lacks direct evidence of how the managers in the central office of the vast estate made their decisions.[1] With the conceptualization open to debate, the question has sometimes been unhelpfully presented as a binary—either rational or non-rational—rather than a matter of bounded rationality in a context of particular cultural values.

The *Natural History* contains a number of economic observations and examples of financial reasoning that shed light on this question, some of which have been cited by historians. Collectively, they do not amount to a coherent system of economic thought, but they do provide insights into how a high-level equestrian functionary with financial responsibilities reasoned in the economic domain.[2] As Mary Beagon put it, Pliny "offers a valuable insight into the mind of a more typical member of the educated Roman élite. These were absorbers rather than the innovators, for whom aspects of Greek learning and philosophy were worked into the fabric of their everyday lives, forming a backdrop of general principles and assumptions, rather than a platform for rigourous intellectual exploration."[3] This chapter will analyze Pliny's scattered comments in several sectors of the economy: primarily agriculture but also mining, urban crafts, and trade. Then we will turn to some general themes that draw the attention of the contemporary discipline of economics: labor, agency, and slavery; prices and currency; investment and consumption; finally, trust and fraud.[4] To the extent that we find that Pliny's ideas and preoccupations differ from those of modern capitalism, the point is not to blame him for a lack of economic rationality but to show how his thought was framed by different values and a bounded rationality.

Agricultural Economics

Agriculture holds the central place in the *Natural History*, not only in its position in the work as a whole but also in its comprehensiveness, systematicity, and practicality of treatment. Agriculture was of course the primary sector of production in the Roman imperial economy, and Pliny's work reflects that. At the end of the final book (N.H. 37.202), Pliny celebrates Italy as the world's best endowed and most productive land, offering "grain, wine, olive oil, wool, linen, cloth, and young cattle." The emphasis here is on the products of agriculture and not the output of urban manufacture, which receives only occasional attention elsewhere (see pp. 93–95).

Pliny assumes a market in land and looks to Cato for guidance on where to invest: seek a farm in an area where the neighbors look healthy, where transportation is available to get crops to market, where the buildings are in good condition, and where the land is well farmed. It is a mistake to buy cheap in the expectation of improving the farm—better to buy from a "good estate owner" (*bonus dominus*; N.H. 18.27–28). This advice can be described as rational but is nowhere near precise enough to qualify as instructions on how to calculate return on investment to maximize profit.

Pliny directly raises the question of how to maximize productivity in farming: "In what way are lands cultivated most usefully" (*Quonam igitur modo utilissime colentur agri*; N.H. 18.39)? To answer he again does not offer a method of calculating return on investment but turns to a gem of wisdom (*oraculum*): "from bad to good" (*malis bonis*). To explain this cryptic comment, he turns to the precepts of the forefathers: by *malis* they meant the "cheapest lands" (*vilissimos*) and their chief aim was "minimal expenses" (*minimum impendii*). This seems to be inconsistent with Cato's advice not to buy cheap in the hope of improving the estate. Pliny then expands with other traditional, commonsense wisdom: don't buy anything you can supply yourself; don't waste time during the day on work that can be done at night, or waste time during work days on tasks that can be done on holidays, or don't do indoor work during hours when outdoor work in the fields is possible (N.H. 18.40). This is sensible advice, but it does not amount to a sophisticated assessment of how to optimize return on investment, Pliny's stated aim.[5]

Rather than an analytic approach to finding a strategy to cultivate most profitably (*utilissime*), the *Natural History* in the typical Roman fashion offers model illustrations (*exempla*).[6] Three of the longest illustrate Pliny's thinking.

Lucius Tarius Rufus, who, though of extremely humble birth, by his soldierly efficiency won a consulship, though in other respects a man of old-fashioned economy [*antiquae parsimoniae*], spent the whole of the money he had accumulated through the generosity of Divus Augustus, about 100 million sesterces, in buying up farms in Picenum and farming them to win glory, with the result that his heir refused to accept the estate [on account of its financial failure]. Is it our opinion then that this policy means ruin and starvation? Nay rather, I vow, it is that moderation is the most valuable criterion of all things. To farm well is necessary, to farm best [*optime*] is injurious [*damnosum*], unless farming with his own offspring or others dependent on him. There are some crops which it does not pay the landlord to harvest if the cost of labor is reckoned, and olives are not easily made to pay; and some lands do not repay diligent farming—this is said to be the case in Sicily, and consequently newcomers find themselves deceived. (N.H. 18.37–38)

I confess that I find the lessons of this *exemplum* confusing. In what sense did Tarius Rufus fail because he farmed his Picenum lands "best"? Was it that he invested too many resources in lands of poor quality? Was it the choice of olives as the main crop? Or was it that he himself was not present to manage the estate? All three resonate with advice found elsewhere in the *Natural History* and other Roman authors. The dictum "moderation in all things is the most useful" (*modum iudicem rerum omnium utilissimum*) fits well in the ancient advice literature exhorting moderation, but it is not obvious that it is a formula for maximizing profit. It fits better in a framework of bounded rationality aimed at minimizing risk, that is, satisficing.[7]

In contrast to Tarius Rufus's failure Pliny relates two *exempla* of success in farming, Q. Remmius Palaemon and C. Furius Chresimus. Palaemon, a famous *grammaticus* of the mid-first century CE, bought farms ten miles from Rome for 600,000 sesterces, a low price owing to the neglect typical of this area; the soils of these farms were not better than the other poor soils nearby. Palaemon was motivated, according to Pliny, not by "virtue of spirit" (*virtus animi*) but by his notorious vanity. To manage the cultivation, he employed Sthenelus of slave descent, whose diligent trenching of the vineyards produced a "barely believable miracle" (*vix credibile miraculum*). Within eight years, Sthenelus had the vines yielding grapes that sold for 400,000 sesterces on the vine and inspired in Seneca a "passion" (*amor*) to buy the estate at four times the price

Palaemon paid for it (N.H. 14.48–52). This story has a number of interesting details. First is the low price of agricultural land within ten miles of Rome owing to neglect and poor soils. Second is the means that Sthenelus used to improve the yield: traditional, diligent labor, not innovative techniques or tools. Third are the motives of Palaemon and Seneca for purchasing the farms: vanity in search of glory in the former case, and passion in the latter. Neither is said to be motivated by maximizing profit. Indeed, fourth, Pliny's evaluation of the profit realized by Palaemon is simple and crude insofar as it takes no account of the investments in labor, tools, and other costs beyond the initial investment in the land, as well as forgone interest.[8]

This *exemplum* has been cited as evidence for Roman aristocrats' interest in agricultural investment for profit, and it is. But it also raises questions about the market and investment. If the path to "barely believable profit" was as straightforward and obvious as diligence, why did the land prices remain low? In a fluid market savvy investors should have been eager to buy to realize a profit, thus raising land prices. Isn't this story, at least as Pliny tells it, an illustration of a different set of cultural values in the sense that the ultimate motive was not maximizing profit for either Palaemon or Seneca? For classical scholars one other amusing detail is that Palaemon's "indolent" (*pigra*) neighbors rushed to catch a view of his miraculous yield and explained their own comparatively lackluster yield by Palaemon's "profound literary learning" (*litteris altioribus*; N.H. 14.51). Pliny finds the neighbors' explanation as implausible as we would, and he understands plain old hard work (not sophisticated economic rationality or innovative methods) to be the key to great success.

A similar lesson about the path to great profit in agriculture can be drawn from the *exemplum* of C. Furius Chresimus, a freedman.[9] He too aroused the envy of his neighbors by his "much larger yields" (*largiores multo fructus*) than those of much bigger estates in the area. As a result, he was brought to trial by the magistrate in charge of public order, the *curule aedile*, on the charge of using "magic spells" (*veneficia*) to coax away the crops from his neighbors' fields. As his defense Chresimus exhibited in court his "farming apparatus" (*instrumentum rusticum*), including his well-cared-for slaves (*familia valida*), his excellent iron tools and heavy mattocks, his heavy-duty plowshare, and well-fed oxen. These, he said, were his alleged magic spells, along with his long days and nights of work. He won a unanimous vote for acquittal. Pliny's conclusion of the vignette: "The fact is that husbandry depends on expenditure of labour, and this is the reason for the saying of our forefathers that on a farm the best fertilizer is the master's eye" (*profecto opera inpensa cultura constat et ideo maiores fertilissimum in agro oculum domini esse dixerant*; N.H. 18.41–43).

The themes in this story are familiar and accentuated by the drama of the trial: diligence and sound investment in the traditional farming apparatus (including slaves) yield enviable profits. Here as in the Palaemon example the surrounding farms were underperforming.[10] Chresimus was an outlier in incredible productivity because he followed the wisdom of the ancestors in the attention to his slaves, animals, and equipment. Innovation and calculations of return on investment played no part in the narrative. We will return to the implication of the comment about the fundamental importance of the "master's eye."

Pliny makes a point of the "small farm" (*agello*) of Chresimus from which he realized a large yield through attentiveness and long hours of work. This story sets the stage for the sharp contrast with his famous condemnation of great estates (*latifundia*): "in old times it was thought that to observe moderation in the size of a farm was of primary importance, inasmuch as the view was held that it was more satisfactory to sow less land and plough it better; and I observe that Virgil was of this opinion. And if the truth be confessed, large estates have been the ruin of Italy, and are now proving the ruin of the provinces too—half of Africa was owned by six landlords, when the emperor Nero put them to death" (N.H. 18.35). Whatever the doubts about the true extent of *latifundia*, it is clear that Pliny's condemnation here is based more on moral sentiment and poetic authority than on explicit economic analysis of return on investment.[11]

In addition to general wisdom and venerated authors such as Cato and Virgil, the *Natural History* offers more specific observations about profits from agriculture. The advantages of raising the shrub *cytisus* are that it can yield 2,000 sesterces per *iugerum* (roughly two-thirds of an acre) as feed for cattle or swine, can be harvested very cheaply even by a "boy or an old woman" (*puer anusve*), and protects cattle from all diseases (N.H. 13.130–32). In viticulture the best grapes are produced from vines trained on trees, and in particular grapes from the tops of the trees (N.H. 17.199). The quality of the grapes deteriorates if the vines are pruned only every other year as a means of labor savings—it is a false savings because the wine commands lower prices (N.H. 17.213). Pliny advises against delays in the grape harvest, motivated by greed, in the hope of higher prices; the responsible estate owner (*aequus paterfamilias*) follows the timing of Nature, and this turns out to be "most profitable" (*lucrosissimum*; N.H. 18.320). It is doubtful that this conclusion was based on analysis of data. In antiquity wine was valued not only for its taste but also for its medicinal value. Pliny reports that wines from different regions were marketed for different treatments (N.H. 14.59). Though he himself devotes a whole book to viticulture, Pliny is not altogether pleased by the attention given to wine since "it perverts the mind, produces madness, and is responsible for thousands of crimes," and in any case Nature has provided water as a free, alternative drink (N.H. 14.137).

Another major sector of agricultural production for the market was oleoculture. Cato's general advice was to plant the variety of olive trees pronounced best in the locality, which is consistent with his advice to observe neighboring farms when deciding whether to purchase an estate (N.H. 15.20). Pliny points to the challenge of making olive cultivation profitable: sometimes the labor costs of harvesting outweigh the revenue from sales (N.H. 18.38). However, the alternatives to costly olive-picking created bigger problems. The practice of allowing ripe olives to fall to the ground minimized labor costs, but the savings was more than off-set by the decline in quality. The practice of knocking the olives off the trees by striking them with poles was discouraged on the grounds that it would harm the trees (N.H. 15.11). These are sensible recommendations made for the sake of profit. In addition, Pliny notes the introduction of new varieties of grapes and olives, in many cases the beneficial result of exchange across the empire.[12]

Book 19 is devoted to non-cereal crops (which Pliny claims were neglected by other authors) and contains some explicitly financial observations. The crops include both other foods and fibers. Among the former, we are told that the Egyptians had a variety of radish that they preferred to sow over wheat, both because it brought a higher "profit" than wheat and because the tax demanded by the state was less (N.H. 19.79).[13] On the other hand, saffron was an unprofitable crop in Italy because of the tiny amounts produced. More generally, Pliny laments the fact that inequality of wealth in Roman society created a market for luxury foods that were consumed to mark status.[14] One has to be impressed that around Ravenna luxury asparagus weighed in at three spears to a pound. Pliny characterized these luxury foods as "monstrosities of the stomach" (*prodigia ventris*; N.H. 19.52–54). Among the non-edibles, flax is presented as the first of the plants that warrant attention on account of "price and usefulness" (*pretio usuque vitae*; N.H. 19.2). Esparto grass used to make rope for ship's rigging and for mechanical devices in construction is a marvel (*miraculum*) grown around Carthago Nova but only within thirty miles of the sea because "the costs of transport prohibited longer distance" (*longius vehi impendia prohibent*; N.H. 19.30). Overland transportation costs were a fundamental constraint on the Roman economy, here explicitly considered by Pliny.

Various possibilities for profit in animal husbandry draw comments. Pliny notes that the highest price paid for an animal was 400,000 sesterces for an ass to use as breeding stock for mules (N.H. 8.167–70). (He adds the interesting fact that Maecenas served donkey foals at banquets.) At a more pedestrian level, Pliny advises that beekeeping is very profitable because the expenses are slight (N.H. 21.70). But the "greatest profit" (*maxime quaestu*) comes from raising horses for chariot racing (N.H. 18.263).

Pliny's thinking about the economics of agriculture does not strike me as entirely consistent. He shows a sensitivity to prices and a concern for profit; at some points he takes into account labor costs, and he reports on the availability of an increasing number of varietals. The *Natural History* reflects a well-developed market for luxury produce. On the other hand, much of the advice is conservative and backward-looking, based on the wisdom of the ancients or poets—essentially traditional commonsense rules of thumb rather than analysis and justified by the superior yield that Cato reported. Pliny's ideal owner was the sensible *paterfamilias* who managed in concert with Nature and was motivated by virtue not avarice, someone who managed "well," not "best."

Mining

Pliny was clearly impressed by the technical achievements of the mining operations in Spain and offers some economic facts, all with a heavy moral overlay. He describes the methods of gold mining and expresses wonder that the deep tunneling exceeds the works of the Giants (N.H. 33.68–70). The cost of the 100-mile water channels was even more expensive and required elaborate engineering feats over the rugged landscape. The bottom line was said to be production of 20,000 pounds of gold (worth 94 million sesterces) per year from Asturia, Callaecia, and Lusitania (N.H. 33.78). Pliny covers the mining of other metals including silver, lead, and iron. A "remarkable fact" about Spanish lead mines with economic consequences is that after being abandoned they "revive more productively" as indicated by the increase in rent for the Salutariensian mine in Baetica from 800,000 sesterces per year to 1,020,000 sesterces (N.H. 34.164–65). Pliny's analysis is interesting: he understands that the magnitude of the rent is an indicator of the productivity of the mines but does not consider the demand side of the pricing or the costs to evaluate return on investment.

State rental of mines was just one aspect of institutional intervention in mining. Pliny reports that though Italy was well endowed with minerals, mining in Italy had long been prohibited by the Senate and was regulated elsewhere. The censors permitted the public contractors (*publicani*) to employ no more than 5,000 men in the gold mines in Victumulae (N.H. 33.78). After the conquest of Britain, the Romans had more easily available lead there on the surface, but a law limited the amount that could be mined (N.H. 34.164). Pliny does not offer an explanation of these regulations, nor what economic effect they may have had on prices.[15]

More broadly, the *Natural History* starts from a moral stance on mining, which is characterized as an "insult to the sacred mother" (*indignatio sacrae parentis*; N.H. 33.1). After gold, silver mining is "the next insanity," yet there is little appreciation on Pliny's part for the utility of coinage in facilitating exchange (N.H. 33.95). In contrast to precious metals, the mining of iron is given short shrift despite its importance in economic production.[16] Similarly, the treatment of stone and quarrying is more concerned with luxury marble than "stones used by craftsmen" (*operarii lapides*), which receive only a dozen lines on varieties of whetstones (N.H. 36.164). Though Pliny states in his prefatory letter to Titus that he aims to write for artisans to provide useful knowledge (*utilitas*), that is belied by the balance of the content.

Crafts

As is appropriate for a preindustrial economy, the *Natural History* treats agriculture at much greater length and in a more focused way than the crafts. Here and there Pliny does highlight particular cities that were "ennobled" by their fame for special, manufactured products.[17] The cities recognized as achieving renown (*nobilitas*) for their pottery are Arretium, Surrentum, Hasta, Pollentia, and Modena in Italy; Saguntum in Spain; and Tralles and Pergamum in Asia Minor (N.H. 35.161). It is interesting that Pliny uses the language of honor (*nobilitantur*) here rather than the language of financial success. That same vocabulary of *nobilitas* appears to describe the cities associated with the best garum, which commands a higher price than any other liquid except unguents. Pompeii, Leptis, Antipolis, Thurii, and Delmatia are praised (*laudantur*) for their garum (N.H. 31.94). And Sidon was renowned (*nobilis*) for its workshops making glass, especially mirrors (N.H. 36.193). In contrast to the fine arts, no names of individuals are associated with the fame of these products.[18] In a sense, Pliny is recognizing the economic value of what we today would call "brand" and does so in the language of the aristocratic value system of the Romans.

In preindustrial economies textiles are typically the second largest sector after food production, and it was in this sector that the Industrial Revolution emerged. So it is not surprising that among the urban crafts Pliny gives most attention to textiles, though not in an organized way.[19] His list of great inventions credits the Egyptians with weaving and the Lydians with dyeing (N.H. 7.196); elsewhere Pamphile of Cos is (sarcastically) celebrated for inventing the process to make silk (N.H. 11.76) and the Phrygians are said to have discovered embroidery (N.H. 8.196). Pliny's special concern for luxury prompts him to give extended attention to purple dye, its sources from the sea, its formula for dyeing, and its cost (N.H. 9.125–41). Elsewhere he observes that a cheaper, land-based alternative for purple dye, *coccum*, was found in Transalpine Gaul; he includes this detail, despite the fact that dyeing is not one of the liberal arts, in order to deprive luxury by this cheaper substitute (*utilitas*; N.H. 22.4).[20] Fulling to clean and finish cloth is mentioned briefly in six passages scattered across Books 7, 19, 28, and 35. A comparison of Pliny's "facts" about fulling and the entry for fulling in Chambers's *Cyclopaedia* of the early eighteenth century provides perspective on the former's organization, or lack thereof, and will be discussed in chapter 6.

Other stray comments about crafts can be found in the *Natural History*. In the description of the animal kingdom we are told that hedgehog skin was valued for leatherworking (N.H. 8.135). One of the more interesting economic facts about craft production that Pliny thought worth mentioning was the disaggregation of the production of luxury chandeliers: the upper parts were made in Aegina and the lower parts in Tarentum. Pliny's comment is not an economic explanation but a recognition that the two places deserve "joint credit" (*iuncta commendatio*; N.H. 34.10). He summarizes his two books on metals (N.H. 33 and 34) in the following way: "We have now practically indicated the nature of metals, in which wealth [*opes*] consists, and of the substances related to them, connecting the facts [*res*] in such a way as to indicate at the same time the enormous topic of medicine and the obscurities of the workshops [*officinarum tenebrae*] and the scrupulous subtlety of carving and shaping and dyeing" (N.H. 35.1). The association of the negative connotations of *tenebrae* with workshops suggests a different set of values than those of the early modern encyclopedists described in chapter 6.

Trade

In addition to Pliny's celebration of the Pax Romana for facilitating trade within the empire, the *Natural History* contains several much-cited remarks about trade beyond the frontiers. The comments on trade with India are scattered across four books. Book 6 describes in detail the trade route from Egypt to India, prefacing this "fact" with the famous lament that India drains (*exhauriente*) the Roman Empire of 50 million sesterces per year.[21] Pliny claims that the merchants marked up the imported luxury goods one-hundredfold (N.H. 6.101). Though he does not explain this important economic fact directly, his description of the length and risks of the trade route provides a rationale for the mark-up. Alternatively, his fact may be wrong or the market may have been very imperfect, allowing traders to command an exorbitant margin of profit. Despite the steep mark-up Pliny asserts that this trade was less rewarding than farming, but the basis for this assertion is not stated (N.H. 14.52). In the discussion of copper and lead Pliny notes that India lacked these two metals and traded gems and pearls for them (N.H. 34.163).

The Arabs are said to be the "richest peoples" (*gentes ditissimae*) in the world because they control the trade between the Roman Empire and Parthia and accumulate wealth "by commerce and by banditry" (*commerciis aut latrociniis*). And in anticipation of mercantilism, Pliny adds that they have become the richest by selling what they capture from the sea and forests and buying nothing in return (N.H. 6.162). The epithet "fortunate" (*felix*) for Arabia arouses Pliny's moral outrage: "a country with a false and ungrateful appellation, as she puts her happiness to the credit of the powers above, although she owes more of it to the power below. Her good fortune has been caused by the luxury of mankind even in the hour of death, when they burn over the departed the products which they had originally understood to have been created for the gods" (N.H. 12.82).[22] Pliny totals the cost of these luxury imports from the Arabian peninsula, India, and China at a minimum of 100 million sesterces and casts partial blame on the women of the empire and their demand for luxuries (N.H. 12.84).[23]

Overseas trade aroused sharp ambivalence in Pliny—a sense of "great wonder" (*maius miraculum*) as well as deep fear (N.H. 19.3). He appreciates the technical feat of transporting obelisks and marble to Rome (N.H. 36.69–71) but decries the luxury of ostentatious display of columns.[24] While he has a basic understanding of the economics of trade and gives some quantitative "facts," the conflation of the moral with the economic leaves the analysis fragmentary and superficial.

Medicine

Requiring licenses to practice medicine is a relatively recent phenomenon dating back to the late nineteenth century in the United States; in ancient Rome it was unregulated. Pliny takes every opportunity to cast aspersions on doctors and, as noted in chapter 4, is particularly incensed by the fees in the hundreds of thousands of sesterces that they draw as they change daily the potions they offer

(N.H. 29.11). After Hippocrates "there was no limit to the profit [*modus quaestus*]" they could command.

Labor and Agency

In the final culmination of his magnum opus Pliny extols Italy as the "fairest" land in the world in all respects, starting with her people, "her men, women, generals, soldiers, and slaves," and ranks Spain second in part for its "training of slaves" (*exercitio servorum*; N.H. 37.201–2). In earlier books the well-known legends about Rome's ancient heroes working their own modest estates are repeated to set the stage for a familiar narrative of decline that is implied in the anecdotes about the jealous, underachieving neighbors of Palaemon and Chresimus. For Pliny the decline was partially explained by the labor force: "nowadays bound feet, condemned hands and branded faces do the farm-work, although Tellus (Earth) who is addressed as our mother and whose cultivation is spoken of as worship is not so dull that when we obtain even our farm-work from these persons one can believe that this is not done against her will and to her indignation. And we are surprised that we do not get the same profits [*emolumenta*] from the labor of slave-gangs [*ergastulorum*] as used to be obtained from generals" (N.H. 18.21). Of course, Pliny is channeling the moral indignation of Tellus here, but there is also a kernel of economic truth rooted in modern-day economists' principal-agent problem—that is, the challenge of motivating and monitoring an agent, especially an involuntary agent such as a chained slave. Some of the wisdom of the venerable ancients addressed this issue by recommending careful oversight by the master. So Cato recommended building a comfortable villa that would attract the master from the city to visit the estate on the grounds that "'the master's face does more good than the back of his head'" (N.H. 18.31). This dictum is repeated in a slightly different form a little later in Book 18 in the story about Chresimus's victory in court: his slave staff was well kept, and his diligence illustrated the saying that "the best fertilizer is the master's eye" (N.H. 18.43). Mago, the authoritative Carthaginian source for the Roman agronomists, emphasized the need for careful oversight of an involuntary labor force (N.H. 18.35).

Though this is a familiar point, it needs to be underlined because some recent treatments of Roman slavery leave the impression that it was a largely voluntary institution and slaves were mainly motivated with positive incentives.[25] There were certainly some slaves in this fortunate position—think of the emperor's slave Drusillanus with his ton of silver serving platters[26]—but this is not the sort of institution that Pliny has in mind with his assorted details about rural and domestic slaves. Among the medicinal uses of hyacinth root was the well-known practice of slave dealers: "applied in sweet wine it checks the signs of puberty and does not let them develop" (N.H. 21.170). Pliny leaves it to the imagination why a slave dealer would want to inhibit sexual development of a young slave; certainly, the slave envisaged was not an adult able to make voluntary decisions. Slave dealers also used terebinth resin, "an ointment for rubbing over whole bodies of their slaves to correct thinness" (N.H. 24.35), and silversmith's powder was used to whiten the feet of herds of slaves imported from overseas (N.H. 35.119–201). In the list of medicinal uses of animal parts Pliny includes gladiators' blood, drunk by epileptics "as though it were a draught of life. . . . the patients think it most effectual to suck from a man himself warm, living blood, and putting their very lips to the wound to drain the very life" (N.H. 28.4). These dying gladiators were likely slaves.[27]

The *Natural History* offers a general comment and a few specific details of acts of resistance by slaves that would have reduced their profitability.[28] "Angry slaves" (*irati servi*) burned down M. Scaurus's Tusculum villa containing extravagant luxuries at a cost of 30 million sesterces (N.H. 36.17). The Vestal Virgins reportedly had a spell to spot runaway slaves but only if they were still in the city (N.H. 28.13). More generally in the discussion of uses of signet rings, Pliny laments that "nowadays even articles of food and drink have to be protected against by means of a ring—a foreign rabble in one's home, so that an attendant to tell people's names now has to be employed even in the case of one's slaves. . . . Nowadays we acquire sumptuous viands only to be pilfered in the home and at the same time acquire people to pilfer them, and it is not enough to keep our keys themselves under seal: while we are fast asleep or on our death-beds, our rings are slipped off our fingers" (N.H. 33.26–27). All these details taken together hardly suggest a slave society in which slaves were typically motivated by positive incentives. As one might expect, given the relationship between master and slave, Pliny's emphasis is on policing a coerced and resistant labor force, one in which the institutional costs of oversight were salient.[29]

Pliny's wandering curiosity prompted him to relate a few other odd items involving a slave. In a slave-to-riches story Clesippus, a humpback slave fuller, was auctioned off with a lampstand to one Gegania; for "the sake of ridiculing entertainment" (*causa ludibrii*) his new mistress exhibited him nude at a party; she formed a passion for him and bequeathed to him her wealth (N.H. 34.11). To restrain his gluttony, the very wealthy late Republican senator Lucius Lucullus "gave charge over himself to a slave to enforce control, and he, an old man who had celebrated a triumph, suffered the very deep disgrace [*ultimo probro*] of having his hand kept away from the food even when feasting in the Capitol, with the added shame of obeying his own slave more readily than himself" (N.H. 28.56). These vignettes reflect a society in which labor has to be understood in a hierarchical culture of honor and shame designed to humiliate slaves, in an institution not devoted solely to economic production.[30]

The topics of slave labor and of women's labor intersect in Pliny's tale of Rhodopis and her pyramid in Egypt. "The smallest and most greatly admired of these pyramids was built by Rhodopis, a mere prostitute. She was once a fellow-slave of Aesop, the sage who composed the Fables; our amazement is all the greater when we reflect that such wealth was acquired through prostitution" (N.H. 36.82). This story reminds us of several important facts about slave and female labor that do not fit neatly into the New Institutional economists' representation of slavery in the ancient world that generally focuses exclusively on adult, male, urban slaves. First, many, possibly most, slaves were women, for whom prostitution was a common occupation.[31] Second, it was a great miracle, in Pliny's view, that prostitution made Rhodopis rich enough to build a pyramid, a "stupid ostentation" (*stulta ostentatio*); more usually, prostitution was a sordid, demeaning occupation.[32]

Pliny stereotyped women in their capacities as both producers and consumers. The domestic tasks of cooking and textile production were coded female in the *Natural History*.[33] The mythical inventor of weaving was Arachne, and the inventor of silk was Pamphile of Cos (N.H. 11.76). This gender coding was rooted in a broader value system of honor and shame, implied by Pliny's comment that in contrast to wool "spinning flax was respectable even for men" (*linum nere et viris decorum est*; N.H. 19.18). Pliny claims that in the absence of professional bakers in Rome before 171 BCE, baking was "the work of women" (*opus mulierum*; N.H. 18.107).[34] In the arts some women painters were notable for their portraits of women, which fetched high prices (N.H. 35.147–48). More ominously, Pliny reports that the common people (*vulgus*) believed that eclipses were caused by "magical charms and herbs," which he characterizes as the "sole expert knowledge of women" (N.H. 25.10). These occasional mentions of women's labor are framed within a context of the Roman male values of honor and shame: in parallel with the notice that Scipio Nasica was judged the best man (*vir optumus*), we are told that Sulpicia was voted the "most chaste woman" (*pudicissima femina*; N.H. 7.120). As so often later in European history, women's labor is underappreciated and underreported in the *Natural History*—a mistake repeated by some historians of the Roman Empire even today.[35]

The Greeks were blamed as the source of the plight of luxury, and Pliny portrayed women as the consumers demanding luxuries from the east.[36] Pompey was said to have brought back to Rome from his eastern campaign a taste for pearls and displayed in his triumph a portrait of himself made of pearls, those "monstrosities" (*prodiga*) meant for women (N.H. 37.15). The luxury items associated with women were not limited to pearls: the hierarchy of value of gems was settled by a women's edict (*senatusconsultum mulierum*; N.H. 37.85). That most fleeting of extravagances, perfume, was a female luxury: "their highest recommendation is that when a woman passes by, her scent may attract the attention even of persons occupied in something else—and their cost is more than 400 denarii per pound" (N.H. 13.20). While men indulged in wasteful displays of silver, women are mentioned sarcastically in association with certain deplorable uses. "Women use silver to wash in and scorn sitting-baths not made of silver, and the same substance does service both for our viands and for our baser needs. If only Fabricius could see these displays of luxury—women's bathrooms with floors of silver, leaving nowhere to set your feet" (N.H. 33.152–53). Women as consumers in the household have attracted attention in recent decades as economists have tried to understand demand more deeply by disaggregating the different consumers of the household. Pliny's stereotype hardly amounts to a serious attempt to analyze gendered consumption.

Prices and Currency

Like classical economists, Pliny was very interested in prices, though for quite different reasons.[37] For moral reasons the *Natural History* is particularly focused on the highest prices for extravagant luxuries, whereas the classical economists theorized about how prices in the market came to be fixed by supply and demand. Pliny does make some general, sensible comments about price-setting. In the realm of agriculture he recognizes that disasters drive up prices (N.H. 18.272).[38] In commerce "we are not unaware that the prices of articles which we have stated at various points differ in different places and alter nearly every year, according to shipping costs or the terms on which a particular merchant has brought them, or as some dealer dominating the market may whip up the selling price. . . . Nevertheless I have found it necessary to state the prices usual at Rome, in order to give an idea of a standard value of commodities" (N.H. 33.164). This passage shows a sensitivity to basic economic considerations of transportation costs, assumed to be by sea (*navigatione*), and to market manipulation. Pliny also recognizes that the expectations of economic actors about the future affect price-setting: so greedy businessmen watch the signs of the coming winter; if it is cloudy, they anticipate a wet winter and raise the prices of cloaks; but if it is clear, they expect a cold winter and raise the prices of other clothes (N.H. 18.225).

The *Natural History*'s list of high prices is an eclectic collection, including some true oddities. In the past the highest price paid for a slave was 700,000 sesterces for a *grammaticus* teaching language and literature, but now slave actors command the highest prices (N.H. 7.128). In Pliny's cynical and moralizing view, the taste of wealthy Romans for gourmet food made slave cooks costly: "People in their complaints about luxury used to protest that cooks were being bought at a higher price per man than a horse; but now the price of three horses is given for a cook, and the price of three cooks for a fish, and almost no human being has come to be more valued than one that is most skillful in making his master bankrupt" (N.H. 9.67). Exotic imported ingredients such as pepper commanded high prices deserving scorn: "to think that its only pleasing quality is pungency, and that we go all the way to India to get this. Who was the first person who was willing to try it on his food, or in his greed for an appetite was not content merely to be hungry? Both pepper and ginger grow wild in their own countries and nevertheless they are bought by weight like gold or silver" (N.H. 12.29). As an example of an indulgent individual, Pliny notes with disgust the cost of the culinary extravagance of Clodius Aesop's casserole of songbirds at 100,000 sesterces (N.H. 10.141).

Among the highest prices noted for animals were the 400,000 sesterces for an ass noted above (N.H. 8.167ff.) and 600,000 for a white nightingale (N.H. 10.83). The fact that small plots at Cordoba and Carthage could bring in 6,000 sesterces for artichokes for the table aroused Pliny's indignation (N.H. 19.152). The extraordinary cost of amber resulted in a price for a small human figurine that was higher than that of living, vigorous slaves (N.H. 37.49). These excessive prices and others served as grist for Pliny's moral mill and are not data for genuine economic analysis. They were selected in part to express Pliny's sense of moral irony.

Other passages exhibit a wish to analyze and to explain prices. This is particularly evident in several discussions about what makes art expensive. The reasons put forward at different points are the skill of the artist, the value of the materials, and the scarcity value. The great Greek painters of the past—Apelles, Aetion, Melanthius, and Nicomachus—executed their works in just four colors (white, yellow, red, and black), and those pictures sold for "the wealth of towns." More and varied pigments are now available, but no picture can be said to be renowned (*nobilis*). "Everything was better in the days when resources were less. The reason for this is that, as we said before, it is the value of materials and not of spirit [*animi*] that people are now looking for" (N.H. 35.50). An illustration of the monetary value added by craftsmanship (*manipretium*) was Gaius Gracchus's purchase of some silver figures of dolphins at 5,000 sesterces per pound—that is, well over ten times the value of the silver content (N.H. 33.147). As in so many other facets of Roman society, Pliny saw a decline in the skill of craftsmen. "Formerly copper used to be blended with a mixture of gold and silver, and nevertheless artistry was valued more highly [*ars pretiosior erat*] than the metal; but nowadays it is a doubtful point whether the craftsmanship or the material is worse, and it is a surprising thing that, though the prices paid for the works of art have grown beyond all limits, the importance attached to this craftsmanship of working in metals has quite disappeared. For this, which formerly used to be practiced for the sake of glory—consequently it was even attributed to the workmanship of the gods, and the leading men of all nations used to seek fame by this method also—has now, like everything else, begun to be practiced for the sake of profit [*quaestus*]" (N.H. 34.5). Similarly, in the art of silver-chasing

Pliny names famous artists of the past and bemoans the fact that "all of a sudden this skill so declined that it is now only valued in the old specimens, and reputation attaches to engravings worn with use even if the figure cannot be discerned" (N.H. 33.157).

Interestingly, one of the examples of a highly skilled artist was the woman painter Iaia who in the early first century BCE painted mostly portraits of women; her artistic skill surpassed "the most celebrated portrait painters of the day, Sopolis and Dionysius, whose pictures fill the galleries" (N.H. 35.148). In judging quality, according to Pliny, the Roman aesthetic appreciated verisimilitude. In the shrine of Juno on the Capitoline there was a (literally) invaluable "bronze figure of a hound licking its wound, the miraculous excellence and verisimilitude are shown by the fact of its dedication in that place but also by the method taken for pledging security for it; for as no sum of money seemed to equal its value, the government enacted that its custodians should be answerable for its safety with their lives" (N.H. 34.38). Unfortunately, it went up in flames along with the Capitol at the hands of the Vitellians. These examples concerning the valuation and pricing of art are scattered across three books. On the one hand, by implication they demonstrate certain recognizable principles of pricing—the cost of the inputs, the demand as influenced by the perceived quality of the craftsmanship, and the limited and scarce supply of antiques. On the other hand, these principles are implied and are not elaborated in any systematic way.

The reasoning about prices for works of art is more moral than economic, and the same can be said about Pliny's discussion of inflation in the cost of living. A rant about the increasingly costly, ostentatious houses and their furnishings concludes with an assertion about poetic justice: "fires punish luxury" (*incendia puniunt luxum*; N.H. 36.110).

At the end of the final book of the *Natural History*, just before his invocation of *Parens Natura*, Pliny once again displays his preoccupation with high prices. To summarize his "things worth knowing," he lists the items commanding the highest price in a series of categories, starting with things from the sea (pearls); from earth's surface (rock-crystal, then other gems); from things growing from earth (plants for dyes and scents); from animals on land that breathe (ivory is most valuable, then tortoise shell); from animal hides (pelts dyed in China and the Arabian she-goat's tufts of hair); and from birds (nothing except plumes for helmets and the grease of the Commagene goose). And finally, "not to be over-looked is that gold, about which all mortals are mad [*insaniunt*], barely comes in tenth place in price; silver, with which gold is pur-chased, almost twentieth" (N.H. 37.204).

This strikes me as an odd way to end a monumental compila-tion whose avowed purpose was "usefulness" for craftsmen and farmers—a list of the most costly exotic luxuries, most of which very, very few Romans would have ever seen. What usefulness would they have derived from the notice that the grease of the Commagene goose or the hair tufts of the Arabian she-goat were the most expensive items by weight in the bird and animal catego-ries? To note gleefully that gold ranks only tenth in the firmament of most costly substances and silver only twentieth, rather than their usefulness as media of exchange, strikes me as especially strange for a man who had spent much of his adult life in high-level administrative positions with financial responsibilities. It would be as useful as today comparing the price of an ounce of Caspian caviar ($135/oz.) with the price of the same weight of silver ($15/oz.).

In his book on precious metals Pliny does devote a lengthy dis-cussion to a history of coinage (N.H. 33.42–47). Book 33 starts from a denunciation of mining for precious metals with the coun-terfactual: how blameless, blissful, indeed, pleasurable life would be if man desired only what was on the surface of the earth (N.H. 33.3). That is to say, life would be happier without mining for gold: "how far happier was the age when goods themselves were ex-changed for goods," as attested by Homer and by the early Roman laws imposing fines priced in cattle (N.H. 33.6). The man who coined a "denarius from gold" committed a "crime" (*scelus*; N.H. 33.42). Zehnacker provides a thorough account of Pliny's history of coinage, noting that in spite of its mistakes it gives insights into Pliny's economic thinking.[39] To my mind, one of those insights is that Pliny was more interested in the etymology of the vocabulary associated with money than in the economic considerations that motivated policies to introduce silver coins at a particular weight and value or the economic consequences of drastically cutting the weight or purity of coins to alleviate state debt. The conclusion to this short history was a moral one: from the invention of coins came the origin of greed along with usury and profitable laziness (N.H. 33.48).[40] The hideous consequence of this "hunger for gold" was that Gaius Gracchus's friend Septumuleius turned in the head of the murdered Gaius with the mouth filled with lead in order to claim a greater reward for its weight in gold. Not only is Pliny's understanding of gold and silver coinage primarily moral, it is not clear that he fully comprehends the fungible quality of money, for he expresses wonder that centuries earlier the conquering Romans imposed the tribute in silver rather than gold (N.H. 33.51).[41]

Investment and Consumption

At the dawn of the Industrial Revolution Adam Smith's *Wealth of Nations* (Book 3) presented a historical analysis titled "Of the Different Progress of Opulence in Different Nations." Like Pliny before him, Smith was interested in productive investment and consumption of luxuries. The similarities and differences in their views offer insight and perspective for the *Natural History*. The *exempla* of Palaemon and Chresimus illustrated the profits to be made by diligent investment in agriculture. The legendary heroes of early Rome proved to Pliny's satisfaction that small farms, carefully tended, were more productive investments than extensive estates. Seventeen centuries later Smith echoed these basic generalizations about the propensities to invest in improvements by small and large proprietors.

> An improved farm is equally advantageous and more durable than any of those machines, frequently requiring no other repairs

than the most profitable application of the farmer's capital employed in cultivating it. . . . It seldom happens, however, that a great proprietor is a great improver. . . . If he was an economist, he generally found it more profitable to employ his annual savings in new purchases than in the improvement of his old estate. To improve land with profit, like all other commercial projects, requires an exact attention to small savings and small gains, of which a man born to a great fortune, even though naturally frugal, is very seldom capable. . . . The situation of such a person naturally disposes him to attend rather to ornament which pleases his fancy than to profit for which he has so little occasion. The elegance of his dress, of his equipage, of his house, and household furniture, are objects which from his infancy he has been accustomed to have some anxiety about. . . . Compare the present condition of those estates with the possessions of the small proprietors in their neighbourhood, and you will require no other argument to convince you how unfavourable such extensive property is to improvement.[42]

Pliny and Smith share the view that investment in agriculture is more productive than investment in commerce or industry. In Pliny's view Cato's yield "conclusively proved that the merchant does not obtain more profit by rashly trespassing on the seas nor by going as far as the coast of the Red Sea or of the Indian Ocean to seek merchandise, than is yielded by a diligently tended homestead [*sedulum ruris larem*]" (N.H. 14.52).[43] (Note the religious connotations of the vocabulary.) And like Smith, Pliny holds the view that a taste for luxuries will motivate wealthy landowners to spend their income on useless indulgences: Smith criticizes expenditure on "menial servants," which brings to mind Pliny's ironic rhetorical question about how many domestic slaves would be required to carry the one-ton collection of silver serving platters of the imperial slave Drusillanus (N.H. 33.145).[44]

In other important respects, however, Smith diverged from Pliny. Whereas Pliny's historical evolution was broadly one of decline in productivity from small farms to unproductive *latifundia*,

Smith's was a story of "the natural progress of opulence." And whereas Pliny denounced "stupid ostentation" and the consumption of luxuries that increased the cost of living,[45] Smith (following John Houghton, Nicholas Barbon, and David Hume) came to see that limited demand for luxuries was a crucial factor stimulating "the invention and production of manufactured goods designed for 'the gratification of the senses.'"[46] Smith reasoned that this in turn encouraged the growth of towns producing these goods:[47] "when they [aristocratic estate owners] spend them [profits] in maintaining tradesmen and artificers, they may, all of them taken together, perhaps maintain as great, or, on account of the waste which attends rustic hospitality, a greater number of people than before. . . . Each tradesman or artificer derives his subsistence from the employment, not of one, but of a hundred or a thousand different customers. Though in some measure obliged to them all, therefore, he is not absolutely dependent upon any one of them."[48]

These quotations provide a glimpse of Smith's systematic analysis of the economic relations between improvements in rural production, luxury consumption, and the growth of towns resulting in the "progress of opulence." He understood that "luxury spending is double edged. In so far as it drives out feudal 'hospitality' it can have all the desirable incentive and political effects that Hume described, but in so far as it displaces savings, it slows growth."[49] Pliny's *Natural History* contains no such systematic thinking, gives little attention to "tradesmen and artificers," sees no positive side to the growth of manufacturing, and (rightly) attributes the increase in opulence to Roman conquest and imperial rule rather than an increase in productivity.

Pliny does make one curious observation about stopping an investment based on profit and loss. Caligula hoped to find a process to refine Syrian orpiment to produce gold but found that so little gold was produced that it yielded a financial loss, despite the fact that orpiment was priced at only four denarii per pound—such were the rewards of greed (N.H. 33.79). Here again Pliny's conclusion was an ironic, moral one.

Though he does not explicitly connect them to improved productivity, Pliny assesses in very positive terms the investments in public infrastructure.[50] Among the most significant changes during the Industrial Revolution was the improvement in the urban public health infrastructure through construction of sewers and attention to the purity of the water supply. Though the scientific understanding of disease transmission was limited, Pliny admired the building of Rome's famous sewer, the Cloaca Maxima, as "the greatest work of all" (*opus omnium maximum*; N.H. 36.104). Similarly, he expressed wonder at the "unsurpassed miracle" of the aqueducts built at huge cost but (unlike luxuries) of "true value" (*vera aestimatio*; N.H. 36.121–23). Among other public works, Pliny mentions Claudius's building of the harbor at Ostia and the draining of the Fucine Lake by a "multitude of workmen" at an "indescribable cost." From a modern point of view, Pliny rightly recognizes the value of public works, but in place of a sober economic analysis of that value, he jubilantly wonders at the "miracles."

Trust and Fraud

As economists have become more attentive to culture's influence on economic performance, a major focus has been on the role of trust. Noting that the same institutional framework can yield different results, some have argued that social trust can reduce transaction costs, as less energy and resources need to be devoted to monitoring and enforcing contracts and agreements. In ancient Rome the Edict of the Aediles regulated a limited set of transactions in the marketplace—in particular, the sale of slaves and domestic animals—but as Wim Broekaert and Taco Terpstra have recently argued, most enforcement of commercial transactions was informal.[51] They point out some institutions and practices, such as religious cults and the ordering of witnesses to contracts, that may have nurtured social trust and hierarchical obligation without formal enforcement by the state.

Pliny does not make any such explicit connection, but he has a lot to say about trust and fraud. As is typical of the *Natural History*,

much of it is about oddities or in a moralizing vein. Far from thinking that Roman institutions engendered increasing trust over time,
Pliny believed that there was a decline of innocence from the age
of the ancients degenerating to "extremely ingenious fraud" in
"every part of life" (N.H. 33.125). "A very great number of crimes
[*scelera*] connected with money are carried out by means of rings.
To think what life was in the old days, and what innocence existed
when nothing was sealed" (N.H. 33.26). As the Romans lost their
innocence, and trust could no longer be assumed, the use of the
signet ring for contracts became the norm. Pliny reasons that
"the employment of a signet-ring must have begun to be much
more frequent with the introduction of usury. This is proved by
the custom for the common men, among whom even at the present day a ring is whipped out when a contract is being made; the
habit comes down from the time when there was as yet no speed-
ier method of guaranteeing a transaction [*arra*], so we can safely
assume that with us money began first and signet-rings came in
afterwards" (N.H. 33.28).

The *Natural History* is filled with fraud alerts to warn readers
about adulterated products and ways to detect them. Here is a
sampling. Balsam was a highly prized scent and was collected by
Rome as tribute: "in no commodity are there practiced more pal-
pable frauds, for a *sextarius* of balsamum which is sold by the fiscus
at 300 denarii, is resold for 1,000, so vast is the profit to be derived
from increasing this liquid" (N.H. 12.123).[52] The result of the scarcity and high price of saffron is that "nothing is adulterated as
much" (*adulterator nihil aeque*; N.H. 21.32). Pliny feels unable to
comment on the quality of wine from Narbonensis because the
merchants there have set up workshops to adulterate the wine
with coloring, herbs, and drugs (N.H. 14.68). The great names in
Italian wines are so regularly adulterated that even the wealthy
never really taste the genuine stuff, so low have moral standards
sunk (N.H. 23.33).[53] Quicksilver (mercury) used in gilding was not
plentiful, so people adulterated it with egg white—"the same
fraudulence that is so extremely ingenious in every part of life has

devised an inferior material [*viliorem materiam*]" (N.H. 33.125). Cinnabar (mercury oxide) was used by painters for a red pigment and was adulterated with goat's blood or crushed service-berries. The genuine article cost 50 sesterces per pound (N.H. 33.117).[54] The pigment indigo was adulterated by staining pigeons' droppings with genuine indigo (N.H. 35.46). Touchstones were used for testing gold and silver content, and silver was tested by placing a shaving on a white-hot shovel and observing the color. "But fraud has found its way into every test; if the shovels are kept in men's urine the silver shaving is so stained by it during the process of being burnt, and counterfeits whiteness" (N.H. 33.127). As for opals "there is no stone which is harder to distinguish from the genuine when it is counterfeited in glass; the only test is by sunlight" (N.H. 37.83).[55] In general, gems are subject to counterfeiting, and treatises on dyeing them were written; no other fraud is "more lucrative" (N.H. 37.197). And though Pliny strongly disapproves of such luxuries, "I will demonstrate the method of detecting false [gems], since it is right that even luxury should be protected against frauds" (N.H. 37.198).

Pliny believed that the practice of medicine in particular was rife with deceptive claims for potions: "the frauds of men and the profits of ingenuity led to the invention of those workshops, in which each person is promised his own life at a price" (N.H. 24.4). The Romans by their conquests have given up their simple, natural remedies for costly, exotic, imported concoctions that do not fulfill the promises (N.H. 24.5). Today doctors "rely on fashionable druggists' shops which spoil everything with fraudulent adulterations" (N.H. 34.108), while dishonest herbalists also withhold portions of their plant remedies to perpetuate the illnesses of their customers in order to encourage return business (N.H. 21.144).[56]

In general, fraudulent adulterations were devalued, but Pliny notes with irony a unique exception: "it is a remarkable thing that in this [debased coins] alone among arts spurious methods are objects of study, and a sample of a forged denarius is carefully

examined and the adulterated coin is bought for more than genuine ones" (N.H. 33.132).

The *Natural History* contains little evidence that the Roman
state introduced formal regulations to suppress fraud apart from
the Edict of the Aediles regarding the sale of slaves and animals
with defects, but Pliny reports one very curious exception, hedge-
hogs: "The animal itself is not, as most of us think, superfluous for
the life of mankind, since, if it had not spines, the softness of the
hides of cattle would have been bestowed on mortals to no purpose: hedgehog skin is used for dressing cloth for garments. Even
here fraud has discovered a great source of profit by monopoly,
nothing having been the subject of more frequent senatorial
edicts, and every emperor without exception having been ap-
proached by complaints from the provinces" (N.H. 8.135).

Altogether, Pliny's preoccupation with fraud would not seem
to attest to a high level of social trust in the marketplace, though
in view of the heavy moral overlay one should be cautious about
drawing conclusions regarding actual practice. There is also a more
general, abstract respect in which the *Natural History* reflects a
deficit of social trust. In early modern Europe the Republic of Letters constituted a community of intellectuals that circulated,
tested, and corroborated new discoveries—an informal marketplace of ideas that engendered acceptance and trust in the experimental development of new knowledge.[57] The *Natural History*
does not attest such a community where trust provided a cohesive
intellectual force to evaluate new discoveries, to sift out untruths,
and to constitute accepted knowledge, and so marvels abound,
subject to Pliny's personal and seemingly erratic skepticism.

Conclusion

Motivated by the goal of usefulness, Pliny included observations
about profitability and productivity in his compilation of more
than 20,000 "things worth knowing." Though the emergence of the
discipline of economics was still seventeen centuries in the future,

Pliny's thinking gives some insights into the culture-framing decisions about productivity at the time. It would be a mistake to use Pliny's thoughts to generalize about the whole Roman population, but he does come from a stratum that owned a sizable share of the capital of the empire, making his attitudes and assumptions consequential.[58]

The lack of quantitative data narrowly limited Pliny's potential for evaluating returns on investments or avenues to increase productivity. And yet he did not attempt anything as complex as Columella's famous calculation of return on investment in a vineyard.[59] Nevertheless, he had an interest in profitability and made observations based on recognizable economic principles of scarcity, risk, supervision of agents, and transportation costs. His economic reasoning was inevitably bound up in a set of cultural values. These included moral values regarding the sanctity of Mother Nature, the moral vocabulary of honor and shame, and a belief in a direct connection between morality and profitability, all set within a narrative of decline of both morality and productivity. In addition, Pliny valued prudence over risk, safe profits over maximum profits. To claim that Pliny and fellow Romans made economic decisions based on a different set of values and a bounded rationality is not to blame them but to suggest that their values differed in some degree from those of modern capitalism.[60]

Beyond differences in his moral framework, Pliny's economic reasoning is colored by his penchant for the sensational, the ironic, and the unique. Apart from a few statements, he is not at all interested in patterns of mundane interactions that drove investment, production, and consumption in the economy as a whole. There is very little on the dynamics of the ordinary craft economy, despite the claim to be writing the *Natural History* for the usefulness of artisans.

6

"Utility" and the Afterlife of the *Natural History*

IN HIS DEDICATION to the emperor Titus Pliny wrote that he intended his comprehensive collection of "things worth knowing" to be of use (*utilitas*) to farmers (*agricolae*) and artisans (*opifices*). I take that profession at face value in part because he regularly employs some form of the word *utilis* in subsequent books to describe the most pragmatic advice. How did later generations actually use the monumental work? Unsurprisingly, we have no direct evidence for the practical application of the 20,000 "things worth knowing" by later generations of Roman farmers and artisans who left virtually no written record, but it is worthwhile to look selectively at the shifting ways in which the *Natural History* powerfully shaped texts produced in later antiquity and the Middle Ages and became "one of the most influential . . . compilations of Greco-Roman learning . . . [and] the largest known collection of natural facts."[1] After more than a millennium of respectful copying and excerpting, the Renaissance saw the scientific authority of Pliny increasingly called into doubt, and a new model for comprehensive collections of knowledge emerged. A comparison of the first alphabetically arranged encyclopedias of early eighteenth-century England—the predecessors of Diderot and D'Alembert's *Encyclopédie*—with the *Natural History* points to a conclusion with major implications: Pliny's book was excerpted and usable in pieces for centuries after publication, but it did not have the utility envisioned by the early modern encyclopedists for their works. The *Natural History* neither supported innovation nor contributed to a "culture of growth" in the Roman Empire.

As noted before, Aulus Gellius's *Attic Nights*, written a century after the *Natural History*, includes the earliest surviving mentions of Pliny's great work, references that acknowledge Pliny's learning but also note his penchant for unbelievable "tales" (*fabulae*). The very nature of the *Attic Nights* excludes the prospect of finding in it evidence of practical uses of Pliny's "facts." One might think of looking outside the elevated literary culture depicted by Aulus Gellius for practical applications, but the corpus of papyri also offers no evidence of use—not surprising in view of the interests represented in the corpus.[2] Unfortunately, not much can be made of the lack of evidence for the utility of the *Natural History* over the generations immediately after Pliny's death, but there is no affirmative support for claims of some modern scholars that the *Natural History* was widely used in the generations immediately following Pliny's death.

Late Antique and Medieval Reception
of the *Natural History*

This relative silence began to change in the third century CE with the production of books drawing heavily on Pliny's work. In her history of the reception of the *Natural History* Aude Doody sees these books as "severe examples of the tendency to read Pliny's subject areas as distinct and separate; they provide a concretisation of the process of reading and excising that acts as a metaphor for less dramatic specialist encounters with the text."[3] Of course, Pliny himself in his dedication indicated that he expected to be read selectively for particular uses, and the thematic collections of excerpts facilitated that goal in a way that Pliny himself did not.

The first of the specialist distillations was Solinus's work on geography, *Collectanea rerum mirabilium* or *Polyhistor*. The date and identity of Solinus are not precisely known, but a linguistic argument places him in the third century, certainly before Ammianus Marcellinus's reference to him in the later fourth century. The *Natural History* accounts for about three-quarters of the *Collectanea*, drawn mainly from Pliny's Books 3–6 on geography and more selectively from twenty other books. Through his selections from Pliny Solinus produced a work of geography and marvels less than one-tenth the length of the *Natural History*, achieving "almost unrivalled popularity" in the Middle Ages and the early modern period, and becoming "the chief Latin geographer to a millennium."[4] This exalted reputation did not endure: among German scholars of the nineteenth century Solinus's dependence on Pliny earned him the sobriquet "Pliny's ape" and the *Collectanea* the appraisal of "wretched" and "trivial."[5] In a more vivid characterization Mary E. Milham described the work as "the most miraculous world view ever put forth in Europe."[6] More recently Kai Brodersen has sought partially to rehabilitate Solinus's achievement of presenting space in a map.[7] That was one aspect of Solinus making the *Natural History* more useful. Another, as Brodersen points out, was simply that by being selective "Solinus condensed Pliny's massive work to a manageable size."[8] For any reader interested in geography Solinus's 33,000-word opus would have been far easier to acquire and to consult than Pliny's 400,000 words.

What Solinus did by way of extracting and organizing in the field of geography in the third century, the anonymous *Medicina Plinii* did for medicine not long after. And like the *Collectanea*, the *Medicina Plinii* was copied again and again, enjoying enormous popularity and influence through the Middle Ages.[9] It comprised more than 1,100 remedies in three books, the first two books ordered by human physiognomy from head to foot and the third for illnesses affecting the whole body.[10] For each illness the symptoms were given and then followed by the remedies. The organization of the *Medicina Plinii* required piecing together "facts" spread across the *Natural History*, as illustrated by Pliny's forty remedies scattered in ten books for rabid dog bites.[11] Like the *Collectanea*, the utility, as explained in the preface, lay in the compression and intuitive organization, thus "instructing lay people in treating themselves, especially when travelling, and so to avoid corrupt doctors."[12] The full thirty-seven books of the *Natural History* were simply too bulky and unwieldy to be useful in the same way regardless of Pliny's professed intention to be "useful."[13]

Through the Middle Ages the *Natural History* was widely used, quoted, and excerpted by learned scholars. On the basis of his exhaustive study of manuscript copies and commentaries, Charles Nauert Jr. concluded that Pliny's work "offered at least some information, and often the best information available, on almost any topic that an ancient, medieval, or Renaissance student of nature might want to know. It was, in fact, the great authority which all writers on natural history made the foundation of their own works; and this situation had barely begun to change even as late as 1600."[14] In the medieval scribal culture the very length of the *Natural History* meant that "probably most manuscripts covered only part of the text. . . . In addition to manuscripts containing all of Pliny's work or several of its books, the Middle Ages produced many manuscripts of excerpts."[15] Leading scholastic figures of the High Middle Ages such as Roger Bacon and Albertus Magnus used Pliny, and the reliance of the major encyclopedists of the thirteenth and fourteenth centuries on the *Natural History* was second only to Aristotle.[16]

Despite this influence the *Natural History* was "not a part of the regular arts or medical curriculum in medieval schools. . . . [It was] a source of information, at a rather low level of sophistication."[17] Robert of Crichlade in the twelfth century did try to make the text more usable in the schools by compressing the thirty-seven books into nine. But "during the eleventh and twelfth centuries, as schools multiplied in cathedrals and non-monastic communities, there was a revived study of the dormant past of Classical Literature, and Latin translations from the Greek and Arabic made available many Classical texts that had been lost to the west for centuries. As a result Pliny was superseded in the more active and advanced parts of science. Aristotle's scientific works enabled a much more systematic study of the physical universe to be undertaken, and his more advanced logical treatises gave a training in intellectual method that was to lead to genuine scientific experiment as opposed to the cruder *experimentum,* or experience, of Pliny."[18] This mixed reception of Pliny—relatively widespread (if partial) copying but limited respect for his science—may explain the surprising "lack of commentaries (as distinguished from marginal glosses and brief readers' notes)."[19]

The Renaissance and the Decline of Pliny's Scientific Authority

The extraordinarily long lives of the *Natural History* and the *Medicina Plinii* lasted through the Renaissance, but their scientific validity very gradually began to be challenged, in the first instance by Niccolò Leoniceno's *De Plinii et plurium aliorum medicorum in medicina erroribus* (Concerning the errors in medicine of Pliny and many other doctors; 1492).[20] The ensuing fierce debates had both philological and scientific strands to establish Pliny's original Latin as an authentic text and to verify scientifically the "facts."[21] With regard to the latter, Franciscus Massarius's commentary on Book 9 (on aquatic animals), published in 1537 but likely written a decade earlier, is of particular interest because the dedication noted that the commentary had special value based on personal observation rather than book learning alone.[22] In the same vein and at about the same time, as Doody shows in fascinating detail, the *Medicina Plinii* was used in Alban Thorer's edition (1528) as a living text to be updated with new "facts" and in a way that would not have been possible with the whole *Natural History* on account of its scatter of "things worth knowing" about any given malady.[23] The book of extracts had a practical utility in a way that the full work did not in an era of increasing recognition that the text of the *Natural History* required revision that was based on observation.

Early Modern Encyclopedias and a Culture of Growth

With the advance of experimental science in the seventeenth century the authority of Pliny's comprehensive collection of knowledge declined and a new genre of encyclopedia emerged.[24] A comparison and contrast between the first alphabetically organized encyclopedias of John Harris (1704) and Ephraim Chambers (1728) and Pliny's *Natural History* offer insights into a shift in the goal of "utility" and a revolution in the "culture of growth" associated with the pivotal figure of Sir Francis Bacon (1561–1626). Bacon famously articulated a program for "the attainment of material progress through propositional and prescriptive knowledge feeding off one another and creating a self-reinforcing (auto-catalytic) feedback loop that changed the economic history of the world."[25] Though not without opposition, the idea of *limitless* improvement through new useful knowledge that would enhance even the lives of the poor gradually came to dominate the intellectual culture of England by 1700.[26] The early English encyclopedists saw themselves as part of that program and sowed the seeds for Diderot's *Encyclopédie*.

Economic historians have recently shown a geographical correlation between the dissemination of the *Encyclopédie* and economic growth based on the idea that the *Encyclopédie* was an indicator of "upper-tail knowledge" and human capital that fueled the discoveries and innovations essential to sustained growth.[27] Today the earlier English encyclopedias are much less well-known and less thoroughly studied than Diderot and D'Alembert's *Encyclopédie*, but in their time they were repeatedly revised and widely distributed.

John Harris was a clergyman whose life (1666–1719) spanned the decades in which Isaac Newton was publishing his fundamental research in mathematics, optics, mechanics, and gravitation. In 1704 Harris published the first volume of his *Lexicon Technicum: or, An Universal English Dictionary of Arts and Sciences: Explaining not only the Terms of Art, but the Arts Themselves.* The second volume appeared in 1710, and together they comprised over one million words and many diagrams. Among the entries was Newton's otherwise unpublished research on the chemistry of acids. The *Lexicon Technicum* went through multiple editions in the following decades. His contribution to knowledge was recognized on November 30, 1709, when Harris was elected first secretary of the Royal Society (on which, more below).

A generation later in 1728 Ephraim Chambers published his more ambitious *Cyclopædia: or, An Universal Dictionary of Arts and Sciences; containing the Definitions of the Terms, and Accounts of the Things signify'd thereby, in the several Arts, both Liberal and Mechanical, and the several Sciences, Human and Divine: the Figures, Kinds, Properties, Productions, Preparations, and Uses, of Things Natural and Artificial; the Rise, Progress, and State of Things Ecclesiastical, Civil, Military, and Commercial: with the several Systems, Sects, Opinions, andc. among Philosophers, Divines, Mathematicians, Physicians, Antiquaries, Criticks, andc. The Whole intended as a Course of Antient and Modern Learning.* Chambers came from the world of instrument makers, having been apprenticed to a globe maker. His encyclopedia was a great success, being reissued in expanded and revised editions over the next sixty years.[28]

Dedications. Pliny, Harris, and Chambers all dedicated their works to members of the ruling family of their day—Pliny to Titus Flavius Vespasianus, Harris to Prince George of Denmark (husband of Queen Anne), and Chambers to King George II. But the tone of the dedications is quite different. Pliny had served in the army with Titus and addressed his letter to him in a tone of playful deference, familiarity, and flattery. He characterizes his prefatory letter as "audacious" (*procax*) and refers to his own "sauciness" (*petulantia*). In contrast to his own lack of talent, Pliny praises Titus for his eloquence and literary talent, which require him to "descend" to the literary level of the *Natural History*. In the context of this mock-modesty, Pliny complains that part of his challenge is to give *auctoritas*, "legitimacy," to new things.

By contrast, Harris's dedication to Prince George is couched in terms of direct and extravagant flattery: "I justly esteem it a Peculiar Happiness to me, that You were pleas'd to Accept the Patronage of this Work: For hereby You exempt me from the hardship which attends most Dedicators, of Inventing the Vertues they Celebrate. But tho' Your Intrinsick and Real Worth takes away all Possibility of Flattery, yet being convinced that whatever I can say, falls short of giving You Your just Due, as I should at ascribing more than be deserved, to another." There is nothing familiar or playful about this dedication, but a more telling contrast is that Harris then praises Prince George not for his literary talent and taste but for his "Noble Mind in Studies of the greatest Use and Benefit to Mankind here, Mathematicks and Mechanicks." The cultural shift from the classical emphasis on literary erudition and taste to unapologetic praise of interest in mathematics and mechanics (engineering) is clear and telling.[29]

Chambers's dedication to King George II expresses the culture of growth in explicit and exuberant terms. "Your Majesty commands a People capable of everything . . . extending your Dominions by new Settlements . . . some in increasing your People's Wealth, by new Trades: Others will be employed in enlarging our Knowledge, by new Discoveries in Nature, or new Contrivances of Art. . . . Methinks I see Trophies erecting to your Majesty in the yet undiscover'd Regions of Science; and Your Majesty's Name inscribed to Inventions at present held impossible." Chambers resorts to a direct comparison with Rome to express his optimism: "the Time seems at hand, when we are no longer to envy Rome her Augustus and Augustan Age, but Rome in her turn shall envy ours."[30] The contrasts with Pliny's dedication to Titus are striking. Chambers feels no need to lament the difficulty of ascribing authority to the new. On the contrary, he celebrates the future of "inventions" now "held impossible." As we have seen, Pliny's attitude to "contrivances" was one of suspicion of moral decline (see p. 52). Chambers echoes Pliny's hope for improvement in the human condition through "new discoveries in nature" but differs in his positive view of wealth and his recognition that the crafts and contrivances will also generate improvements. For Pliny contrivances had a negative impact insofar as they were not in harmony with Nature.

Conceptions of the work. All three compilers saw their works as a solution to the challenge of too many books for any one person to master.[31] But from there the conceptions diverge in a revealing way. Pliny conceived of the *Natural History* as a treasure chest to store ancient knowledge in order to preserve it from loss. His worry stemmed from his belief that his contemporaries lacked sufficient respect for the old knowledge and were forgetting it. For Harris and Chambers the rationale for distilling the excess of books in their own day was to provide a manageable summary of prior research to serve as a platform for future discovery.[32] Chambers drew a sharp contrast between the Schoolmen, whose aim was a mastery of the classics of ancient and Christian thought, and the modern directions of new discovery. The old (i.e., the Schoolmen) will be more perfect because it only has to "compare, order, methodize what is ready to hand."

> [The new has] likewise to *find*. After which, all the labour to do likewise still remains. . . . The former takes nature in all her simplicity; the latter adds art to her and thus brings nature into consideration in all her diversity: the former chiefly considers natural bodies in their integral state; the latter divides and analyses them. . . . The latter can scarce ever arrive at perfection, since experiments are endless. . . . The modern is yet wild, and unascertained: 'tis not arrived at the maturity of method. . . . Not but the rules and methods of the antients are, in some measure, applicable to the new, and will go a good way towards the arranging of it; but the present philosophers seem too warm

and sanguine for such a business; and the farther they go on to dig materials, still the more difficult will the ranging of them be. This a man may be positive of, he never will see half the experiments and observations already made, employed in a system of physics. . . . The bare acquisition of new ideas is no real advantage, unless they be such as are adapted to the circumstances of our wants, and occasions, or capable of being made so.

Though Chambers does not mention Pliny here, the *Natural History* may directly or indirectly stand as the illustration of the ancient insofar as it was intended as a comprehensive compilation of knowledge and did not pursue experimental investigation of the new.[33]

The rationale for Chambers's monumental effort was laid out in these terms:

In effect, a reduction of the body of learning is growing every day more and more necessary; as the objects of our knowledge are increasing, books becoming more numerous, and new points of dispute and enquiry turning up. For want of this, the sciences remain in great measure at a stand, or can advance only imperceptibly; since the whole life of those who should make discoveries, is spent in learning what is already found out. Hence, such improvements as are occasionally made, rarely arrive at any maturity but terminate in hints and imperfect openings, or in queries and proposals for farther enquiry. Most of the late discoveries in the sciences remain thus crude and imperfect; the whole vast systems of microscopical plants and animals, and the telescopic worlds, of attraction, magnetism, electricity, and the like, remain, as it were in embryo.[34]

Organization. Pliny's organization of "facts" follows a broadly rational sequence of cosmos, geography, animals, plants, and minerals, but within those rubrics particular, useful facts could be hard to find despite the *Summarium* of Book 1 (see chapter 2).[35] One of the hallmarks of Harris's *Lexicon Technicum* was the alphabetic arrangement of topics so familiar to us from the standard, printed editions of recent encyclopedias.[36] That arrangement together with cross-references allowed readers to navigate the million words to put together a coherent description of subjects. Chambers's *Cyclopaedia* followed Harris's lead, and the consequences will be illustrated below by an excursus comparing Pliny's and Chambers's treatment of the topic of "fulling" (the scouring and milling of woolen cloth).

Acknowledgement of sources. Pliny writes that he has excerpted his 20,000 "things worth knowing" from 100 authors, which is a vast undercount. His *Summarium* names his authorities by book, as well as his topics:

> I have done so because it is, in my opinion, a pleasant thing and one that shows an honorable modesty [*ingenui pudoris*], to own up to those who were the means of one's achievement, not to do as most of the authors to whom I have referred did. For you must know that when collating authorities I have found that the most professedly reliable and modern writers have copied the old authors word for word, without acknowledgement. . . . Surely it marks a mean spirit and an unfortunate disposition to prefer being detected in a theft to repaying a loan. (N.H. pr.21–23)

The implication of this passage is that Pliny did not generally view writers of his own day as adding much to the store of knowledge of the "old authors" whose works they were plagiarizing.

Harris's acknowledgments reveal a marked difference in attitude. He wants to be right up-to-date: he apologizes that his first volume (1704) did not include Newton's work on optics because it came out after the sheets for the printer were finished, and he includes some of Newton's otherwise unpublished work. Unlike Pliny, Harris has such a respect for artificers that he goes out of his way to name them:

And as I have usually taken particular care to give all Authors their just due, from whom I have taken any considerable part of my Materials, without Partiality, so I have designedly done Justice to such Ingenious and Industrious Artificers, as do truly serve the greatest Encouragement for their Skill and Accuracy in the making of those Instruments: Such are Mr. John Rowley, Mathematical Instrument-maker . . . : Mr. Yarwell, and Mr. Marshal, Perspective Makers . . . : Mr. Hawkesbee, who makes Air-Pumps . . . : And Mr. John Patrick . . . , who makes all Kinds of Barometers and Thermometers. . . . And I can't here omit mentioning the Ingenious Mr. Wilson . . . , because those Sheets about the Microscope were Printed off before I had seen Mr. Wilson or his Glasses: But I must now do him that Justice to Say, That of all the Microscopes I have ever seen for Commodiousness, various Uses, Portability and Cheapness; I never met with anything like Mr. Wilson's Glasses.

Harris's awareness that progress in the discovery of new knowledge depends on instrumentation sets him apart from Pliny, who does not honor artisans by name and does not view instruments and their makers as vital to the discovery of new knowledge.[37]

Attitude toward subject matter. A comparison of the topics covered in the *Natural History*, the *Lexicon Technicum*, and the *Cyclopaedia* shows similarities of content but also stark and important differences in attitude toward the subject matter. To offer a sampling, all three works have things to say about meteorology, mineralogy, phytology, zoology, anatomy, astronomy, medicine, agriculture, geography, navigation, and the arts. In addition, Harris and Chambers have a strong interest in mathematics and the physical sciences, which the *Natural History* lacks, apart from astronomy. As Harris writes in his dedication, "I have been very Full and Particular in the Mathematicks, because 'tis the only Solid Foundation on which a Useful Enquiry into Nature and all Physical Learning, can possibly be built; and because 'tis also of the greatest Use and

Advantage to Mankind in all respects." In physics "we are chiefly indebted to that Prodigious Mathematician, Mr. Isaac Newton." The topics of Electricity, Solidity, Elasticity, Effluviums, Magnetism, Light, and Colours are treated, as are the "Mathematical and Philosophical Instruments: Globes, Quadrants, Telescopes, Microscopes, Baroscopes, Hygroscopes, and Air-Pumps." Chambers too covered topics in mathematics and the physical sciences neglected by Pliny.[38]

Pliny's lack of interest in the principles of mathematics and physical sciences is of a piece with his lack of interest in systems of knowledge and causation (see p. 61).[39] This feature of Pliny's intellectual scope and (to judge by the decline in numbers of mathematicians) Roman imperial culture more broadly may have been a serious obstacle to developing a "culture of growth." Mokyr's fundamental premise about early modern Europe is that "the essence of Schumpeterian growth is based on the manipulation of natural regularities and phenomena and thus au fond should be seen as a game against nature."[40]

Harris's esteem for the physical sciences, the scientists, and the instruments that made experimental discoveries possible has no parallel in the *Natural History* for at least two reasons. First, as Paparazzo argued, "the 'physics = praxis' [that is, applied physics] referred to by Conte would fall under the heading of the *uulgares* [common, lowly], or even the *sordidae* [sordid]."[41] Second, Pliny characterized his own contents as boring stuff (*sterilis materia*) and indicated that his peers were laughing at him for his efforts (N.H. 22.14–15).

Cultural context. John Harris was not only a pioneer in the English encyclopedic tradition, he was elected first secretary of the Royal Society, which had been founded in 1660. The scientific societies of seventeenth- and eighteenth-century Europe were important for circulating, testing, and validating ideas and for elevating the esteem for leading scientists. The scholarly societies had their roots in sixteenth-century French academies.[42] James Dowey has recently argued that they became part of "the world's first substantial infrastructure for research and development. . . . learned societies, 'mechanics institutes', masonic lodges and public libraries . . . steadily reduced the cost of access to useful knowledge."[43] A unique aspect of Harris's and Chambers's world was the Republic of Letters, a private order institution that brought together scientists and scholars from different nations of Europe in a collective and competitive enterprise of discovery of useful knowledge.[44] The "Republic of Letters provided an institution in which innovation, even radical innovation, was not only not frowned upon but even encouraged."[45]

The *Natural History* records Asinius Pollio's institution of public libraries in Rome (in connection with portrait-statues [N.H. 35.10]) but gives no hint that Pliny participated in any private order institution or society promoting the discovery and dissemination of useful knowledge. His nephew's description of his work habits suggests that his uncle was a loner whose work was supported by slave assistants but not part of an intellectual network sharing and testing ideas. The competitive display of knowledge in imperial Rome, as described by Aulus Gellius in his *Attic Nights*, seems to have been based on precise memory of authoritative literary texts rather than the production of new experimental discoveries (see excursus, chapter 4). The younger Pliny's letter about his uncle's *opera* (N.H. 3.5.17) reports that his uncle could have sold his notebooks for 400,000 HS, and he declined. But there is no reason to think that the would-be buyer, Larcius Licinus, planned to put those notebooks to any scientific use—they were trophies.

Conclusion

Harris's *Lexicon* and Chambers's *Cyclopaedia* embodied the values and attitudes of the culture of growth: their optimistic view was that new discoveries of useful knowledge could improve the human condition through "inventions at present held impossible."

These inventions would enable an ever greater manipulation of Nature. And in doing so Britain would be the envy of the Romans. By contrast, Pliny held a pessimistic view that greed distracted the Romans from new investigations. Furthermore, the advance of knowledge did not aim to manipulate or control Nature. As Roger French summarized: "No one in antiquity strove through philosophy to manipulate nature. . . . Natural philosophy had understanding nature as one of its goals, but since this aim did not include manipulation, it did not use technology."[46]

Aude Doody has argued convincingly that it is a mistake to interpret Pliny in the context of the genre of the encyclopedia, which had not yet been established.[47] So it might be argued that it is wrongheaded to compare the *Natural History* with the *Lexicon* and the *Cyclopaedia*. But it is those very differences that alert us to important features of Pliny's work, despite the fact that his professed purpose was usefulness. It might also be argued that Pliny was just one author, and it would be a mistake to draw any more general conclusions. Pliny was certainly idiosyncratic, but unless we believe that he was completely obtuse about the preferences of Titus, his dedication associating Titus with literary eloquence rather than with Prince George's mathematics and mechanics surely provides some insight into an imperial culture that did not celebrate growth through technical progress.

Excursus: Fulling as an Illustration Comparing Pliny's *Natural History* and Chambers's *Cyclopaedia*

As pointed out in the previous chapter, one of the main non-agricultural sectors in premodern societies was textile production. In that process fulling serves the purpose of cleaning and finishing the cloth, and it has recently received a thorough study.[48] Fulling is treated in both Pliny's *Natural History* and Chambers's *Cyclopaedia*, and a comparison of the two offers an insight into differences of organization, content, and tone. The *Natural History* contains six references to fulling scattered across four books;[49] the *Summarium*, intended to guide readers to the "facts" for which they were searching, does not list fullers or fulling as contents in any of the four books. By contrast, Chambers has an entry entitled "Fulling," which is straightforward to find because it is in alphabetical order under "F."

The contents of the two encyclopedias also display a clear contrast. Pliny's first five references to fulling give stray "facts":

- the name of the alleged inventor (Nicias of Megara) in a long list of inventors (N.H. 7.196);
- fullers' use of a kind of flax in a longer discourse about flax (N.H. 19.13);
- fullers' demonstration of the efficacy of urine to ward off gout in a list of maladies remedied by human urine (N.H. 28.66);[50]
- the use of camel urine by fullers (N.H. 28.91);
- the type of sulfur used in fulling (N.H. 35.175).

In the final reference in a section on different uses of various types of earth Pliny gives a somewhat more detailed description, running to ten lines or so, of the stages and ingredients of the fulling process including the application of Cimolian earth to brighten the colors (N.H. 35.197–98). Even this longer description says nothing of the equipment or labor required.

Chambers's entry, on the other hand, provides a systematic description, starting with a definition of fulling and a cross-reference to the similar process of milling (grain).[51] I give the whole entry here as an example to highlight the contrast.

Fulling, the art, or act of cleaning, beating, and pressing cloths, staffs, stockings, to render them stronger, closer, and firmer; call'd also milling. See mill.

Pliny, lib.7. cap.16. assures, that one Nicias, the son of Hermias, was the first inventor of the art of fulling: And it appears by an inscription, quoted by Sir G. Wheeler, in his travels thro' Greece, that this same Nicias was a Governour in Greece, in the time of the Romans.

The fulling of cloths, and other stuffs, is perform'd by a kind of Watermill; thence call'd fulling, or scouring mill.

These mills, excepting in what relates to the mill stones and hopper, are much the same with corn mills. And there are even some, which serve indifferently for either use; corn being ground, and cloths full'd by the motion of the same wheel.

Whence, in some places, particularly France, the fullers are call'd millers; as grinding corn, and milling stuffs at the same time.

The principal parts of the fulling mill, are, the wheel, with its trundle; which gives motion to the tree, or spindle, whose teeth communicate it to the pestles, or stampers, which are hereby raised, and fallen alternately according as its teeth catch on, or quit a kind of latch in the middle of each pestle. The pestles and troughs are of wood; each trough having at least two, sometimes three pestles, at the discretion of the master, or according to the force of the stream of water.

In these troughs are laid the cloths, stuffs, etc. intended to be fulled: then, letting the current of water full on the wheel, the pestles are successively let fall thereon, and by their weight and velocity stamp, and press the stuffs very strongly; which by this means become thickned and condensed.

In the course of the operation, they sometimes make use of urine; sometimes fullers earth, and sometimes soap.

To prepare the stuffs, to receive the first impression of the pestle, they are usually laid in urine; then in fullers earth, and water; and lastly in soap, dissolv'd in hot water.

Soap alone would do very well; but this is expensive; though fullers earth, in the way of our dressing, is scarce inferior thereto' but then it must be well clear'd of all stones and grittinesses, which are apt to make holes in the stuff.

As to urine, 'tis certainly prejudicial, and ought to be entirely discarded; not so much on account of its ill smell, as of its sharpness, and saltness; which is apt to render the stuffs dry and harsh.

The true method of fulling with soap, is deliver'd by Mons. Colinet, in an authentic memoir on that subject, supported by experiments made by order of the Marquis de Louvois, the Super-Intendent of the Arts and Manufactories of France. The substance of which we shall here subjoin.

METHOD OF FULLING CLOTHS AND
WOOLEN STUFFS, WITH SOAP.

A colour'd cloth, of about 45 Ells, is to be laid, in the usual manner, in the trough of a fulling mill; without first soaking it in water, as is commonly practised in many places.

To full this trough of cloth, 15 pounds of soap are requir'd; one half of which is to be melted in two pails of river or spring water, made as hot as the hand can well bear it. This solution is to be pour'd by little and little upon the cloth, in proportion as 'tis laid in the trough: and thus it is to be fulled for at least two hours; after which it is to be taken out, and stretch'd.

This done, the cloth is immediately return'd into the same trough; without any new soap; and there full'd two hours more. Then taking it out, they wring it well, to express all the grease and filth.

After this second fulling, the remainder of the soap is melted, as the former, and cast at four different times, on the cloth; re-membering to take out the cloth every two hours, to stretch it, and undo the plaits and wrinkles it has acquired in the trough. When they perceive it sufficiently full'd, and brought to the quality and thickness required, they scour it out for good, in hot water, keeping it in the trough, till it be quite clean.

As to white cloths; in regard these full more easily, and in less time, than colour'd ones, a third part of the soap may be spared.

FULLING of stockings, caps, etc. should be performed somewhat differently; viz. wither with the feet, or the hands; on a kind of rack, or wooden machine, either arm'd with teeth of the same matter, or else horse, or bullocks teeth.

The ingredients made use of herein, are urine, green soap, white soap, and fullers earth. But the urine also reckoned prejudicial here.

Note, woven stockings, etc. should be full'd with soap alone: for those that are knit, earth may be us'd with the soap.

Indeed, 'tis frequent to full these kinds of works with the mill, after the usual manner of cloth, etc. But that is too coarse and violent a manner, and apt to damage the work, unless it be very strong. See Stockings.

It is obvious that the ease of finding the entry and the step-by-step treatment make Chambers's entry genuinely useful, whereas it is hard to imagine any would-be fuller searching through the thirty-seven books of the *Natural History* to find facts that could be employed in his craft, especially since the *Summarium* gives no hint that fulling is addressed at all.

Conclusion

THE ROLE of culture in promoting *sustained* economic growth is not a settled question among economists, but whatever the cause and effect, such growth in the long term must be underwritten by repeated technical improvements in production.[1] As Joel Mokyr has emphasized, *institutional* improvements for growth such as the Pax Romana are not necessarily durable and can be reversed, whereas invention and innovation based on advances in knowledge provide a foundation for sustained growth.[2] This was recognized by the early modern political economists William Petty and Samuel Hartlib.[3] At an intuitive level, the elder Pliny recognized the value of investigation (*inquisitio*) and expressed regret that in his own day pursuit of profit through trade was active while pursuit of new knowledge was not. The *Natural History*, taken as a whole, provides a window into the mindset of wealthy Romans regarding discovery and its implications for economic production. In some basic respects Pliny's observations anticipated those of the great political economists of the eighteenth century, and in others his fundamental values and attitudes were quite different.

The *Natural History* as a whole, in my view, deserves more attention than it has received as a witness to Roman attitudes regarding innovation, investment, and what might be broadly labeled a culture of growth. Its overt purpose was very different from that of a work like Cicero's *De Officiis* (I.150–51), which has been repeatedly criticized as evidence for Roman attitudes regarding low-status occupations. The *De Officiis* expresses the moral values and sense of propriety of a very small, wealthy, educated elite; there is good evidence that that sense of propriety did not represent

Roman culture from top to bottom. Pliny is a different sort of witness, not only because he had more experience of practical affairs beyond politics but also because he claims to be writing with the aim of "usefulness" (*utilitas*) and for a broader audience extending from the emperor to the working class of farmers and artisans. Of course, that does not mean that Pliny's worldview can be taken as the general or dominant view held by all Roman imperial society, which was too variegated to make such a concept of a unitary ideology plausible. But the *Natural History* adds an important dimension to our understanding of the cultural context of the Roman economy.[4] And although Pliny came from the upper 1 percent of the population of the empire, Walter Scheidel estimates that the 1 percent controlled perhaps 80 percent of the surplus production above subsistence, making the financial attitudes and decisions of that tiny minority especially influential in directing the flow of capital investment.[5]

I have argued that there are two reasons why historians should pay attention to this textual evidence. First, none of the recent efforts to substitute proxies in order to assess the aggregate or per capita performance of the economy can survive scrutiny. Despite the increasing scientific sophistication in gathering and analyzing material data, whether from the Greenland icecap or Italian graveyards, the correlation of the proxies with broad economic performance remains very doubtful. The accumulation of archaeological reports will certainly continue to enhance our understanding of the development of material prosperity in particular regions and of certain social groups, but there remain huge methodological obstacles to generalizations about trends in productivity and well-being for the empire as a whole. We can only guess at certain fundamental features affecting economic production, such as the balance between the urban and rural populations or between free and slave labor, and it is hard to imagine how those uncertainties might ever be resolved. Therefore, my view is that texts remain a useful complement, with appropriate circumspection, for understanding the dynamics of the Roman economy, and the *Natural History* holds a special interest among Latin texts on account of its aim to provide a *comprehensive* compilation of *useful* knowledge (not to mention the mundane fact that it has survived).

Mokyr has argued that a culture of growth emerged in early modern Europe that provided the essential foundation for sustained economic growth and industrialization resulting in the Great Enrichment. The features of that culture of growth were an increasing knowledge of Nature, which established a *broadly vetted* consensus about the *regularities* as demonstrated by replicable *experiments* with *quantified* results, often using more and more precise *instruments*; the demonstrated regularities could then be exploited to *manipulate* Nature for increased productivity and the *enrichment* of humans.

Of these features, Pliny clearly shared the goal of disseminating an exhaustive knowledge of Nature with the express purpose of *honoring* rather than *manipulating* Mother Nature. Pliny did not see himself as adding to that store of knowledge; rather, it was his sacred duty to preserve it, and to preserve it without systematic vetting or much discrimination.[6] That is, he aimed to include everything he read, especially from the venerated ancients, without necessarily judging the truth of his "things worth knowing," and certainly without experimentation with improved instruments to verify a commonly held body of knowledge.[7] Indeed, as far as we know, Pliny did not participate in any learned communities comparable to the Republic of Letters to provide critical testing of scientific claims; his effort seems to have been solo. The learned communities described by Aulus Gellius were interested mostly in matters of language and verified claims by reference to authoritative texts and philosophical argument. For Pliny under the influence of Stoic thought, Nature was sacred and mysterious, not to be measured to find exploitable regularities.[8] And without an interest in regularities, there was not much need for mathematics or measurement.

That is not to say that Pliny was uninterested in discovery/invention and innovation. On the contrary, one of the *Natural*

History's longest discourses on any subject is the inventory of great discoveries and their inventors in Book 7. Scholars today debate the level of innovation in the Roman economy, which is bound to be a matter of subjective judgment—after all, it is not clear-cut precisely what would qualify as "significant" or a "major break-through," much less what would qualify as a lot, or a scarcity, of technical advances as a whole.[9] On the one hand, there can be no doubt that inventions and technical improvements such as the water mill and glass-blowing were disseminated across the empire.[10] Any judgment about the rate of innovation should also take account of the fact that the time period extends to many centuries, and the population was in the scores of millions.[11] To my mind, it is striking that Pliny's inventory of scores of technical inventions in Book 7 contains not a single one by a Roman, and the over-whelming majority are prehistoric (that is, not within the previous half millennium).[12] In the principal sector of production, agriculture, Pliny's recommendations for profitability are more often *oracula*, that is, tried and true precepts, rather than innovation or calculation. He gives little sense of an intentional process of discovery and innovation beyond exploring new territories. Invention was a matter of accident or a gift of Mother Nature—there is no hint of a concept of deliberate "research and development" in the thirty-seven books.

Though Pliny's express purpose was utility, the length of his treatment of different discoveries/inventions does not seem to be governed by the magnitude of economic impact. The discussion of the (millennia-old) invention of papyrus is appropriately lengthy, given the critical importance of the technology of written communication, but it is hard to understand why the water mill and *opus caementicium* receive shorter shrift than Columella's year-round cucumber. The explanation must be that Pliny was not focused on the *manipulation* of Nature for the *enrichment* of the human race. But Pliny was perceptive enough to see that competition motivated invention in the Hellenistic kingdoms, a motivation that in his view was lost under the majesty of Roman rule.

Pliny's early eighteenth-century successors in the encyclopedic tradition bring into sharp relief some important characteristics of the *Natural History*. In the tradition of Francis Bacon their forward-looking optimism that new knowledge leading to new inventions would open prospects "now thought to be impossible" was not within Pliny's horizons.[13] The importance that John Harris and Ephraim Chambers attributed to mathematics and the physical sciences—so important to sustained innovation—is not evident in the *Natural History*. Harris and Chambers viewed their works as a means efficiently to disseminate the knowledge necessary for future innovations in an age when the proliferation of books made mastery of them all impossible. The invention of the printing press made such dissemination feasible, as is manifested in the many updated editions published through the decades of the eighteenth century.[14] The culmination of the encyclopedic genre was Diderot and D'Alembert's *Encyclopédie*, the distribution of which has been associated with economic growth. Some scholars have suggested that Pliny's *Natural History* also served to disseminate technical knowledge, but I know of no direct evidence to show that it actually served that purpose during the century or more after publication.[15] The first mention after the younger Pliny's letters is to be found in Aulus Gellius's *Attic Nights* and does not reflect an interest in the work for technical advice by practitioners. Indeed, the problems with locating any sought-after "fact" in the 400,000-word work must have been discouraging.

In the end, from a modern point of view the *Natural History* is a mixed bag, ranging from insights anticipating contemporary economics to the frivolous and absurd. Pliny could see that the Roman Empire promoted Smithian growth through peace and public infrastructure that nurtured trade. And he noticed that it discouraged Schumpeterian growth by creating an environment in which lack of competition depressed incentives for investigation and innovation. His more specific financial advice was a mixture of shrewd commonsense and venerable tradition. We will never have the data to measure the impact on growth, but Pliny points to institutions and investments such as urban infrastructure that surely did encourage prosperity, as well as others such as *latifundia* and chained slave-gangs, which he believed to be detrimental.

It is ironic that the *Natural History* had no detectible impact in the generations immediately after its publication but was regarded as authoritative and widely referenced in late antiquity, the Middle Ages, and Renaissance. It was one of the first classical works published in the new age of the printing press in the fifteenth century and was published thereafter in many editions. In the course of the sixteenth century the attitude toward the *Natural History*, as well as other ancient scientific works, began to shift from efforts to establish authentic texts embodying classical authority to efforts to establish the scientific truth.[16] With this shift Pliny's reputation declined, and in 1600 the English physicist and physician William Gilbert avoided quoting the errors of the magnum opus, likening them to "'evil and noxious plants [which] ever have the most luxurious growth.'"[17] At a distance of four centuries from Gilbert we are no longer worried about the noxious influence of the *Natural History* and can assess it in a less judgmental tone as one witness to Roman cultural values and attitudes that influenced the imperial economy.

One closing thought. As alien as much of the *Natural History* seems in an age of modern science, Pliny's moral advocacy of respect for Nature and his outraged criticism of heedless exploitation in pursuit of wealth surely resonate among a generation deeply concerned by environmental degradation and climate change.

LATIN TEXTS

LATIN: FOR THE translations of the *Natural History* in the preceding chapters the Latin texts from the Loeb and Budé editions are provided below. Where the editions agree, the text is introduced with Loeb and Budé. Where the Budé edition differs, the text is introduced with Loeb and (Budé) and the Budé variants are given in parentheses.

Page

Page

45   N.H 28.67: Loeb and (Budé): sua cuique autem, quod fas sit dixisse, maxime prodest, confestim perfuso canis morsu, echinorumque spinis inhaerentibus (et) in spongea lanisve inposita aut adversus rabidi canis morsus cinere ex ea subacto, contraque serpentium ictus.

45   N.H. 28.82: Loeb and Budé: Lais et Salpe canum rabiosorum morsus et tertianas quartanasque febres menstruo in lana arietis nigri argenteo bracchiali incluso.

45   N.H. 28.84: Loeb and (Budé): inter omnes vero convenit, si aqua potusque formidetur a morsu canis, supposita (subposita) tantum calici lacinia tali, statim metum eum discuti, videlicet praevalente sympathia illa Graecorum, cum rabiem canum eius sanguinis gustatu incipere dixerimus.

45   N.H. 28.104: Loeb and Budé: carnes si edantur, contra rabidi canis morsus efficaces esse, etiamnum iocur efficacius.

46   N.H. 28.75: Loeb and Budé: eius quae marem peperit lacte gustato canes rabiosos negant fieri.

46   N.H. 29.98: Loeb and (Budé): In canis rabidi (rabiosi) morsu tuetur a pavore aquae canini capitis cinis inlitus vulneri (volneri), oportet autem comburi omnia eodem modo . . . in vase fictili novo argilla circumlito atque ita in furnum indito. idem et in potione proficit. quidam ob id edendum dederunt. aliqui et vermem e cadavere canino adalligavere menstruave canis in panno subdidere calici aut intus ipsius caudae pilos combustos inseruere vulneri (volneri) . . . est limus salivae sub lingua rabiosi canis qui datus in potu hydrophobos fieri non patitur, multo tamen utilissime iocur eius qui in rabie momorderit datur, si fieri possit, crudum mandendum, sin minus, quoquo modo coctum, aut ius coctis carnibus. est vermiculus in lingua canum qui vocatur a Graecis lytta, quo exempto infantibus catulis nec rabidi fiunt nec fastidium sentiunt. idem ter igni circumlatus datur morsis a rabioso ne rabidi fiant. et cerebello gallinaceo occurritur. sed id devoratum anno tantum eo prodest. aiunt et cristam galli contritam efficaciter inponi et anseris adipem cum melle. Saliuntur (salliuntur) et carnes eorum qui rabidi fuerunt ad eadem remedia in cibo dandae. quin et necantur catuli statim in aqua ad sexum eius qui momorderit, ut iocur crudum devoretur ex iis.

49   N.H. 27.146: Loeb and Budé: artesque salutares inseruit et visceribus.

50   N.H. 14.1: Loeb and (Budé): quis enim non communicato orbe terrarum maiestate Romani imperii profecisse vitam putet commercio rerum ac societate festae pacis, omniaque etiam quae ante (antea) occulta fuerant in promiscuo usu facta? (14.2)

50   N.H. 3.39: Loeb and (Budé): sparsa congregaret imperia ritusque molliret et tot populorum discordes ferasque linguas sermonis commercio contraheret ad colloquia (conloquia) et humanitatem homini daret, breviterque una cunctarum gentium in toto orbe patria fieret.

Page

50–51 N.H. 11.240: Loeb: Laus caseo Romae, ubi omnium gentium bona comminus iudicantur, e provinciis Nemausensi praecipua, e Lesure Gabalicoque pagis.

51 N.H. 11.242: Loeb: tradunt Zoroastren in desertis caseo vixisse annis xx ita temperato ut vetustatem non sentiret.

51 N.H. 22.1: Loeb and (Budé): Implesse poterant miraculum sui natura atque tellus reputanti (reputantium) vel prioris tantum voluminis dotes totque genera herbarum utilitatibus hominum aut voluptatibus genita. sed quanto plura restant quantoque mirabiliora inventu! illarum (Illa) enim maiore in parte cibi aut odoris decorisve commendatio ad numerosa experimenta duxit, reliquarum potentia adprobat nihil ab rerum natura sine aliqua occultiore causa gigni.

51 N.H. 24.1: Loeb and Budé: Ne silvae quidem horridiorque naturae facies medicinis carent, sacra illa parente rerum omnium nusquam non remedia disponente homini, ut medicina fieret etiam solitudo ipsa.

53 N.H. 29.24: Loeb and (Budé): ex rebus LIIII componitur, inter nullas pondere aequali et quarundam rerum sexagesima denarii unius imperata (imperatur).

54 N.H. 33.50: Loeb and Budé: Antonium triumvirum aureis usum vasis in omnibus obscenis desideriis, pudendo crimine etiam Cleopatrae . . . Antonius solus contumelia naturae vilitatem auro fecit.

54 N.H. 34.138: Loeb and Budé: optumo pessimoque vitae instrumento est, siquidem hoc tellurem scindimus, arbores serimus, arbusta tondemus, vites squalore deciso annis omnibus cogimus iuvenescere, hoc extruimus tecta, caedimus saxa, omnesque ad alios usus ferro utimur, sed eodem ad bella, caedes, latrocinia, non comminus solum, sed etiam missili volucrique, nunc tormentis excusso, nunc lacertis, nunc vero pinnato, quam sceleratissimam humani ingenii fraudem arbitror, siquidem, ut ocius mors perveniret ad hominem, alitem illam fecimus pinnasque ferro dedimus. quam ob rem culpa eius non naturae fiat accepta.

55 N.H. 6.89: Loeb and Budé: Sed ne Taprobane quidem, quamvis extra orbem a natura relegata, nostris vitiis caret: aurum argentumque et ibi in pretio, marmor testudinis simile, margaritae gemmaeque in honore; multo praestantior est totus luxuriae nostra cumulus. ipsorum opes maiores esse dicebant, sed apud nos opulentiae maiorem usum.

55 N.H. 9.104: Loeb and Budé: populatio morum atque luxuria non aliunde maior quam e concharum genere proveniat.

56 N.H. 21.45: Loeb and Budé: in quibus unguento vicisse naturam gaudens luxuria vestibus quoque provocavit eos flores qui colore commendantur.

Page

56   N.H. 13.20: Loeb and Budé: unguenta ilico expirant ac suis moriuntur horis.

56   N.H. 10.141–42: Loeb and Budé: nulla alia inductus suavitate nisi ut in iis imitationem hominis manderet, ne quaestus quidem suos reveritus illos opimos et voce meritos.

57   N.H. 35.49: Loeb and Budé: iuvatque pugnaturos ad mortem aut certe caedem speciose vehi.

58   N.H. 37.12: Loeb and Budé: Victoria tamen illa Pompei primum ad margaritas gemmasque mores inclinavit, sicut L. Scipionis et Cn. Manli ad caelatum argentum et vestes Atticas et triclinia aerata, sicut L. Mummi ad Corinthia et tabulas pictas.

58   N.H. 7.1: Loeb: Principium iure tribuetur homini, cuius causa videtur cuncta alia genuisse natura magna, saeva mercede contra tanta sua munera, ut non sit satis aestimare, parens melior homini an tristior noverca fuerit.

65   N.H. 35.166: Loeb and Budé: quis enim satis miretur pessumam eius partem ideoque pulverem appellatam in Puteolanis collibus opponi maris fluctibus, mersumque protinus fieri lapidem unum inexpugnabilem undis et fortiorem cotidie, utique si Cumano misceatur caemento?

66   N.H. 32.1: Loeb and Budé: quo maiore hominum ingenio in ulla sui parte adiuta est quam velis remisque?

66   N.H. 19.6: Loeb and Budé: nulla exsecratio sufficit contra inventorem . . . cui satis non fuit hominem in terra mori.

66   N.H. 9.39: Loeb and Budé: prodigi et sagacis ad luxuriae instrumenta ingenii.

67   N.H. 9.66: Loeb and Budé: M. Apicius ad omne luxus ingenium natus in sociorum garo . . . necari eos praecellens putavit.

68   N.H. 27.1–2: Loeb and Budé: quantoque maior copia herbarum dicenda restat, tanto magis adorare priscorum in inveniendo curam, in tradendo benignitatem subit. nec dubie superata hoc modo posset videri etiam rerum naturae ipsius munificentia, si humani operis esset inventio. nunc vero deorum fuisse eam apparet aut certe divinam, etiam cum homo inveniret.

69   N.H. 25.17: Loeb and Budé: nuper cuiusdam militantis in praetorio mater vidit in quiete ut radicem silvestris rosae quam cynorrhodon vocant blanditam sibi aspectu pridie in frutecto mitteret filio bibendam.

69   N.H. 27.6: Loeb and Budé: quae si quis ulla forte ab homine excogitari potuisse credit, ingrate deorum munera intellegit.

69   N.H. 37.60: Loeb and Budé: cuius hoc invento quove casu repertum? aut quae fuit coniectura experiendi rem inmensi pretii in foedissimo animalium? numinum profecto talis inventio est et hoc munus omne, nec quaerenda ratio in ulla parte naturae, sed voluntas!

Page

70–71 N.H. 2.117–18: Loeb and (Budé): quo magis miror orbe discordi et in regna, hoc est in membra, diviso tot viris curae fuisse tam ardua inventu, inter bella praesertim et infida hospitia, piratis etiam omnium mortalium hostibus transituros fama terrentibus (transitus famae tenentibus), ut hodie quaedam in suo quisque tractu ex eorum commentariis qui numquam eo accessere verius noscat quam indigenarum scientia, nunc vero pace tam festa, tam gaudente proventu literarum (rerum) artiumque principe, omnino nihil addisci nova inquisitione, immo ne veterum quidem inventa perdisci. non erant maiora praemia in multos dispersa fortunae magnitudine, et ista plures sine praemio alio quam posteros iuvandi eruerunt. [Namque] mores hominum senuere, non fructus, et inmensa multitudo aperto quodcumque est mari hospitalique litorum omnium adpulsu navigat, sed lucri, non scientiae, gratia; nec reputat caeca mens et tantum avaritiae intenta id ipsum scientia posse tutius fieri.

72 N.H. 14.2–4: Loeb and (Budé): illud satis mirari non queo, interisse quarundam (quarumdam) memoriam atque etiam nominum quae auctores prodidere notitiam. quis enim non communicato orbe terrarum maiestate Romani imperii profecisse vitam putet commercio rerum ac societate festae pacis, omniaque etiam quae ante (antea) occulta fuerant in promiscuo usu facta? at, Hercules, non reperiuntur qui norint multa ab antiquis prodita: tanto priscorum cura fertilior aut industria felicior fuit, ante milia annorum inter principia litterarum Hesiodo praecepta agricolis pandere orso subsecutisque non paucis hanc curam eius; unde nobis crevit labor, quippe cum requirenda <u>iam</u> sint non solum postea inventa, verum etiam ea quae invenerant prisci, desidia rerum internicione (internecione) memoriae indicta. cuius vitii causas quis alias quam publicas mundi invenerit? nimirum alii subiere ritus circaque alia mentes hominum detinentur et avaritiae tantum artes coluntur. antea inclusis gentium imperiis intra ipsas, ideoque (adeoque) et ingeniis, quadam sterilitate fortunae necesse erat animi bona exercere, regesque innumeri honore artium colebantur et in ostentatione has praeferebant opes, immortalitatem sibi per illas prorogari arbitrantes; quare (qua re) abundabant et praemia et opera vitae. posteris laxitas mundi et rerum amplitudo damno fuit.

76 N.H. 29.9: Loeb and Budé: nullius histrionum equorumque trigarii comitatior egressus in publico erat, cum Crinas Massiliensis arte geminata, ut cautior religiosiorque, ad siderum motus ex ephemeride mathematica cibos dando horasque observando auctoritate eum praecessit, nuperque HSc̄ reliquit.

77 N.H. 22.14–15: Loeb and Budé: sed quis non mores iure castiget? addidere vivendi pretia deliciae luxusque. numquam fuit vitae cupido maior nec minor cura . . . immo vero plerisque ultro etiam inrisui sumus ista commentantes atque frivoli operis arguimur.

Page

79   N.H. 7.73: Loeb: in plenum autem cuncto mortalium generi minorem in dies
     fieri propemodum observatur, rarosque patribus proceriores.

85   N.H. 37.202: Loeb and Budé: quidquid est quo carere vita non debeat, nusquam
     est praestantius: fruges, vinum, oleum, vellera, lina, vestes, iuvenci.

86–87 N.H. 18.37–38: Loeb and (Budé): L. Tarius Rufus infima natalium humilitate
     consulatum militari industria meritus, antiquae alias parsimoniae, circiter |m̄|
     HS. liberalitate divi Augusti congestorum (congestum) usque ad detrectatio-
     nem heredis exhausit agros in Piceno coemendo colendoque in gloriam. in-
     ternicionem ergo famemque censemus? immo, Hercules, modum iudicem
     rerum omnium utilissimum. bene colere necessarium est, optime damno-
     sum, praeterquam subole sua colono aut pascendis alioqui colente. domino
     aliquas messes colligere non expedit si conputetur inpendium operae, nec
     temere olivam, nec quasdam terras diligenter colere, sicut in Sicilia tradunt,
     itaque decipi advenas.

89   N.H. 18.35: Loeb and Budé: Modum agri in primis servandum antiqui puta-
     vere, quippe ita censebant, satius esse minus serere et melius arare, qua in
     sententia et Vergilium fuisse video. verumque confitentibus latifundia perdi-
     dere Italiam, iam vero et provincias—sex domini semissem Africae posside-
     bant, cum interfecit eos Nero princeps.

90   N.H. 14.137: Loeb and Budé: quod hominis mentem mutet ac furorem gignat,
     milibus scelerum ob id editis.

95   N.H. 35.1: Loeb and Budé: Metallorum, quibus opes constant, adgnascen-
     tiumque iis natura indicata propemodum est, ita conexis rebus, ut immensa
     medicinae silva officinarumque tenebrae et morosa caelandi fingendique ac
     tinguendi subtilitas simul dicerentur.

96   N.H. 12.82: Loeb: falsi et ingrati cognominis, quae hoc acceptum superis ferat
     cum plus ex eo inferis debeat. beatam illam fecit hominum etiam in morte
     luxuria quae dis intellexerant genita inurentium defunctis.

97   N.H. 18.21: Loeb and (Budé): at nunc eadem illa vincti pedes, damnatae ma-
     nus inscriptique vultus exercent, non tam surda tellure quae parens appellatur
     colique dicitur ut ipso opera ab his adsumpto non invita ea et indignante
     (ipso honore his adsumpto, ut non invita ea et indignata) credatur id fieri.
     et nos miramur ergastulorum non eadem emolumenta esse quae fuerint
     imperatorum!

97   N.H. 18.31: Loeb and Budé: frontemque domini plus prodesse quam occipi-
     tium non mentiuntur.

98   N.H. 21.170: Loeb and Budé: quae e vino dulci inlita pubertatem coercet et
     non patitur erumpere.

98   N.H. 24.35: Loeb and Budé: inlinitur eadem calida . . . et totis corporibus
     mangonum maxime cura ad gracilitatem emendandam.

Page

98   N.H. 28.4: Loeb and Budé: sanguinem quoque gladiatorum bibunt, ut viventibus poculis, comitiales [morbi] . . . illi ex homine ipso sorbere efficacissimum putant calidum spirantemque et vivam ipsam animam ex osculo vulnerum.

98–99   N.H. 33.26–27: Loeb and Budé: nunc cibi quoque ac potus anulo vindicantur a rapina . . . in domo turba externa ac iam servorum quoque causa nomenclator adhibendus . . . nunc rapiendae conparantur epulae pariterque qui rapiant eas, et claves quoque ipsas signasse non est satis. gravatis somno aut morientibus anuli detrahuntur.

99   N.H. 28.56: Loeb and Budé: L. Lucullus hanc de se praefecturam servo dederat, ultimoque probro manus in cibis triumphali seni deiciebatur vel in Capitolio epulanti, pudenda re servo suo facilius parere quam sibi.

99   N.H. 36.82: Loeb and Budé: minimam ex iis, sed laudatissimam, a Rhodopide meretricula factam. Aesopi fabellarum philosophi conserva quondam et contubernalis haec fuit, maiore miraculo, tantas opes meretricio esse conquisitas.

101   N.H. 13.20: Loeb and (Budé): summa commendatio eorum ut transeunte femina odor invitet etiam aliud agentes (agentis)—exceduntque quadringenos denarios librae!

101   N.H. 33.152–53: Loeb and Budé: feminae laventur et nisi argentea solia fastidiant, eademque materia et cibis et probris serviat? videret haec Fabricius et stratas argento mulierum balineas ita, ut vestigio locus non sit.

101–2   N.H. 33.164: Loeb and Budé: Pretia rerum, quae usquam posuimus, non ignoramus alia aliis locis esse et omnibus paene mutari annis, prout navigatione constiterint aut ut quisque mercatus sit aut aliquis praevalens manceps annonam flagellet . . . poni tamen necessarium fuit quae plerumque erant Romae, ut exprimeretur auctoritas rerum.

102   N.H. 9.67: Loeb and (Budé): qui in conquestione luxus cocos (coquos) emi singulos pluris quam equos queritabant; at nunc coci trium horum pretiis parantur et cocorum (coquorum) pisces, nullusque prope iam mortalis aestimatur pluris quam qui peritissime censum domini mergit.

102   N.H. 12.29: Loeb: sola placere amaritudine, et hanc in Indos peti! quis ille primus experiri cibis voluit aut cui in appetendi aviditate esurire non fuit satis? utrumque silvestre gentibus suis est et tamen pondere emitur ut aurum vel argentum.

103   N.H. 35.50: Loeb and Budé: omnia ergo meliora tunc fuere, cum minor copia. ita est, quoniam, ut supra diximus, rerum, non animi pretiis excubatur.

103   N.H. 34.5: Loeb and (Budé): quondam aes confusum auro argentoque miscebatur, et tamen ars pretiosior erat; nunc incertum est, peior haec sit an materia, mirumque, cum ad infinitum operum pretia creverint, auctoritas artis extincta est. quaestus enim causa, ut omnia, exerceri coepta est quae gloriae solebat— ideo etiam (autem etiam) deorum adscripta operi, cum proceres gentium claritatem et hac via quaererent.

Page

104   N.H. 33.157: Loeb and Budé: subitoque ars haec ita exolevit, ut sola iam ves-
tustate censeatur usuque attritis caelaturis si nec (si ne) figura discerni possit
auctoritas constet.

104   N.H. 35.148: Loeb and Budé: artis vero tantum, ut multum manipretiis ante-
cederet celeberrimos eadem aetate imaginum pictores Sopolim et Diony-
sium, quorum tabulae pinacothecas inplent.

104   N.H. 34.38: Loeb and Budé: canem ex aere volnus suum lambentem, cuius
eximium miraculum et indiscreta veri similitudo non eo solum intellegitur,
quod ibi dicata fuerat, verum et satisdatione; nam quoniam summa nulla par
videbatur, capite tutelarios cavere pro ea institutum publice fuit.

105   N.H. 37.204: Loeb and Budé: non praetereundum est auro, circa quod omnes
mortales insaniunt, decumum vix esse in pretio locum, argento vero, quo
aurum emitur, paene vicensimum.

105   N.H. 33.6: Loeb and Budé: quanto feliciore aevo, cum res ipsae permutaban-
tur inter sese.

107   N.H. 14.52: Loeb and Budé: efficacibus exemplis non maria plus temerata
conferre mercatori, non in Rubrum litus Indicumve merces petitas quam
sedulum ruris larem.

110   N.H. 33.26: Loeb and (Budé): denique vel (ut) plurima opum scelera anulis
fiunt. quae fuit illa vita priscorum, qualis innocentia, in qua nihil signabatur!

110   N.H. 33.28: Loeb and Budé: celebratior quidem usus cum faenore coepisse
debet. argumento est consuetudo volgi, ad sponsiones etiamnum anulo exili-
ente, tracta ab eo tempore, quo nondum erat arra velocior, ut plane adfirmare
possimus nummos ante apud nos, mox anulos coepisse.

110   N.H. 12.123: Loeb and Budé: nec manifestior alibi fraus, quippe milibus de-
narium sextarii, empti vendente fisco tricenis denariis, veneunt: in tantum
expedit augere liquorem.

110–11 N.H. 33.125: Loeb and Budé: sed eadem fraus, quae in omni parte vitae inge-
niosissima est, viliorem excogitavit materiam.

111   N.H. 33.127: Loeb and Budé: sed experimento quoque fraus intervenit.
servatis in urina virorum vatillis inficitur ita ramentum obiter dum uritur
candoremque mentitur.

111   N.H. 37.83: Loeb and Budé: nullos magis fraus indiscreta similitudine vitro
adulterat. experimentum in sole tantum.

111   N.H. 37.198: Loeb and Budé: nos contra rationem deprendendi falsas demon-
strabimus, quando etiam luxuriam adversus fraudes muniri deceat.

111   N.H. 24.4: Loeb and Budé: postea fraudes hominum et ingeniorum capturae
officinas invenere istas in quibus sua cuique homini venalis promittitur vita.

111   N.H. 34.108: Loeb and Budé: credunt Seplasiae omnia fraudibus corrumpenti.

Page

111–12 N.H. 33.132: Loeb and Budé: mirumque, in hac artium sola vitia discuntur et
falsi denarii spectatur exemplar pluribusque veris denariis adulterinus emitur.

112 N.H. 8.135: Loeb and Budé: ipsum animal non, ut remur plerique, vitae hominum supervacuum est, si non sint illi aculei, frustra vellerum mollitia in
pecude mortalibus data: hac cute expoliuntur vestes. magnum fraus et ibi
lucrum monopolio invenit, de nulla re crebrioribus senatus consultis nullo-
que non principe adito querimoniis provincialibus.

124 N.H. pr.21–23: Loeb and (Budé): est enim benignum, ut arbitror, et plenum
ingenui pudoris fateri per quos profeceris, non ut plerique ex his (iis) quos
attigi fecerunt. scito enim conferentem auctores me deprehendisse a iuratis-
simis et proximis veteres transcriptos ad verbum neque nominatos . . .
obnoxii profecto animi et infelicis ingenii est deprehendi in furto malle quam
mutuum reddere.

NOTES

Preface

1. Murphy 2004, 32.

Introduction

1. Morris 2013.

2. Gudger 1924; Isager 1991, 10.

3. Slack 2014; Mokyr 2016; McCloskey 2016.

4. Mokyr 2016.

5. Squicciarini and Voigtländer 2015.

6. Doody 2010 suggests that we think of the *Natural History* as "encyclopedic" in the sense of a comprehensive store of existing knowledge, though not an "encyclopedia."

7. Beagon 1992; Healy 1999; Murphy 2004, on which, see Doody 2010, 132. For a broad and insightful interpretation, see Conte 1994. Two articles have explored aspects of Pliny's economic thought: Zehnacker 1979 on the history of coinage and Lao 2011 on luxury consumption. Howe 1985, 561: "As if taking their cue from its shapelessness, most scholars of the *Natural History* seem more concerned with selected passages than with the work as a whole."

8. Naas (2002, 6) notes the various disciplines (such as astronomy, geography, and art) that Plinian scholars have explicated; economics is missing from the list, and Naas comments that the economic aspect of the empire is subordinated to the political and moral in the *Natural History* (9).

9. This is the way that the *Natural History* is used, e.g., by M. I. Rostovtzeff in his great *Social and Economic History of the Roman Empire* and by M. I. Finley in *The Ancient Economy*. Eric Roll in his classic *History of Economic Thought* refers to Pliny's comment on the deleterious effects of *latifundia* and on why gold was precious; it is interesting that Roll gave Pliny more credit than he deserved in the comment, "Pliny may be said to have carried a little farther the discussion of money by pointing out the qualities which make gold a particularly suitable medium of exchange" (29). In

fact, Pliny's discussion of the special qualities of gold that give it value contains nothing specifically about exchange (N.H. 33.58–63). Curiously, Flohr's recent essay on Roman innovation (2016) cites Pliny repeatedly for specific inventions but does not address Pliny's general pessimism about lack of *inquisitio*.

10. Humphrey, Oleson, and Sherwood 1998. The *Natural History* is cited by Flohr (2016) as evidence for a culture of innovation.

11. E.g., McConnell et al. 2018; Harper 2017.

12. Murphy 2004, 30.

13. Mokyr (2016, 306) defends the value of historical comparisons for understanding "the outcomes of the different cultural systems generating and disseminating intellectual innovations"—in his case the differences between early modern Europe and China.

14. Doody 2010.

Chapter 1. Proxies for Economic Performance in the Roman Empire

1. Hopkins 1980, 103. Hopkins was very careful to hedge his claim in several ways. The phrase "general prosperity" was "purposefully vague" because "how can we know about the distribution of wealth?" In addition, his emphasis on structure and proxies for aggregate production was not meant to imply that "the Romans' own economic thoughts or writings should be neglected" (101n1).

2. Gibbon 1776–88, chap. 3 at 85.

3. Morris 2014, 41. For recent studies of enrichment from Roman imperialism, see Kay 2014 and Tan 2017.

4. E.g., Acemoglu and Robinson 2012; Hubbard and Kane 2013. Verboven 2015 offers a critique of the application of New Institutional Economics to the Roman economy.

5. Hopkins 1980, 106, 109.

6. Hopkins 1980, 116.

7. Hong et al. 1994; Rosman et al. 1997.

8. Hopkins 2017, 520. The inefficiency is evident in the high level of vaporization of lead in the process.

9. De Callataÿ 2005, 370–72. Kay 2014 makes a convincing case for economic growth in mainland Italy during the era of relentless Republican conquest in the last two centuries BCE, citing increases in the money supply and lead pollution; it would be interesting to know how the notable *decline* in lead pollution during the first century BCE, discussed below, would be explained.

10. Fogel and Costa 1997.

11. Jongman 2007, 195. Verboven 2015, 49 and Verboven 2018, 350 accept the Antonine Plague as contributing to the breakpoint.

12. Scheidel 2009, 46.

13. Scheidel 2009, 49–53. The article also points to weaknesses in generalizations from fish-salting factories, stature, and urbanization.

14. Scheidel 2009, 52.

15. Scheidel 2009, 62.

16. For increased inequality of wealth from Republican imperialism, see Tan 2017.

17. Wilson 2009, 71–73; also Wilson 2014.

18. Wilson 2009, 73; also Wilson 2014.

19. Wilson 2009, 74; also Wilson 2014.

20. MacMullen 1982, 244; Wilson (2014, 165) partially takes account of Mac-Mullen's point, noting underrepresentation of inscriptions during the Republic, but he still tentatively claims that "within the Roman imperial period . . . things may be broadly comparable across chronological divisions." The basis for the claim of "broadly comparable" is not at all clear, nor in my view is it likely, given the variability described by Laurence, Esmonde Cleary, and Sears (2011, 9); with regard to public baths the authors suggest that "over time bathing facilities were clearly provided in greater number and were more elaborate. This cannot be explained in terms of population growth, and we should resist explanations solely based on increased wealth and ostentation. The cultural trend towards greater bathing facilities in the cities of Italy is just that, a fashion driving a change in the way urban life was experienced and expressed via the grooming of the body" (212). Bodel (2001, 8–10) points out the variation in local epigraphic cultures in the empire, which would make interpretation of counts of inscriptions problematic.

21. Russell (2013, 11–12) argues that "the emergence of stone architecture in Gaul, Spain, Britain and elsewhere . . . was first and foremost connected to public building, itself tied to patterns of elite self-display, a central feature of the way in which the local aristocracy was integrated into wider Roman society . . . [it] was the perfect medium in which the socio-cultural priorities of the status quo were monumentalized; it was an expression of political allegiance, at the same time demonstrating an abnormal control of wealth, resources, and labour."

22. Hanson 2016, 78; Duncan-Jones 1982, 75, 90–91, 157–60. The average cost of the more expensive construction projects in North Africa (36 temples, theaters, and public baths) was ~100,000 HS. Laurence, Esmonde Cleary, and Sears (2011) provide tables of bath and amphitheater construction by century in Italy (table 8.2, p. 213) and North Africa (table 8.3, p. 226). Russell (2013, 19) reports that 54% of imperial building inscriptions from the city of Rome from 180 to 305 CE recorded restorations—in other words, efforts to deal with a challenge familiar to all university administrators: depreciation.

23. Wilson 2009, 81–82. Many of his criticisms are echoed in Wilson 2014.

24. Scheidel (2009, 54) points out that sustained economic growth does not necessarily accompany urbanization.

25. Hanson 2016, 47.

26. Hanson 2016, 70.

27. De Ligt and Bintliff 2020, 3.

28. De Ligt and Bintliff 2020, 8–10.

29. De Ligt and Bintliff 2020, 24.

30. McConnell et al. 2018, followed by another article by McConnell et al. (2019). For bone length and stature, see Jongman, Jacobs, and Goldewijk 2019.

31. Wade 2018; Langin 2018; *Economist* 2019; Kornei 2020.

32. McConnell et al. 2018, 5726.

33. There may have been external shocks to the economy other than the plague. For example, Elliott (2020, 69) shows that records from Egypt suggest low levels of Nile flooding in the 150s and 160s that likely depressed agricultural production. A comparison of the average background lead pollution in the twenty-five years after Augustus's reign (15–39 CE) with a period of twenty-five years a century later (115–139 CE) also shows a decline of 4% and perhaps more surprisingly a decline of 11% from the twenty-five-year average from 129 to 104 BCE, *thus providing no evidence of sustained growth before this alternative shock.*

34. Pavlyshyn, Johnstone, and Saller 2020, 363.

35. Pavlyshyn, Johnstone, and Saller 2020, 363–64.

36. Jongman 2019; Jongman, Jacobs, and Goldewijk 2019.

37. Harper (2017, 67) drew a similar conclusion.

38. Jongman, Jacobs, and Goldewijk (2019, 141) note the underrepresentation of the east but do not note the large shift in representation over time. The likelihood that the "trend" is a compositional effect is reinforced by the conclusion of Killgrove (2019) that trends over time within sites from the region of Rome appear "conflicting or insignificant"—that is, within a closely studied single region there was no discernible secular trend in stature.

39. Terpstra (2019, chap. 6) makes the point that the regional patterns do not support the causal claim that urbanization resulted in shorter stature.

40. E.g., Garnsey 2017.

41. Verboven 2018, 350. It is worth noting that Scheidel and Friesen (2009) met the challenge by suggesting a plausible range. I realize that my critics would say that my "framing the debate over growth in the ancient economy" (Saller 2002, also reprinted as Saller 2005) with the graph showing per capita growth from Roman times to the present suffered from the same fault, but it was qualified by the statement: "Let me stress that it is a heuristic device to clarify the debate" over whether the Roman Empire experienced "significant" per capita growth. That is, were the proponents of growth arguing that they had evidence to show that the hypothesis of 25% growth was too low? And what would that mean in the broader historical context?

42. Verboven 2018, 366.

43. Verboven 2018, 365.

44. Jacobs 1969, 49.

45. Verboven 2018, 365.

46. Bresson (2020, 236–37) points out the issue of variability in regard to the changing climate during the Roman Empire in his review of Harper 2017.

47. Erdkamp 2015, 17.

48. Erdkamp 2019, 426. Ward-Perkins (2001, 376), among others, notes the rolling prosperity that favored one region to replace another in the export of wine and oil, an explanation of which "would require more information than we will ever have. For instance, we would need to know about relative labour-costs across the empire and how they changed through time; about who organized and financed export-trades; and about consumer-perception of different goods and how these perceptions altered." Harris (2011, 29) stresses variability by region and Italy's privileged position. Launaro (2011) finds the peak in Italian agriculture in the Augustan age, followed by stagnation.

49. Erdkamp 2019, 432.

50. Judging the aggregate historical trend is made all the more difficult by the rolling prosperity as one region replaced another as the leader in material signs of increased prosperity. As Pliny noted with regard to reputation of wine, each locality had its own period of fame (N.H. 14.65). Russell (2013, 17) notes the rolling high points of dedications of public buildings by region. Erdkamp (2019, 425) points out more generally that the trends do not show the same chronology in all parts of the empire.

51. For example, Kyle Harper's ambitious book, *The Fate of Rome*, acknowledges financial strains in the empire before 165 CE but sees the Antonine Plague as the turning point toward economic decline (Harper 2017, 21, 61). A subsequent article, Harper 2018, cites the proxy of lead pollution: "The new lead emission study of McConnell et al. (2018) shows how other, new kinds of evidence might be brought to bear (and it suggests that the Antonine plague had sudden and dramatic economic effects)."

52. Verboven 2018, 365.

53. Hausmann et al. 2013, 29: "In short, economic complexity matters because it helps explain differences in the level of income of countries, and more important, because it predicts future economic growth. Economic complexity might not be simple to accomplish, but the countries that do achieve it, tend to reap important rewards."

54. Hausmann et al. 2013, 15–18.

55. Hausmann et al. (2013, 20–23) justify their use of exports on the grounds that international trade data constitute "the only dataset available that has a rich detailed cross-country information linking countries to the products that they produce in a standardized classification. As such, it offers great advantages, but it does have limitations. First, it includes data on exports, not production. Countries may be able to

make things that they do not export. The fact that they do not export them, however, suggests that they may not be very good at them."

56. Hidalgo and Hausmann 2009; Hausmann et al. 2013, 27–42.

57. Hausmann et al. (2013, 27) argue that "economic complexity can explain about 73 percent of the variation in income across all 128 countries."

58. Hausmann et al. 2013, 81.

59. Piketty (2017, 141–73) provides a series of graphs clearly demonstrating the waning importance of agricultural land in contemporary economies and the rising importance of other forms of capital, such as office buildings and technological improvements to industry.

60. See pp. 11–14 for details on the debate between Scheidel and Wilson.

61. This approach has its own issues. As one reviewer of Hidalgo and Hausmann's work has pointed out (Hickson 2017, 31), using the nation as the unit of analysis can elide how production spans national borders. Nonetheless, it is still true that nations form relatively easy units to study, especially since contemporary nation-states often produce robust data sets on exports and GDP.

62. Hausmann et al. (2013, 20) define ubiquity as the number of countries that make a product. Ubiquity scores are introduced to serve as a corrective to the diversity scores because it is theoretically possible that a country might make many products (i.e., have a high diversity score) but that all of these products are relatively simple to make (i.e., require low levels of embedded knowledge and know-how and indicating low complexity). Ubiquity is based on the assumption that if a product is made in fewer places, it is probably more complex.

63. Woolf (2004, 423–24), in a survey of Roman archaeology, questions whether the province is a particularly useful unit of analysis. He writes, "Roman provinces were administrative entities that rarely corresponded to areas of social, cultural, or ecological homogeneity and were not significantly unified by Roman rule."

64. Woolf (2004, 424) and Laurence (2012, 22–23) both praise recent regional syntheses but bemoan a lack of comparative work encompassing multiple provinces.

65. Hidalgo and Hausmann (2009, 10570–71) use three classification systems: (1) North American Industry Classification System (NAICS) developed by Canada, Mexico, and the United States; (2) Standard International Trade Classification (SITC) established by the United Nations; and (3) Harmonized Commodity Description and Coding System (HS) used by the World Customs Organization (WCO). It is obvious that each of these entities has its own interests and biases that certainly influence how they typologize commodities and what products are considered distinct from each other.

66. See Ford 1954 vs. Spaulding 1953 for their famous debate about the nature of typology. Chapman and Wylie (2016, 22–23) provide a detailed synthesis on the use of typology in archaeology today.

67. Compare the publication of the archaic graves in Lyons 1996 to the Late Hellenistic and Republican pottery in Stone 2015.

68. Stone 2015, 416–50.

69. Lyons (1996, 55) was unable to conduct this sort of analysis.

70. Stone 2015, 113–22.

71. Hidalgo and Hausmann 2009, 20.

72. Hausmann et al. 2013, 20.

73. Pliny devotes much more attention to local specialties of agricultural products, but it is not obvious how one would identify *discrete* categories of agricultural products (e.g., grape varietals for wine) requiring special technical know-how.

Chapter 2. Pliny's Purpose, Audience, and Method

1. For an account of the classical encyclopedic tradition and how Pliny fits in, see König and Woolf 2013.

2. D'Arms 1981 and with recent references, Oleson 2008, 5.

3. Syme 1969; Healy 1999, chap. 1.

4. Horden and Purcell 2000.

5. Syme 1969, 224: "Valuable evidence converges, bearing on the habits and quality of the educated class in the provinces of the West. Some were avid for marvels and the exotic, credulous when not superstitious. That did not preclude a keen business sense, exact study of plants and animals and medicine—and a passion for scientific agriculture." Beagon 1992; Healy 1999, chap. 1.

6. Harris (2011, 210–11) concludes that Pliny "does not represent the whole culture, but he will not have been an isolated voice either." See Wallace-Hadrill 1990, 80 on various deprecating judgments of Pliny's Latin.

7. See chapter 6. Conte (1994, 81) describes Pliny's attitude as hostile to "Man's activity as artisan, for his industriousness, in short, for technology"; I would describe the attitude as lack of respect.

8. For Pliny's work habits, see Conte 1994, 69. See Gibson and Morello 2012, chap. 4 for this letter representing the elder Pliny as a model for the younger Pliny.

9. Greenaway 1986, 153. Advocates of literary coherence include Beagon 1992; Naas 2002; Murphy 2004; Gibson and Morello 2011; see Doody 2010, chap. 3 on ideologies underlying the interpretations of the *Natural History*.

10. Vivenza (2012) cites the elder Pliny for several, scattered points: his notion that all wealth derives from the land (28ff.), his criticism of slave labor (31), his celebration of the riches of empire and fear of luxury (34), his connection between the supply of precious metals and prices (36), and his famous condemnation of *latifundia* (38).

11. Von Staden (2013) discusses Pliny's authorial self-presentation.

12. Beagon 1992, v. See also Isager 1991, 25. On Pliny's "quest for totality," see Carey 2006, 18, which Naas 2002 sees as his originality.

13. White 1984, 183, 185.

14. Beagon 1992, 13. Similarly, Howe 1985, 572: "a work valuable for the preliminary purpose of practical education." Fögen 2013, 95: Pliny's position is "that he contributes to the constant growth of learning with his own work."

15. Naas 2002, 473. As Naas observes, the privileging of the marvelous and extraordinary represents an inversion of the relationship between the exceptional and the normal that one might expect in an encyclopedia, making Pliny's work more a "paradoxographie" (2).

16. Murphy 2004, 39–40, 211 (my italics).

17. Lewit 2020, 310, 324. Elsewhere Burton and Lewit (2019, 588) conclude that "Pliny does not say or imply that each of the three main press types described successively improved upon inferior types in a 'step forward.'"

18. Lao 2011, 48: "To the extent that the *Natural History* cannot truly be said to be organized around skills and actions, it is inaccurate to call it a technical work in the traditional sense."

19. Cuomo 2008, 25; Doody 2010, 51.

20. Healy 1999, 40–41, 391.

21. Specifically and rightly denied by Healy (1999, 41, 78). Flohr (2016, 6) claims more generally that "the first-century AD encyclopedia of the elder Pliny exemplifies how not only knowledge itself but also its history became a central part of Roman society and how this knowledge extended far beyond the theoretical realm of philosophy, mathematics, and mechanics into the practical world of applied chemistry, medicine, crafts, and agriculture." But he provides no evidence for the claim. Holmes (2017) offers a more subtle rationale. It seems to me that Al-Nuwayri was more realistic in compiling his massive Mamluk encyclopedia *The Ultimate Ambition in the Arts of Erudition* (completed 1333 CE) for fellow scribes to give them a broad cultural literacy to do their jobs (Muhanna 2018).

22. Pliny's lack of respect for the astronomical knowledge of the peasants is evident in the phrase *quod intellegere vel rustici possint* (N.H. 18.323). Martin (1971, 379) accepts Pliny's claim that he was writing for ordinary farmers, motivated by "une volonté de démocratisation et de vulgarization."

23. Greene 1992, 103. Healy (1999, 78) accepts Pliny's statement that he was compiling *res dignae* "for the man in the street" but does not consider how the man in the street might have gotten access and then found the facts he wanted.

24. Schneider 2007, 167. Doody (2010, 89) sees Pliny's inclusion of the manual crafts as well as aristocratic theory as an effort to democratize knowledge and an inspiration for the *Encyclopédie*.

25. Goodyear 1982, 670; Isager 1991, 24–25; Lewit 2020, 324.

26. Starr (1987) notes the scarcity of evidence for book prices and the comment that a book of Martial's Epigrams, comprising about 4,000 words, sold for 5 denarii or a week's pay for a legionary. The *Natural History* was about 100 times larger, so if the cost of copying were similar, the cost would have been about two years' salary for a legionary. A comparison with the cost of an encyclopedic manuscript in the Mamluk scribal tradition suggests that this estimate of price is the right order of magnitude: Al-Nuwayri's *The Ultimate Ambition in the Arts of Erudition* from the early fourteenth century was about five times the size of the *Natural History* and cost about five times the annual salary of a librarian at the time (Muhanna 2018, 107).

27. Lloyd (1983, 116, 149) notes the gap.

28. The *Cyclopaedia* cost 4 guineas or about one month's average wage at the time.

29. Stahl (1962, 122) notes that Pliny and his fellow compilers were "the great authorities" in the eyes of medieval and Renaissance men of science, who regarded them "with awe and veneration."

30. Aulus Gellius, *Attic Nights* 3.10.17. Healy 1999, 46; Paparazzo 2011, 109.

31. See Murphy 2003, 302 for the number of authorities. See Scarborough 1986, 68 for compiling compilations of *medicinae*; Scarborough counts more than 900, many of which "are in the purely magical or folkloristic class" (59).

32. Doody (2010, 111) notes that using the *Summarium* would have been a "slow process." Muhanna (2018) points out that Al-Nuwayri in *The Ultimate Ambition in the Arts of Erudition* is also reluctant to judge the truth of the items in his compilation, but this seems to me to make more sense for Al-Nuwayri because his purpose was scribal cultural literacy rather than pragmatic usefulness to farmers and craftsmen for whom the truth was essential to effectiveness.

33. The importance of "propositional knowledge" for technical progress is stressed by Mokyr 2016.

34. On the importance attached to scientific instruments by the early modern encyclopedists, see chapter 6.

35. Headrick (2000, 49), analyzing the technologies of knowledge dissemination in the early modern era, suggests the contrast: "Science does not just accumulate data and find patterns in nature; it also seeks to explain these patterns. Yet finding patterns requires classifying and naming natural phenomena. Hence classification and nomenclature are the foundation upon which explanations can be built and influence those explanations. Linnaeus classified plants into genera in order to bring some clarity and logic into their naming, but his classification avoided the issue of explanation."

36. French (1994, 208) concluded: "Even if we adopt an historically relativist position and argue that rationality is the use of chains of argument (whether right or wrong) and one person's superstition may be another's religion, then Pliny is still less using argument than piling up examples." (I cannot help but think that Pliny was

compiling "facts" for the ancient equivalent of a contestant on the contemporary quiz show *Jeopardy*.)

37. Stahl 1962, 258ff. Also, Reynolds 1986, 7. Doody (2010, 89) views this welter of facts as a democratizing virtue of Diderot.

38. Stahl 1962, 119; Healy 1999, 62.

39. See excursus at the end of this chapter for additional discussion of rabid dog bite.

40. N.H. 28.10. Schilling 1978, 279; Pederson 1986. Pliny is critical of claims of senators and equestrians to have easily penetrated as far as Mount Atlas: "it is too true, that men in high station, when they are disinclined to take the trouble of inquiring into the truth, through a feeling of shame at their ignorance are not averse to be guilty of falsehood; and never is implicit credence more readily given, than when a falsehood is supported by the authority of some personage of high consideration. For my own part, I am far less surprised that there are still some facts remaining undiscovered by men of the equestrian order, and even those among them who have attained senatorial rank, than that the love of luxury has left anything unascertained; the impulse of which must be great indeed, and most powerfully felt, when the very forests are ransacked for their ivory and citron-wood, and all the rocks of Gætulia are searched for the murex and the purple" (N.H. 5.12).

41. Beagon 1992, 237; Nutton 1986, 37–39; Healy 1999, chap. 6. Pliny sees it as his mission to refute the *Magicas vanitates* because their "most fraudulent of arts" has been valued around the world for ages (N.H. 30.1). For the *vanitas* of the Magi, see also N.H. 37.54 and 118; the use of "tortoise-stone" for prophetic powers is among the *mendacia Magorum* (N.H. 37.155; see also 37.192).

42. Beagon 1992, 66.

43. Lloyd 1983, 139. Similarly, Joyce Reynolds noted that "the information collected and retailed was not all second hand; autopsy played a part; but there do not seem to have been any planned programmes of observation of particular categories of phenomena and still less anything designed to produce explanations. Facts were enough; apparently for everyone, certainly for Pliny" (1986, 7). Also, Murphy 2004, 4n9.

44. Pederson 1986, 170.

45. N.H. pr.15. Stahl 1962, 112; Schilling 1978, 280–81. Lloyd 1983, 146: "The heavy, in places total, dependence on literary sources, the sometimes garbled versions of these, the erratic way in which Pliny may or may not include the reservations and criticisms of the authorities he relies on, all add up to a rather strong indictment of his work in this field." Murphy 2004, 4: "more a product of literary tradition than direct observation." More broadly, Lauwers (2015, 28) notes the "highly conservative" quality of the standard rhetorical and philosophical schooling.

46. Taub 2017, 28.

47. White 1970, 28.

48. The contrast here with the underlying principle of the early modern Republic of Letters is worth noting: the latter was a network that crossed ethnic and national boundaries on the grounds that nationality was irrelevant to scientific authority.

49. Lloyd 1983, 143. Morton (1986) also concludes that Pliny's botany represents a decline from Theophrastus. Stahl (1962, 258–59) generalizes: "The more gifted of Roman intellectuals of the classical period failed to appreciate the systematic character of scientific disciplines and showed no disposition to master any of the Greek sciences."

50. Harris 2011, 210ff.

51. Headrick 2000, 166.

52. Doody 2010, 26–27.

53. Schilling 1978, 275. Doody (2010, 26–27) points to hierarchies within some lists, for example, based on size, but that was not a universal organizing principle. Murphy (2004, 29) suggests that Pliny, influenced by his rhetorical training, organized his material by analogy and contrast, rather than scientific logic. Just one illustration of the cognitive drift in the text: "In the territory of Fidenæ, in the vicinity of the City, the storks have no young nor do they build nests: but vast numbers of ringdoves arrive from beyond sea every year in the district of Volaterræ. At Rome, neither flies nor dogs ever enter the temple of Hercules in the Cattle Market. There are numerous other instances of a similar nature in reference to all kinds of animals, which from time to time I feel myself prompted by prudent considerations to omit, lest I should only weary the reader. Theophrastus, for example, relates that even pigeons, as well as peacocks and ravens, have been introduced from other parts into Asia, as also croaking frogs into Cyrenaica" (N.H. 10.79). According to Muhanna 2018, Al-Nuwayri's *The Ultimate Ambition in the Arts of Erudition* was more disciplined in offering the reader cross-references.

54. Doody 2001. Headrick (2000, 165) posits the same two types of reader for the early modern encyclopedias.

55. Doody 2001.

56. Doody (2001) imagines a reader in search of a cure for a headache. For Books 34 and 36 the *Summarium* offers an undifferentiated list of 257 and 89 *medicinae*, respectively, and then an undifferentiated list of dozens of ailments and body parts that these scores of *medicinae* are meant to treat.

57. Oikonomopoulou 2016, 981. Also, König and Woolf 2013, 45; Riggsby 2007, 93–98 and 2019, 24–29.

58. For example, Healy's chapter titled "Chemistry" (1999, 116): "A positive and selective approach, however, may produce a more constructive picture of [Pliny's] contribution" than allowed for by Greenaway 1986, 148. But of course, Pliny's ancient readers would not have had Healy's knowledge to select the "positive" and hence useful.

59. Humphrey, Oleson, and Sherwood 1998, 338–39.

60. French 1994, 199.

61. Stahl 1962, 112.

62. Further discussion of Pliny's attitude to venerable knowledge in chapter 4, and of Harris's and Chambers's, in chapter 6.

63. The preoccupation with rabies is easier to understand if we remember that even today in the absence of regular vaccination of dogs an estimated 31,000 human deaths due to rabies occur annually in Asia, with the majority—approximately 20,000—concentrated in India. India has the highest rate of human rabies in the world primarily due to stray dogs (Harris 2012).

64. French and Greenaway 1986; Beagon 1992; Healy 1999; Murphy 2004; Gibson and Morello 2011. *Greek and Roman Technology: A Sourcebook* does not include any of the passages discussed in this excursus. French (1994, 203) briefly discusses dogs and dog bites.

65. Steele 1973, 299: "Pliny, the Roman historian, recognized rabies as a contagious disease of dogs, which was transmitted to man. The innumerable cures cited by Pliny indicate that the disease must have been quite common in the Roman empire." Baer 2007 mentions several of Pliny's cures.

66. As Doody (2010, 63) observes, "It would be difficult to guess from most work on Pliny just how dense and unreadable most of the *Natural History* appears."

67. Mithridates's commentary on potions was so highly thought of that Pompey had his freedman Laenas translate it (N.H. 25.7).

68. On antipathy and sympathy in the *Natural History*, see Conte 1994, 92.

69. The ash of the skull of a rabid dog sprinkled in drink is also a remedy for pains in the side: N.H. 30.53.

70. Neville 2004, 5. So also, Wasik and Murphy 2012, 34–35: "Things totter off the rails with Pliny the Elder."

71. The *Summarium* does list three remedies that could be made from a rabid dog in the list of cures from animals in Book 29 but does not link them to the illness of rabies.

72. Chambers's *Cyclopaedia* has entries under "C" for "Canine madness" and under "A" for "Alysson."

Chapter 3. *Parens Natura* and Smithian Growth

1. Mokyr 2016; Spolaore 2020.

2. Sellars 2006, 92–93. Seneca's similar, but less pragmatic, view was summarized by Bury (1920, 14): "Seneca believed in a progress of knowledge and recognised its value. Yes, but the value which he attributed to it did not lie in any advantages which it would bring to the general community of mankind. He did not expect from it any improvement of the world. The value of natural science, from his point of view, was

this, that it opened to the philosopher a divine region, in which, 'wandering among the stars,' he could laugh at the earth and all its riches, and his mind 'delivered as it were from prison could return to its original home.'"

3. Wallace-Hadrill 1990; Beagon 1992; Conte 1994, 76. See also Paparazzo 2011, which details the Stoic roots of Pliny's thought and shows how the premise of the four elements yields some nonsensical explanations.

4. Schilling 1978, 275.

5. Wallace-Hadrill 1990, 85.

6. For the ethic of reciprocity in the Roman Empire, see Saller 1982.

7. Beagon 1992, 59.

8. Harris 2000 provides a balanced summary; see Tchernia 2016 for a fuller assessment.

9. Isager 1991, 50.

10. Beagon 1992, 65.

11. Wallace-Hadrill 1990, 87–88; Conte 1994, 79.

12. Beagon 1992, 42. Also Isager 1991, 34.

13. Forbes 1950, 5.

14. Wallace-Hadrill 1990, 86; Beagon 1992, 40–41.

15. N.H. 33.3 with Beagon 1992, 40–41.

16. N.H. 36.1–3; Isager 1991, 144–45.

17. Cleopatra's shame is noteworthy because elsewhere the story of her imaginatively conspicuous consumption of dissolved pearls is condemned as among the *summa luxuriae exempla* (N.H. 9.119).

18. Cohen 1991; Lendon 2011.

19. Ash 2011, 14; Beagon 1992, 40.

20. Zehnacker 1979, 178. Contrast the lengthy entry in Chambers's *Cyclopaedia* that characterizes iron unambiguously as of "great use." Pliny's discussion of gold is four times the length of that of iron; by contrast, Chambers's entry for iron is twice that of gold.

21. Beagon 1992, especially 190–94; Wallace-Hadrill 1990, especially 86–92.

22. N.H. 6.89–91. Despite suffering from the vice of luxury, Taprobane was in other respects idealized by Pliny: "In this island no slavery exists; they do not prolong their sleep to day-break, nor indeed during any part of the day; their buildings are only of a moderate height from the ground; the price of corn is always the same; they have no courts of law and no litigation. Hercules is the deity whom they worship; their king is chosen by the people, an aged man always, distinguished for his mild and clement disposition, and without children. If after he has been elected king, he happens to become the father of children, his abdication is the consequence; this is done that there may be no danger of the sovereign power becoming hereditary. . . . The king, if he is found guilty of any offence, is condemned to death; but no one slays

him; all turn their backs upon him and refuse to hold any communication or even discourse with him. . . . They take great delight in fishing, and especially in catching turtles; beneath the shells of which whole families find an abode, of such vast size are they to be found. These people look upon a hundred years as a comparatively short life. Thus much have we learned respecting Taprobane." Slack (2014, 202) points to a similar moral discourse in early modern England.

23. One may sympathize with Pliny's condemnation of flavoring wines with aromatic ingredients as a travesty of Nature (N.H. 14.115 and 130). See N.H. 15.105 for another condemnation of mixing Nature's ingredients in pursuit of novel tastes.

24. Conversely, *publicani* wiped out silphium in the province of Cyrenaica because they could realize greater profit by grazing on the land where silphium had grown (N.H. 19.38–39). The demand for coral drove up the price to the point that it became scarce and was hardly seen in its place of origin (N.H. 32.23). Healy (1999, chap. 19, especially p. 372) notes Pliny's attention to the environmental damage done by mining for luxuries.

25. Isager 1991, 142.

26. Wallace-Hadrill 1990, 92. Also Zehnacker 1979, 179.

27. Russell 2013, 4.

28. The Greeks, "sources of all vices" (*genitores vitiorum omnium*), introduced that perverse luxury of using olive oil in the gymnasium, and even worse, then selling it used (N.H. 15.19). "Important remedies have been made by the profit-seeking Greeks even with human offscouring from the gymnasia; for the scrapings from the bodies soften, warm, disperse, and make flesh, sweat and oil forming an ointment. This is used as a pessary for inflammation and contraction of the uterus. So used it is also an emmenagogue; it soothes inflammations of the anus and condylomata, likewise pains of the sinews, dislocations, and knotty joints" (N.H. 28.50). See also Carey 2006, 23.

29. Schilling 1978, 276.

30. Beagon 1992, 44.

31. Murphy 2004, 15. Carey 2006, 38: "a simultaneous progress of knowledge and military advancement."

Chapter 4. Innovation and Economic Growth in the *Natural History*

1. Reprinted in Hume (1777) 1985, 113.

2. Beagon 1992, 59.

3. Mokyr 2016, 5.

4. Mokyr 2016, xiii.

5. Mokyr 2016, 27. On the culture of *improvement* through useful knowledge in early modern England, see Slack 2014.

6. Mokyr 2016, 7.

7. Naas 2002, 293 on man as the culmination of Nature and Pliny's interest in exceptional men.

8. See Beagon 2005, 416–72 for introduction and commentary on this section. Naas (2002, chap. 6) offers an extensive interpretation of Book 7 but does not comment on the striking chronology of the inventions; indeed, she interprets N.H. 7.191–215 as Pliny's commentary on the human condition without noticing that many of the inventors were gods.

9. Not that I think that daily shaving is weird—what is strange is its inclusion in a list of major discoveries. See Naas 2002, 321–22 on Pliny's inclusion of barbers and beards.

10. Beagon 1992, chap. 2.

11. Bacon's utopian vision in his novel *New Atlantis* imagines a process in which men collected past experiments, others ("pioneers") then tried new experiments, which were in turn compiled by others, and then the benefactors "bend themselves, looking into the experiments of their fellows, and cast about *how to draw out of them things of use and practice for man's life and knowledge*" (my italics). Though this is utopian, it offers a conception of a feedback loop from experimental science to application that is lacking in the *Natural History*.

12. Greene (2009, 804) quotes Pliny's lament about the lack of recent innovation but believes that it was unwarranted.

13. Casson (1971, chap. 6) discusses the hypotheses for how the larger ships could possibly have been configured and notes that Augustus reverted to smaller warships.

14. White 1984, 10: "the Greeks and Romans inherited from earlier civilizations not only such inventions as fire, writing and the wheel, but four out of five fundamental technical devices for the redirection of muscular effort, namely the lever, the wedge, the windlass and the pulley; the fifth, the screw, was, as far as we know, an innovation of the third century B.C." Ash (2011, 8) makes the interesting point that "Pliny romanticizes as natural scientists" both generals and soldiers, which makes sense in the context of his view that discovery was about finding new things in Nature.

15. Given the dominance of the Greeks in this inventory, it is hard to understand Pliny's conclusion that Italy is superior in the arts and illustrious examples of genius (*artium praestantia, ingeniorum claritatibus*; N.H. 37.201). French (1994, 239) observed: "Overall the impression that Pliny gives is of the Romans adopting industrial processes, or perhaps in some cases simply their products, from older and more widespread Hellenistic centres." Lloyd (1983, 139) lists some of Pliny's mentions of inventions.

16. Beagon (1992, 166) suggests that Pliny is more interested in inventions than Columella, but his accounts of particular inventions are hardly proportionate to their importance (see p. 136).

17. Beagon 1992, 84.

18. He assures the reader that his interest in wine is for its effects on human health and is motivated by *Romana gravitas* and his "appetite for the *artes liberales*" (N.H. 23.32).

19. See Purcell 1985 on varietals of grapes. Lewit (2020, 333) makes the point that the screw press did not represent an improvement in efficiency and did not replace the lever press.

20. See Wilson 2020 on the spread in use of water mills.

21. Mokyr (2016, 143) acknowledges recent research on the spread of water mills in the Roman Empire but puts it in perspective: "Yet none of this distracts from the technological achievements of medieval Europe such as the invention of heavy ploughs, mechanical clocks, spectacles, wind mills, iron-casting, fire-arms, and the shipping design and navigational equipment that eventually allowed Europeans to cross large oceans."

22. White 1984, 84, 106; Flohr 2016, 15; Lancaster 2005.

23. Naas 2002, 322.

24. Healy (1999, 356) comments that Pliny makes a number of basic mistakes in his description of glass-making.

25. Less dramatically, Pliny credits Gaul with the invention of mattresses made of flax.

26. Isager 1991.

27. Pliny credits Carians of the fourth century BC with cutting thin slabs of marble to use as veneers (N.H. 36.47) and characterizes the unknown discoverer as having *importunum ingenium*, "misplaced talent" (N.H. 36.51).

28. Elsewhere Apicius is noted as the "foremost spendthrift" (*altissimus gurges*) for his culinary judgment that flamingo tongue had the finest flavor (N.H. 10.133).

29. Purcell 2003 provides a thoughtful account of the history of Roman foodways, based heavily on Pliny's *Natural History*.

30. N.H. 11.76; silk clothing also contributed to the loss of *virtus* in men who used it to bear up under the cuirass. See Lao 2011, 43.

31. Healy (1999, 114) qualifies "Pliny's contribution to science and technology" with the phrase "however unsophisticated, and irrespective of any understanding of the principles underlying observed phenomena, chemical reactions, or the physical properties of matter."

32. Beagon 1992, 63–64.

33. Magnes discovered magnetite when the nails in his sandals and the tip of his staff stuck to it on Mount Ida (N.H. 36.127).

34. Beagon 1992, 65.

35. Conte 1994, 85.

36. Lloyd 1983, 139. Also, Isager 1991, 43.

37. Lloyd 1984, 327.

38. Doody 2010, 51.

39. Terpstra 2020. The importance of competition in the eighteenth century was noticed by David Hume (Mokyr 2016, 290).

40. Stahl 1962, 29.

41. Many have commented on this passage, e.g., Isager 1991, 35; Beagon 1992, 56; Conte 1994, 74; and Taub 2017, 79–80.

42. Scheidel 2019; Terpstra 2020. Murphy (2004, 69–70) found Pliny's observation paradoxical. Greene (2009, 804) cites this passage and notes a similar pessimism in Frontinus, which, he argues, the fourth-century *De rebus bellicis* by an anonymous author belies. This is a telling counterexample, and the only one offered: it was written some three centuries later, and it is unclear how many of the inventions could have been implemented. I would say that this example confirms Pliny's pessimism about first-century *inquisitio*.

43. Slack 2014, 171, 179. The connection between the economy and state power had already been made in France and Italy in the later sixteenth century (242)—a connection that we do not find in the *Natural History*. Perhaps the closest analogue from the ancient Mediterranean was Xenophon's *Poroi*, which, interestingly, was framed as a policy in an environment of competing Greek city-states; Xenophon's advice for increasing the resources and power of Athens was not innovation for higher productivity but more slaves to mine silver and more metics.

44. N.H. 25.1 offers a similar observation of decline in the field of herbal medicines: "The more highly esteemed plants of which I am now about to speak, and which are produced by the earth for medicinal purposes solely, inspire me with admiration of the industry and laborious research displayed by the ancients. Indeed there is nothing that they have not tested by experiment or left untried; no discovery of theirs which they have not disclosed, or which they have not been desirous to leave for the benefit of posterity. We, on the contrary, at the present day, make it our object to conceal and suppress the results of our labours, and to defraud our fellow-men of blessings even which have been purchased by others."

45. Wallace-Hadrill 1990, 95; Murphy 2004, 69–70; Lao 2011.

46. Keyser and Irby-Massie 2008, 938.

47. Keyser and Irby-Massie 2008, 4.

48. Bresson 2014, 69.

49. E.g., Schneider 2007, 146; Cuomo 2007, 4; Flohr 2016.

50. Mokyr 2016, chap. 8, especially 109. A new study by Feingold and Svorenčík (2020) demonstrates a broader diffusion of Newton's *Principia* upon publication than previously realized.

51. Naas 2002, 294: "hommes hors du commun."

52. Beagon 2005, 50–51.

53. See Mokyr 2016, 268 for the contrast with early modern Europe: in Britain "a scientist (Newton) and later an engineer (Watt) became symbols of a national spirit and a heroism that had nothing to do with the battlefield and everything to do with the creation of useful knowledge."

54. N.H. 7.92. In this respect Pliny rated Pompey more highly for his defeat of the pirates (N.H. 7.93).

55. Conte (1994, 70) observed that that Pliny's heroes of science belonged to a past age.

56. Broadly speaking, the evolution of military technology might be seen as a microcosm of the whole—that is, no breakthroughs but incremental improvements. Elton (1994, 494) observed that "the lack of change in weaponry over the period is noticeable. Characterized in simple terms, in the 1st c. B.C. most Roman infantry wore mail, a helmet, and carried a large shield, a sword, and some form of throwing spear. Yet in the 4th c. the equipment was the same. The period was one of minimal technological change and development." Bishop and Coulston (2006, 241) note the improvements in production technique: "The weapons of the early Principate were not at all complex in their construction, yet Roman sword smiths were able to carburize iron, weld different metals together, quench for hardening, and (possibly) temper."

57. Howe (1985, 562–65) observed that the *Natural History* enjoyed little honor until St. Jerome: "no doubt Pliny relegated himself to a peripheral position by choosing to compile an encyclopedia, but his austere choice exacted a certain price, that his work would not immediately command widespread readership and respect."

58. In the geographical tour of the Roman Empire and its neighbors Pliny characterizes several places as wealthy (*dives*): after Italy, Baetica is noted for its wealth indicated by its 175 *oppida* (N.H. 3.7); the Ebro river is *dives* from its *commercium* (N.H. 3.21); Arabia is *dives* with its scents (N.H. 5.65); Pella is *dives* for its water, and Palmyra for its soil (N.H. 5.74, 88); Parthia is *dives* (N.H. 6.111) and an unnamed island off the coast of Africa is *dives* in gold (N.H. 6.198). In order words, wealth comes from trade, agriculture, and natural resources—not manufacture associated with wealth in this survey. Sidon gets a bare mention as *artifex vitri*, "maker of glass" (N.H. 5.76).

59. Lao 2011, 41. On *captatio*, see Champlin 1991, chap. 5.

60. Bang 2012.

61. Isager 1991, 93, 105, 138.

62. Ovid (*Ars Amatoria* 3.113–14) shows how deeply the assumption that predation was the source of wealth had penetrated in Roman culture.

63. Flohr 2016. Other archaeologists emphasizing the growth of the Roman imperial economy include Greene (2000) and Wilson (2002).

64. Scheidel (2007) gives an overview of estimates of the population of the Roman Empire, while in the same volume Schneider (2007) presents a balanced survey of the advances in technology, noting where there was progress and conversely sectors in which "much of the work hardly changed over long periods of time." Paterson (1998, 159) concluded that the growth in the economy was "not accompanied by a transformation in the productivity of labour."

65. Beagon (1992, 10) stresses the optimism, as does Fögen (2013, 95); Isager (1991, 78), the pessimistic side.

66. Isager 1991, 44.

67. Here anticipating Jongman 2019.

68. Howley 2018, 113, 3. Aside from Gellius, Galen cites Pliny very briefly for a remedy for viper bite, a reference for which I thank Susan Stephens.

69. Holford-Strevens 2003, 71. Gellius as a representative of Roman elite culture is of a piece with the broad intellectual culture of elite child-rearing described by Rawson (2003, chap. 5): a heavy emphasis on literature, rhetoric, and mores, with no science or scientific celebrities.

70. N.A. 9.4.13: *vir in temporibus aetatis suae ingenii dignitatisque gratia auctoritate magna praeditus.* N.A. 9.16.1: *aetatis suae doctissimus.*

71. N.A. 10.12, 9.16.1. It should be noted that Gellius's criticisms of the falsehoods (*vana*) in the *Natural History* show that Pliny's earliest-known interpreter found fault with some of the 20,000 "things worth knowing"—this is not to be dismissed as an anachronistic reaction of a modern reader.

72. Holford-Strevens 2003, 165–66: Gellius "never denies his erudition, but insinuates that the great polymath would have done better to learn less and think more." Howley 2018, chap. 3, especially 113.

73. N.A. 4.9.1, 4.16.1, 19.14.1.

74. N.A. 12.1.17.

75. Holford-Strevens 2003, 98–130, quotation from 130.

76. For Herodes Atticus, see N.A. 19.12.1 with Holford-Strevens 2003, 139–44. For Cicero and Hortensius, N.A. 1.5.

77. N.A. 4.17.11: *vir praestanti litterarum scientia.* For discussion, see Howley 2018, 224 and Kaster 1988, 58–59.

78. N.A. 4.7: *praestanti scientia.*

79. N.A. 5.21.9, 10.21.

80. N.A. 11.15, 1.21.2. Other *grammatici* earning approbation: Cn. Matius, *vir eruditus* (N.A. 15.25); Aelius Melissus, *summi quidem loci inter grammaticos* (N.A. 18.6.1); and Domitius, *homini docto celebrique in urbe Roma grammatico* (N.A. 18.7.1).

81. Lao (2008) describes the dinner talk as "competitive and game-like," in which the *res dignae* of the *Natural History* would have been useful.

82. Kaster 1988, 58.

83. N.A. 19.10.

84. Holford-Strevens 2003, 178.

85. N.A. praef.12: *a turpi certe agrestique rerum atque verborum imperitia.*

86. N.A. 1.22, 4.1.

87. N.A. praef.12.

Chapter 5. Pliny's Economic Observations and Reasoning

1. Rathbone 1991.

2. Murphy (2004, 95) makes the general point that "all the ethnographies of the *Natural History* carry out one of the following tasks: they either describe the

limits of geographical knowledge, or they describe extreme forms of the human body, or they portray non-Roman economic behaviors that define Roman culture by contrast."

3. Beagon 1992, v.

4. The Roman monetary unit referred to in this chapter is the sestertius; in Pliny's day the annual salary of a legionary was 900 sesterces.

5. In this, Pliny is similar to other Roman agricultural writers, on which see White 1970. Martin (1971, 376) interprets Pliny as an advocate of traditional polyculture in reaction to Columella, who advocated investment in viticulture: "Cette attitude nettement traditionaliste—voire réactionnaire—en matière économique, nous allons la retrouver tout au long de ce livre XVIII." But this interpretation does not take into account Pliny's three extended *exempla* of agricultural investment, especially Remmius Palaemon's purchase of a run-down estate and his successful investment in viticulture.

6. Schultze 2011.

7. Kehoe 1997, 20.

8. Purcell (1985, 5) discusses the case of Palaemon. Beagon (1992, 168–69) cites the Palaemon story as an example of Pliny advocating the "intelligent organization of work." I see nothing in the narrative about *organization* of labor; rather, the point is attentiveness of oversight, which is commonsense rationality (so Rostovtzeff [1957, 581n25] interpreted the comment).

9. Schultze 2011, 172–78.

10. It is not clear to me how Beagon (1992, 164) can conclude that in Pliny's view "the present-day farmer was not necessarily lagging behind his predecessors in *cura* and *diligentia*"—the *exempla* of Remmius Palaemon and Chresimus are exceptional in their diligence in contrast with their neighbors.

11. On Pliny's dislike of *latifundia*, see Martin 1971, 383. For a more complex view of property sizes, see Garnsey and Saller 2015, 93–97. The view of Rostovtzeff (1957, 98) was that Pliny failed to understand that the worsening conditions for Italian agriculture were related to the development of the western provinces, but he agreed with Pliny about the deleterious effects of *latifundia* (Rostovtzeff 1957, 198; Beagon 1992, 162).

12. N.H. 14.14–15. White 1970, 229.

13. One might conjecture that this is an illustration of how the institution of the tax system distorted incentives to produce suboptimal productivity.

14. Wallace-Hadrill 1990, 92. See chapter 3.

15. The legal limit on lead production in Britain would seem to be an example of a Roman institution that interfered with the market and constrained productivity. Citing Pliny N.H. 34.164, Flohr (2016, 11) claims that the legal limit was motivated by the concern that the silver by-product of lead refining would cheapen the value of silver; Pliny says nothing about the motivation, nor did the British lead ore contain

much silver. Flohr also plausibly suggests that "after glass, lead is the second major Roman addition to the material spectrum of the ancient world. The increased use of lead must be seen as an important innovation with significant impact throughout the Roman world." Lead had been used earlier but not to the same extent. Very recent research by Joanna Moore and colleagues (2021) concludes that the widespread use of lead by the Romans may have been a mixed blessing: "This study provides the first bioarcheological evidence that lead poisoning was a contributing factor to the high infant mortality and childhood morbidity rates seen within the Roman world."

16. Smith et al. (2017, 198) note that iron was "by far the most common metal in use" in Roman Britain.

17. French 1994, 235.

18. It is interesting that in his description of the occupational classes of the more civilized Indian peoples Pliny includes farmers, soldiers, traders, those in government service, and those devoted to "wisdom" (*sapientia*), who were most esteemed (N.H. 6.66). Absent from the list is craftsmen.

19. Flohr 2016, 13: "textile manufacturing—not the smallest sector of the manufacturing economy, nor the least visible—appears a beacon of stability until late antiquity: there are several changes in the organization and scale of the textile economy, but these do not seem to have affected the quality and price of textiles as the basic procedures that cost the most time remained fundamentally unaltered." The connotations of the word "stability" seem unduly positive—"stagnation" might be a more apt description.

20. N.H. 6.201 notes in passing that King Juba established the craft of dyeing with Gaetulian purple on islands off the coast of Mauretania.

21. Beagon (1992, 191) suggests that there is no moral judgment in this comment, but *exhauriente* surely has a negative connotation.

22. If Arabia is blamed for the luxury of scents, the Persians were the first to indulge in the luxury of unguents (N.H. 13.1).

23. Slack (2014, 71) indicates that this same worry was echoed in the seventeenth century: "The East India Company, exporting treasure in return for useless luxuries, was especially vulnerable to the charge that it was 'gainful to the adventurers, . . . with public detriment to the state.'"

24. Isager 1991, 144.

25. Erdkamp (2014) offers an effective critique of this view as expressed in Temin 2013.

26. N.H. 33.145; Pliny also complains that "even slaves nowadays encircle the iron of their rings with gold—other articles they decorate with pure gold" (N.H. 33.23).

27. Kyle 1998, chap. 3. N.H. 11.198 discusses the function of the diaphragm in the human anatomy and notes that when a gladiator dies of a pierced diaphragm, he laughs.

28. See Bradley 2011.

29. Beagon 1992, 162.

30. The distinction between honorable *artes* and servile labor in Greece, according to Pliny, was manifested in the prohibition of teaching slaves the liberal art of drawing (N.H. 35.77); see Isager 1991, 105.

31. Bagnall and Frier 1994, 71, 343: in the Roman Egyptian census returns female slaves outnumber male slaves by two to one.

32. For a study of the realities of Roman prostitution, see McGinn 2004.

33. See Dixon 2001, 117–25 for coding textile work as female.

34. Another traditionally female domestic duty was tending the *hortus* (N.H. 19.57).

35. Saller 2003.

36. Wallace-Hadrill 1990; Vons 2000; Totelin 2017.

37. Lao 2011; Beagon (1992, 192) sees Pliny's attitude toward the prices of luxury goods as more pragmatic than I do: "Yes, overall, he refrains from wholesale condemnation of the luxury trade, as he does of luxury in general. . . . Here again, pragmatism in the form of financial awareness colours his moral criticisms."

38. As an *exemplum* of the value of *scientia* of astronomy and weather in agriculture, Pliny tells the story of Democritus using his knowledge of astronomy to predict that a wet spring would produce a poor olive harvest and so made a fortune by buying up olives in advance (N.H. 18.273).

39. Zehnacker 1979, 177; see also the discussion in von Reden 2010, 188–98 and French 1994, 191.

40. Zehnacker 1979; Isager 1991, 62–63.

41. Pliny's explanation for the high value placed on gold: "gold is the only thing that loses no substance by the action of fire, but even in conflagrations and on funeral pyres receives no damage" (N.H. 33.59).

42. Book 3, chapter 2.

43. Beagon 1992, 161.

44. The Roman jurists had a category of "slaves who don't work" referring to domestic slaves (Saller 2003, 191).

45. N.H. 22.14: *addidere vivendi pretia deliciae luxusque*, which he viewed as detrimental to well-being.

46. Brewer 1998, 80; Slack 2014, 129.

47. Brewer 1998.

48. Book 3, chapter 4.

49. Brewer 1998, 97.

50. Beagon 1992, 55.

51. Broekaert 2017; Terpstra 2019 with review by Saller 2020.

52. Other scents prone to adulteration: myrrh (N.H. 12.18), styrax (N.H. 12.124), and nard (N.H. 13.16).

53. Purcell (1985, 19) discusses the adulteration of wine.

54. Dark ochre is another pigment that is counterfeited (N.H. 15.90).

55. But only a little later in the book (N.H. 37.112) we are told that no gemstone is more easily counterfeited in glass than callaina. And iaspis is also counterfeited in glass (N.H. 37.117), as is leucochrysi (N.H. 37.128).

56. Another medicinal fraud: verdigris (N.H. 34.112).

57. Mokyr (2016, 190), following Shapin (1994, 212ff.), identifies seven criteria for evaluation of knowledge, including "plausibility (consistency with what was already known), the integrity and impartiality of the source, internal consistency, and consistency with multiple other sources reporting on the same matter."

58. Scheidel 2020, 344.

59. Columella, *De re rustica* 3.3, on which see Duncan-Jones 1982, chap. 2.

60. Pliny's preference for prudence over risk is similar to what behavioral economists today describe as a tendency to be motivated more strongly by loss aversion than by risk aversion.

Chapter 6. "Utility" and the Afterlife of the *Natural History*

1. Crombie 1953, 2–3.

2. My thanks to Professor Susan Stephens for her advice on this matter.

3. Doody 2010, 133. Of course, my study here would come under the heading of "specialist encounters."

4. I am relying here on Brodersen 2011, 63, quoting Kimble 1938 and Milham 1980. See also Chibnall 1975, 59.

5. Brodersen 2011, 70.

6. Milham 1980, 205, citing Beazley 1897, 252.

7. Brodersen 2011, 88.

8. Brodersen 2011, 72.

9. Langslow 2000, 64.

10. Doody 2010, 139.

11. See excursus to chapter 2. Hunt (2020, x) provides the first translation of the *Medicina Plinii* into English preceded by an earnest but amusing disclaimer reflecting the truth value of Pliny's remedies: "**Do not try these at home.** The advice outlined in this text was meant for an ancient audience and does not constitute modern medical advice. Not only was the vast majority of ancient medicine ineffectual, in some cases it was injurious to patient health. . . . Yes, these remedies can be considered natural, but natural does not mean safe!" For her commentary on rabies, see pp. 83, 242–46. Doody (2010, 140–42) illustrates the consolidation of scattered "things worth knowing" in *Medicina Plinii* with asp bite.

12. Langslow 2000, 64.

13. Nauert 1980, 302. Interestingly, some eighteenth-century encyclopedia projects failed owing to an impractical ambition to include all knowledge—e.g., Johann

Heinrich Zedler's *Grosses vollständiges Universal-Lexicon* (1732), on which see Headrick 2000, 155.

14. Nauert 1980, 301. For a more recent inventory of the manuscripts of the *Natural History*, see Reeve 2007.

15. Nauert 1980, 303.

16. Nauert 1980, 304.

17. Nauert 1980, 306.

18. Chibnall 1975, 64–65; her chapter describes medieval abridgments tailored to particular uses.

19. Nauert 1980, 306. The earliest important commentary on the whole work by Hermolaus Barbarus contained nearly five thousand textual emendations—an indication of how corrupt the text had become in transmission. Many commentaries were limited to the preface or a few books.

20. Nauert 1979.

21. Loveland and Schmitt 2015, 4.

22. Nauert 1980, 373.

23. Doody 2010, 151–52: "Medicine is the point at which philology gives way to utility, but also the point at which textual criticism is at its most crucial, where providing the right reading means providing the right remedy."

24. Headrick 2000, 150–51. Loveland and Schmitt (2015) document a (surprising?) revival in the prestige of the *Natural History* in the Enlightenment.

25. Mokyr 2016, 71; Scheidel 2019, 478–79. In reviewing Murphy 2004, Beagon 2006 quotes a letter from Sir Francis Bacon in 1622 on the project to replace the *Natural History*, "'which includes a great many things belonging to philology, to fable, to antiquity and not to Nature.'"

26. Slack 2014, especially 92 and 145.

27. Squicciarini and Voigtländer 2015.

28. The *Cyclopaedia* earned Chambers membership in the Royal Society the year after publication in 1728; for evidence that Chambers's work was read and cited in the years soon thereafter, see Bracken 1956. Headrick (2000, 170–71) counts twenty-three editions and reprints of the *Cyclopaedia* from 1728 to 1795 as evidence of "the growing penetration of reference works."

29. Both the *Lexicon Technicum* and the *Cyclopaedia* are not paginated, making precise references impossible. It is worth noting that Quintilian's *Institutes* advocates learning astronomy and geometry—astronomy motivated by the wish to understand poetry (1.4.4) and geometry for the purpose of sharpening the student's logical powers for forensic practice (1.10.34); neither motivation is related to technical advance.

30. The boast that England was surpassing Rome was anticipated by Thomas Sprat and Christopher Wren (Slack 2014, 134).

31. Muhanna (2018) writes that the purpose of Al-Nuwayri's *The Ultimate Ambition* was similar in this respect though different and more realistic than Pliny's *Natural History* in its presumed readership of scribes.

32. Mokyr 2016, 332.

33. Nauert (1979, 72–85) points out that the *Natural History* was introduced as a university textbook in Wittenberg as an anti-scholastic replacement for Aristotle.

34. Slack (2014, 4) underlines the significance of Chambers's use of the word "improvement."

35. Riggsby (2019, 12) points to a few instances of very limited alphabetization in the *Natural History* and offers reasons why ancient authors tended to refrain from this mode of presentation.

36. Headrick 2000, 160.

37. Mokyr (2016, 162) remarks on the connection between the development of scientific instruments and scientific discovery. Headrick (2000, 156) notes the radical innovation of Diderot and D'Alembert in visiting workshops to see firsthand how crafts were practiced.

38. Pliny's lack of interest in mathematics had cultural antecedents, pointed out by Rawson (1985, 156–58): Cicero (*De oratore* 1.10) wrote, "Who is ignorant in how great obscurity of matter, in how abstruse, manifold, and subtle an art they who are called mathematicians are engaged?" See also Conte 1994, 82. Headrick (2000, 62) describes how in the seventeenth century quantitative data began to be collected for an understanding of English society: "Also in that first generation [of British inventors of 'political arithmetic'] was Gregory King (1648–1712), who used the hearth tax records, along with some assumptions about the number of persons per 'hearth,' or household, to estimate the population of England both at the time and well into the future.... the first attempt to quantify society." See also Slack 2014, 2.

39. Healy 1999, chaps. 11 and 12 are devoted to phenomena that later would fall in the fields of chemistry and physics and conclude that "Pliny describes many observed facts which would, centuries later, become incorporated in the Laws of Physics.... Although his degree of originality in this field is limited, Pliny's collation of what was known, in the first century AD, apropos the properties of matter and energy and the relationships between them, is an invaluable contribution to our understanding of the 'science' of that period" (170). Greenaway (1986, 153) concludes that Pliny's chemical tests are "devoid of any real technical basis" and obscured genuine information.

40. Mokyr 2016, 16.

41. Paparazzo 2011, 105.

42. Yates (1947, 278) notes that Florence Rivault in the sixteenth century laid a plan for an academy, "anxious to emphasize the practical utility of such an enterprise."

43. Dowey 2017.

44. Mokyr (2016, 186) describes the fundamental qualities of the Republic of Letters for which the Roman Empire had no equivalents: "The community constituted an elite group of intellectuals and scientists who circulated and checked new knowledge through an epistolary network, the printing press, and local meeting places of scholars." Terpstra (2020) underlines the importance of the competitive environment.

45. Mokyr 2016, 301.

46. French 1994, ix.

47. Doody 2011.

48. Flohr 2013; see also Healy 1999, 219.

49. I believe that I have captured all of the entries on fulling in the *Natural History* but cannot be confident, given the (lack of) organization.

50. The causal connection, understood by Pliny and his readers, is that fullers spent their days stomping clothes in tubs of urine. In his thorough study of fulling, Flohr (2013, 104) claims that the use of urine has been overstated by historians, a claim based partly on the absence of a mention of urine in Pliny, N.H. 35.197–98, but Flohr apparently missed the earlier passages (N.H. 28.66, 91) in which Pliny attributed fullers' resistance to gout to their use of urine and reported camel's urine to be *utilissimam*, "very useful," to fullers. Flohr's oversight in an otherwise extremely thorough study illustrates the challenge that any reader of the *Natural History* would have in finding relevant information.

51. *Cyclopaedia*, "Fulling," vol. 1, 106–7.

Conclusion

1. I accept the argument of Erdkamp (2016) that gains in productivity were possible from changes in social organization but also the conclusion of Mokyr (2016) that such growth runs into diminishing returns in the absence of advances in technology.

2. Mokyr 2018.

3. Slack 2014, 102.

4. Conte 1994, 90 describes the *Natural History* as "a monumental 'culture text.'"

5. Scheidel 2020, 344, where he also estimates the savings rate at a low ~1%.

6. Conte 1994, 72.

7. According to Conte 1994, 73, for Pliny "science is not conceived as an open process" with the result that his opus could be a "stable summation." But Pliny did allow for exploration and new discoveries.

8. Conte (1994, 84) argues it is Pliny's view that "regularity is not of this world."

9. The ambiguity of the meaning of "significant" extends into other economic histories, as noted by Jones (2000, 26): "Work in this subject almost never specifies in advance what level it would accept as significant." For the vacuity of meaning of "significant" in Roman economic history, see Saller 2001.

10. Greene 2000; Wilson 2002, 2020. Malanima (2013, 33–34) offers a calculation of the "modest" contribution to the Roman energy supply by water mills.

11. Flohr (2016) argues that the Roman Empire did enjoy a culture of innovation against Finley 1965, which he takes to be "the standard reference for the 'stagnation-ist' take on ancient technological progress." It is worth noting that Finley did not use the word "stagnation" in the article; his position was "there was more, provided we avoid the mistake of hunting solely for great radical inventions and we also look at developments within the limits of the traditional techniques. There was less—far less—if we avoid the reverse mistake and look not merely for the appearance of an invention, but also for the extent of its employment" (29). Finley acknowledges major inventions such as concrete and the water mill ("a radical invention"), but he did not know the extent of its use. Shaw (2019) offers a stimulating and provocative exploration of Romans' conceptions of the future; his argument that the conceptions for purposes of planning had a short time horizon may well be related to the absence of an idea of indefinite, sustained economic growth through never-ending technical progress.

12. As it happens, in the omission of Roman inventions Pliny anticipated the list of greatest inventions in Fallows 2013.

13. Zagorin 1998, 97: "The major purpose of Baconian natural philosophy is to produce innovations of which nature unaided is not capable"—a prospect of progress not to be found in the *Natural History*.

14. The whole notion of an "updated edition" would have been foreign to Pliny, not only because the absence of the printing press meant that there was no fixed form of presentation of the *Natural History* but also because Pliny was not concerned that the rapid progress of discovery would make revised editions necessary.

15. For what it is worth, the text of the *Natural History* is not found in the inventory of Egyptian papyri, which in any case are more Greek than Latin.

16. Nauert 1979.

17. From the work *De Magnete*, quoted by Mokyr (2016, 152). Doody (2010, 38), described the shift in attitudes toward the *Natural History* in this way: "Bacon's respect for Pliny's authority is coupled with scepticism about his inclusion of fabulous matter, and scorn for his dependence on symbolic systems of thought. The emphasis on experimentalism and objectivity that Bacon pioneered in the philosophy of science was to be instrumental in our misunderstanding of Pliny's project as the *Natural History* gradually came to be seen as unscientific, rhetorical and slightly bizarre. Bacon's irritation with Pliny's mistaken stories is recognisable, but the reasons why he might choose to use Pliny as the key example of how to write *Natural History* are less expected. As the Scientific Revolution takes hold, forgetfulness or derision of the systems of thought to which Pliny's stories belong makes it increasingly difficult to respect his authority as a scholar. The extent to which we have internalised a scientific discourse on nature that has no place for Pliny's *mirabilia*, and expects experimentation rather than reading, is reflected in our chronic misunderstanding of the seriousness of Pliny's scholarship, or the value of his particular claims to originality."

BIBLIOGRAPHY

Acemoglu, Daron, and James A. Robinson. 2012. *Why Nations Fail: The Origins of Power, Prosperity, and Poverty*. New York: Crown Publishers.

Alcock, Susan E. 1993. *Graecia Capta: The Landscapes of Roman Greece*. Cambridge: Cambridge University Press.

Allen, Robert C. 2009. "How Prosperous Were the Romans? Evidence from Diocletian's Price Edict (301 AD)." In *Quantifying the Roman Economy: Methods and Problems*, ed. Alan Bowman and Andrew Wilson, 327–45. Oxford: Oxford University Press.

Ash, Rhiannon. 2011. "Pliny the Elder's Attitude to Warfare." In *Pliny the Elder: Themes and Contexts*, ed. Roy K. Gibson and Ruth Morello, 1–20. Leiden: Brill.

Baer, George M. 2007. "The History of Rabies." In *Rabies*. 2nd ed., ed. Alan C. Jackson and William H. Wunner, 1–22. Amsterdam: Elsevier/Academic.

Bagnall, Roger S., and Bruce W. Frier. 1994. *The Demography of Roman Egypt*. Cambridge: Cambridge University Press.

Bang, Peter F. 2012. "Predation." In *The Cambridge Companion to the Roman Economy*, ed. Walter Scheidel, 197–217. Cambridge: Cambridge University Press.

Beagon, Mary. 1992. *Roman Nature: The Thought of Pliny the Elder*. Oxford: Clarendon Press.

———. 2005. *The Elder Pliny on the Human Animal: Natural History, Book 7*. Oxford: Clarendon Press.

———. 2006. Review of *Pliny the Elder's Natural History: The Empire in the Encyclopedia*, by Trevor Murphy. *Aestimatio: Critical Reviews in the History of Science* 3:31–37.

Beazley, Charles R. 1897–1906. *The Dawn of Modern Geography*. London: John Murray.

Bishop, M. C., and J.C.N. Coulston. 2006. *Roman Military Equipment from the Punic Wars to the Fall of Rome*. 2nd ed. Oxford: Oxbow Books.

Bodel, John. 2001. *Epigraphic Evidence: Ancient History from Inscriptions*. London: Routledge.

Bracken, Harry M. 1956. "Berkeley and Chambers." *Journal of the History of Ideas* 17:120–26.

Bradley, Keith. 2011. "Resisting Slavery at Rome." In *The Cambridge World History of Slavery*, ed. Keith Bradley and Paul Cartledge, 362–84. Cambridge: Cambridge University Press.

Bresson, Alain. 2014. "Capitalism and the Ancient Greek Economy." In *The Cambridge History of Capitalism*, ed. Larry Neal and Jeffrey G. Williamson, 43–74. Cambridge: Cambridge University Press.

———. 2020. "Fates of Rome." *Journal of Roman Studies* 110:233–46.

Brewer, Anthony. 1998. "Luxury and Economic Development: David Hume and Adam Smith." *Scottish Journal of Political Economy* 45 (1): 78–98.

Brewer, Daniel. 2011. "The *Encyclopédie*: Innovation and Legacy." In *New Essays on Diderot*, ed. James Fowler, 47–58. Cambridge: Cambridge University Press.

Brodersen, Kai. 2011. "Mapping Pliny's World: The Achievement of Solinus." *Bulletin of the Institute of Classical Studies* 54 (1): 63–88.

Broekaert, Wim. 2017. "Conflicts, Contract Enforcement, and Business Communities in the Archive of the Sulpicii." In *The Economy of Pompeii*, ed. Miko Flohr and Andrew Wilson, 387–414. Oxford: Oxford University Press.

Burton, Paul, and Tamara Lewit. 2019. "Pliny's Presses: The True Story of the First Century Wine Press." *Klio* 101 (2): 543–98.

Bury, J. B. 1920. *The Idea of Progress; An Inquiry into Its Origin and Growth*. London: Macmillan.

Carey, Sorcha. 2006. *Pliny's Catalogue of Culture: Art and Empire in the Natural History*. Oxford: Oxford University Press.

Casson, Lionel. 1971. *Ships and Seamanship in the Ancient World*. Princeton: Princeton University Press.

Champlin, Edward. 1991. *Final Judgments: Duty and Emotion in Roman Wills, 200 B.C.–A.D. 250*. Berkeley: University of California Press.

Chapman, Robert, and Alison Wylie. 2016. *Evidential Reasoning in Archaeology*. London: Bloomsbury Publishing.

Chibnall, Marjorie. 1975. "Pliny's *Natural History* and the Middle Ages." In *Empire and Aftermath: Silver Latin II*, ed. T. A. Dorey, 57–78. London: Routledge.

Cohen, David. 1991. "The Augustan Law on Adultery: The Social and Cultural Context." In *The Family in Italy from Antiquity to Present*, ed. David I. Kertzer and Richard P. Saller, 109–26. New Haven: Yale University Press.

Conte, Gian B. 1994. *Genres and Readers: Lucretius, Love Elegy, Pliny's Encyclopedia*. Trans. Glenn W. Most with a foreword by Charles Segal. Baltimore: Johns Hopkins University Press.

Crombie, A. C. 1953. *Augustine to Galileo: The History of Science, A.D. 400–1650*. Cambridge, MA: Harvard University Press.

Cuomo, Serafina. 2007. *Technology and Culture in Greek and Roman Antiquity*. Cambridge: Cambridge University Press.

———. 2008. "Ancient Written Sources for Engineering and Technology." In *The Oxford Handbook of Engineering and Technology in the Classical World*, ed. John Peter Oleson, 15–34. Oxford: Oxford University Press.

D'Arms, John H. 1981. *Commerce and Social Standing in Ancient Rome*. Cambridge, MA: Harvard University Press.

De Callataÿ, François. 2005. "The Graeco-Roman Economy in the Super Long-Run: Lead, Copper, and Shipwrecks." *Journal of Roman Archaeology* 18:361–72.

De Ligt, Luuk, and John Bintliff. 2020. Introduction to *Regional Urban Systems in the Roman World, 150 BCE–250 CE*, ed. Luuk de Ligt and John Bintliff, 1–34. Leiden: Brill.

Dixon, Suzanne. 2001. *Reading Roman Women*. London: Duckworth.

Doody, Aude. 2001. "Finding Facts in Pliny's Encyclopedia: The *Summarivm* of the *Natural History*." *Ramus* 30 (1): 1–22.

———. 2010. *Pliny's Encyclopedia: The Reception of the Natural History*. Cambridge: Cambridge University Press.

———. 2011. "The Science and Aesthetics of Names in the *Natural History*." In *Pliny the Elder: Themes and Contexts*, ed. Roy K. Gibson and Ruth Morello, 113–29. Leiden: Brill.

Dowey, James. 2017. "Mind Over Matter: Access to Knowledge and the British Industrial Revolution." PhD diss., London School of Economics and Political Science.

Duncan-Jones, Richard. 1982. *The Economy of the Roman Empire: Quantitative Studies*. 2nd ed. Cambridge: Cambridge University Press.

Economist. 2019. "Arctic Lead Levels Shed New Light on Europe's History." July 11.

Elliott, Colin P. 2020. "Coin Debasement, Climate and Contagion in Second-Century Egypt: Some Intersections." In *Debasement: Manipulation of Coin Standards in Pre-Modern Monetary Systems*, ed. Kevin Butcher, 63–72. Oxford: Oxbow Books.

Elton, Hugh. 1994. "The Study of Roman Military Equipment." Review of *Roman Military Equipment from the Punic Wars to the Fall of Rome (B.T. Batsford, London 1993)*, M.C. Bishop and J.C.N. Coulston. *Journal of Roman Archaeology* 7:491–95.

Erdkamp, Paul. 2014. "How Modern Was the Market Economy of the Roman World?" *Oeconomia* 4–2:225–35.

———. 2015. "Structural Determinants of Economic Performance in the Roman World and Early-Modern Europe: A Comparative Approach." In *Structure and Performance in the Roman Economy: Models, Methods and Case Studies*, ed. Paul Erdkamp and Koenraad Verboven, 17–32. Brussels: Éditions Latomus.

Erdkamp, Paul. 2016. "Economic Growth in the Roman Mediterranean World: An Early Good-Bye to Malthus?" *Explorations in Economic History* 60:1–20.

———. 2019. "War, Food, Climate Change, and the Decline of the Roman Empire." *Journal of Late Antiquity* 12 (2): 422–65.

Erdkamp, Paul, Koenraad Verboven, and Arjan Zuiderhoek, eds. 2020. *Capital, Investment, and Innovation in the Roman World*. Oxford: Oxford University Press.

Fallows, James. 2013. "The 50 Greatest Breakthroughs since the Wheel." *Atlantic*, October 29.

Feingold, Mordechai, and Andrej Svorenčík. 2020. "A Preliminary Census of Copies of the First Edition of Newton's *Principia* (1687)." *Annals of Science* 77 (3): 253–348.

Finley, M. I. 1965. "Technical Innovation and Economic Progress in the Ancient World." *Economic History Review*, n.s., 18 (1): 29–45.

———. 1973. *The Ancient Economy*. Berkeley: University of California Press.

Flohr, Miko. 2013. *The World of the Fullo: Work, Economy, and Society in Roman Italy*. Oxford: Oxford University Press.

———. 2016. "Innovation and Society in the Roman World." In *Oxford Handbooks Online*. Oxford: Oxford University Press.

Fogel, Robert W., and Dora L. Costa. 1997. "A Theory of Technophysio Evolution, with Some Implications for Forecasting Population, Health Care Costs, and Pension Costs." *Demography* 34 (1): 49–66.

Fögen, Thorsten. 2013. "Scholarship and Competitiveness: Pliny the Elder's Attitude towards His Predecessors in the *Naturalis Historia*." In *Writing Science: Medical and Mathematical Authorship in Ancient Greece*, ed. Markus Asper, 83–107. Berlin: De Gruyter.

Forbes, R. J. 1950. *Man, the Maker: A History of Technology and Engineering*. New York: Schuman.

Ford, James A. 1954. "On the Concept of Types." *American Anthropologist* 56 (1): 42–54.

French, Roger. 1994. *Ancient Natural History: Histories of Nature*. London: Routledge.

French, Roger, and Frank Greenaway, eds. 1986. *Science in the Early Roman Empire: Pliny the Elder, His Sources and Influence*. London: Croom Helm.

Garnsey, Peter. 2017. "Dem Bones." In *Text and the Material World, Essays in Honour of Graeme Clarke*, ed. Elizabeth Minchin and Heather Jackson, 199–210. Uppsala: Astroms Editions.

Garnsey, Peter, and Richard P. Saller. 2015. *The Roman Empire: Economy, Society and Culture*. 2nd ed. Berkeley: University of California Press.

Gibbon, Edward. 1776–88. *The History of the Decline and Fall of the Roman Empire*. London: Strahan & Cadell.

Gibson, Roy K., and Ruth Morello, eds. 2011. *Pliny the Elder: Themes and Contexts*. Leiden: Brill.

———. 2012. *Reading the Letters of Pliny the Younger: An Introduction.* Cambridge: Cambridge University Press.

Goodyear, F.R.D. 1982. "Technical Writing." In *The Cambridge History of Classical Literature Volume II*, ed. E. J. Kenney and W. V. Clausen, 667–73. Cambridge: Cambridge University Press.

Greenaway, Frank. 1986. "Chemical Tests in Pliny." In *Science in the Early Roman Empire: Pliny the Elder, His Sources and Influence*, ed. Roger French and Frank Greenaway, 147–61. London: Croom Helm.

Greene, Kevin. 1992. "How Was Technology Transferred in the Western Provinces." In *Current Research on Romanization in the Western Provinces*, ed. Mark Wood and Francisco Queiroga, 101–5. Oxford: Tempus Reparatum.

———. 2000. "Technological Innovation and Economic Progress in the Ancient World: M. I. Finley Reconsidered." *Economic History Review* 53 (1): 29–59.

———. 2009. "Inventors, Invention, and Attitudes toward Technology and Innovation." In *The Oxford Handbook of Engineering and Technology in the Classical World*, ed. John Peter Oleson, 800–818. Oxford: Oxford University Press.

Gudger, E. W. 1924. "Pliny's *Historia Naturalis*: The Most Popular Natural History Ever Published." *Isis* 6 (3): 269–81.

Hanson, J. W. 2016. *An Urban Geography of the Roman World, 100 BC to AD 300.* Oxford: Archaeopress Publishing.

Harper, Kyle. 2017. *The Fate of Rome: Climate, Disease, and the End of an Empire.* Princeton: Princeton University Press.

———. 2018. "Integrating the Natural Sciences and Roman History: Challenges and Prospects." *History Compass* 16:e12520.

Harris, Gardiner. 2012. "Where Streets Are Thronged with Strays Baring Fangs." *New York Times*, August 6.

Harris, William V. 2000. "Trade." In *The Cambridge Ancient History XI: The High Empire, A.D. 70–192.* 2nd ed., ed. Alan Bowman, Peter Garnsey, and Dominic Rathbone, 710–40. Cambridge: Cambridge University Press.

———. 2011. *Rome's Imperial Economy: Twelve Essays.* Oxford: Oxford University Press.

Hausmann, Ricardo, César A. Hidalgo, Sebastián Bustos, Michele Coscia, Alexander Simoes, and Muhammed A. Yıldırım. 2013. *The Atlas of Economic Complexity: Mapping Paths to Prosperity.* Cambridge, MA: MIT Press.

Headrick, Daniel R. 2000. *When Information Came of Age: Technologies of Knowledge in the Age of Reason and Revolution, 1700–1850.* Oxford: Oxford University Press.

Healy, John F. 1999. *Pliny the Elder on Science and Technology.* Oxford: Oxford University Press.

Hickson, Josiah. 2017. "The Atlas of Economic Complexity: A Review." *Newcastle Business School Student Journal* 1 (1): 27–33.

Hidalgo, César A. 2015. *Why Information Grows: The Evolution of Order, from Atoms to Economies*. New York: Basic Books.

Hidalgo, César A., and Ricardo Hausmann. 2009. "The Building Blocks of Economic Complexity." *Proceedings of the National Academy of Sciences* 106 (26): 10570–75.

Holford-Strevens, Leofranc. 2003. *Aulus Gellius: An Antonine Scholar and His Achievement*. Rev. ed. Oxford: Oxford University Press.

Holmes, Brooke. 2017. "The Generous Text." In *Knowledge, Text and Practice in Ancient Technical Writing*, ed. Marco Formisano and Philip van der Eijk, 231–51. Cambridge: Cambridge University Press.

Hong, Sungmin, Jean-Pierre Candelone, Clair C. Patterson, and Claude F. Boutron. 1994. "Greenland Ice Evidence of Hemispheric Lead Pollution Two Millennia Ago by Greek and Roman Civilizations." *Science* 265 (5180): 1841–43.

Hopkins, Keith. 1980. "Taxes and Trade in the Roman Empire (200 B.C.–A.D. 400)." *Journal of Roman Studies* 70:101–25.

———. 2017. *Sociological Studies in Roman History*. Ed. Christopher Kelley. Cambridge: Cambridge University Press.

Horden, Peregrine, and Nicholas Purcell. 2000. *The Corrupting Sea: A Study of Mediterranean History*. Oxford: Blackwell.

Howe, Nicholas Phillies. 1985. "In Defense of the Encyclopedic Mode: On Pliny's *Preface* to the *Natural History*." *Latomus* 44 (3): 561–76.

Howley, Joseph A. 2018. *Aulus Gellius and Roman Reading Culture: Text, Presence, and Imperial Knowledge in the Noctes Atticae*. Cambridge: Cambridge University Press.

Hubbard, Glenn, and Tim Kane. 2013. *Balance: The Economics of Great Powers from Ancient Rome to Modern America*. New York: Simon and Schuster.

Hume, David. (1777) 1985. *Essays, Moral, Political, and Literary*. Edited and with a foreword, notes, and glossary by Eugene F. Miller; with an apparatus of variant readings from the 1889 edition by T. H. Green and T. H. Grose. Indianapolis: Liberty Classics.

Humphrey, John William, John Peter Oleson, and Andrew N. Sherwood, eds. 1998. *Greek and Roman Technology: A Sourcebook: Annotated Translations of Greek and Latin Texts and Documents*. London: Routledge.

Hunt, Yvette. 2020. *The Medicina Plinii: Latin Text, Translation, and Commentary*. London: Routledge.

Isager, Jacob. 1991. *Pliny on Art and Society: The Elder Pliny's Chapters on the History of Art*. Trans. Henrik Rosenmeier. Odense: Odense University Press.

Jacobs, Jane. 1969. *The Economy of Cities*. New York: Random House.

Jones, E. L. 2000. *Growth Recurring: Economic Change in World History*. 2nd ed. Ann Arbor: University of Michigan Press.

Jongman, Willem M. 2007. "Gibbon Was Right: The Decline and Fall of the Roman Economy." In *Crises and the Roman Empire*, ed. O. Hekster, G. de Kleijn, and Daniëlle Slootjes, 183–99. Leiden: Brill.

————. 2019. "The Economic Archaeology of Roman Economic Performance." In *Finding the Limits of the Limes: Modelling Demography, Economy and Transport on the Edge of the Roman Empire*, ed. Philip Verhagen, Jamie Joyce, and Mark R. Groenhuijzen, 95–107. Cham: Springer.

Jongman, Willem M., Jan P.A.M. Jacobs, and Geertje M. Klein Goldewijk. 2019. "Health and Wealth in the Roman Empire." *Economics and Human Biology* 34:138–50.

Kaster, Robert A. 1988. *Guardians of Language: The Grammarian and Society in Late Antiquity*. Berkeley: University of California Press.

Kay, Philip. 2014. *Rome's Economic Revolution*. New York: Oxford University Press.

Kehoe, Dennis P. 1997. *Investment, Profit, and Tenancy: The Jurists and the Roman Agrarian Economy*. Ann Arbor: University of Michigan Press.

Keyser, Paul T., and Georgia L. Irby-Massie, eds. 2008. *The Encyclopedia of Ancient Natural Scientists: The Greek Tradition and Its Many Heirs*. London: Routledge.

Killgrove, Kristina. 2019. "Using Skeletal Remains as a Proxy for Roman Lifestyles: The Potential and Problems with Osteological Reconstructions of Health, Diet, and Stature in Imperial Rome." In *The Routledge Handbook of Diet and Nutrition in the Roman World*, ed. Paul Erdkamp and Claire Holleran, 245–58. London: Routledge.

Kimble, George H. T. 1938. *Geography in the Middle Ages*. London: Methuen.

König, Jason, and Greg Woolf. 2013. "Encyclopaedism in the Roman Empire." In *Encyclopaedism from Antiquity to the Renaissance*, ed. Jason König and Greg Woolf, 23–63. Cambridge: Cambridge University Press.

Kornei, Katherine. 2020. "Ancient Rome Was Teetering. Then a Volcano Erupted 6,000 Miles Away." *New York Times*, June 22.

Kyle, Donald G. 1998. *Spectacles of Death in Ancient Rome*. London: Routledge.

Lancaster, Lynne C. 2005. *Concrete Vaulted Construction in Imperial Rome: Innovations in Context*. Cambridge: Cambridge University Press.

Langin, Katie. 2018. "Rise and Fall of the Roman Empire Exposed in Greenland Ice Samples." *Science*, May 14.

Langslow, D. R. 2000. *Medical Latin in the Roman Empire*. Oxford: Oxford University Press.

Lao, Eugenia. 2008. "Restoring the Treasury of Mind: The Practical Knowledge of the *Natural History*." PhD diss., Princeton University.

————. 2011. "Luxury and the Creation of a Good Consumer." In *Pliny the Elder: Themes and Contexts*, ed. Roy K. Gibson and Ruth Morello, 35–56. Leiden: Brill.

Launaro, Alessandro. 2011. *Peasants and Slaves: The Rural Population of Roman Italy (200 BC to AD 100)*. Cambridge: Cambridge University Press.

Laurence, Ray. 2012. *Roman Archaeology for Historians*. London: Routledge.

Laurence, Ray, Simon Esmonde Cleary, and Gareth Sears. 2011. *The City in the Roman West, c. 250 BC–c. AD 250*. Cambridge: Cambridge University Press.

Lauwers, Jeroen. 2015. *Philosophy, Rhetoric, and Sophistry in the High Roman Empire: Maximus of Tyre and Twelve Other Intellectuals*. Leiden: Brill.

Lendon, J. E. 2011. "Roman Honor." In *The Oxford Handbook of Social Relations in the Roman World*, ed. Michael Peachin, 377–403. Oxford: Oxford University Press.

Lewit, Tamara. 2020. "Invention, Tinkering, or Transfer?: Innovation in Oil and Wine Presses in the Roman Empire." In *Capital, Investment, and Innovation in the Roman World*, ed. Paul Erdkamp, Koenraad Verboven, and Arjan Zuiderhoek, 307–53. Oxford: Oxford University Press.

Lloyd, G.E.R. 1983. *Science, Folklore, and Ideology: Studies in the Life Sciences in Ancient Greece*. Cambridge: Cambridge University Press.

———. 1984. "Hellenistic Science." In *The Cambridge Ancient History Volume VII, Part I: The Hellenistic World*. 2nd ed., ed. F. W. Walbank, A. E. Astin, M. W. Frederiksen, and R. M. Ogilvie, 321–52. Cambridge: Cambridge University Press.

Loveland, Jeff, and Stéphane Schmitt. 2015. "Poinsinet's Edition of the *Naturalis Historia* (1771–1782) and the Revival of Pliny in the Sciences of the Enlightenment." *Annals of Science* 72 (1): 2–27.

Lyons, Claire L. 1996. *Morgantina Studies, Volume V: The Archaic Cemeteries*. Princeton: Princeton University Press.

MacMullen, Ramsay. 1982. "The Epigraphic Habit in the Roman Empire." *American Journal of Philology* 103 (3): 233–46.

Malanima, Paolo. 2013. "Energy Consumption in the Roman World." In *The Ancient Mediterranean Environment between Science and History*, ed. William V. Harris, 13–36. Leiden: Brill.

Martin, René. 1971. *Recherches sur les agronomes latines et leurs conceptions économiques et sociales*. Paris: Les Belles Lettres.

McCloskey, Deirdre Nansen. 2016. "The Great Enrichment: A Humanistic and Social Scientific Account." *Scandinavian Economic History Review* 64 (1): 6–18.

McConnell, Joseph R., Nathan J. Chellman, Andrew I. Wilson, Andreas Stohl, Monica M. Arienzo, Sabine Eckhardt, Diedrich Fritzsche, Sepp Kipfstuhl, Thomas Opel, Philip F. Place, and Jørgen Peder Steffensen. 2019. "Pervasive Arctic Lead Pollution Suggests Substantial Growth in Medieval Silver Production Modulated by Plague, Climate, and Conflict." *Proceedings of the National Academy of Sciences* 116 (30): 14910–15.

McConnell, Joseph R., Andrew I. Wilson, Andreas Stohl, Monica M. Arienzo, Nathan J. Chellman, Sabine Eckhardt, Elisabeth M. Thompson, A. Mark Pollard, and Jørgen Peder Steffensen. 2018. "Lead Pollution Recorded in Greenland Ice Indicates European Emissions Tracked Plagues, Wars, and Imperial Expansion during Antiquity." *Proceedings of the National Academy of Sciences* 115 (22): 5726–31.

McGinn, Thomas A. J. 2004. *The Economy of Prostitution in the Roman World: A Study of Social History and the Brothel.* Ann Arbor: University of Michigan Press.

Milham, Mary E. 1980. "The Renaissance Tradition of Solinus." In *Acta conventus neo-Latini Turonensis*, ed. Jean-Claude Margolin, 205–8. Paris: Librairie Philosophique J. Vrin.

Mokyr, Joel. 2016. *A Culture of Growth: The Origins of the Modern Economy.* Princeton: Princeton University Press.

———. 2018. "The Past and the Future of Innovation: Some Lessons from Economic History." *Explorations in Economic History* 69:13–26.

Moore, Joanna, Kori Filipek, Vana Kalenderian, Rebecca Gowland, Elliott Hamilton, Jane Evans, and Janet Montgomery. 2021. "Death Metal: Evidence for the Impact of Lead Poisoning on Childhood Health with the Roman Empire." *International Journal of Osteoarchaeology.* https://onlinelibrary.wiley.com/doi/pdf/10.1002/oa.3001.

Morris, Ian. 2013. *The Measure of Civilization: How Social Development Decides the Fate of Nations.* Princeton: Princeton University Press.

———. 2014. *War! What Is It Good For? Conflict and the Progress of Civilization from Primates to Robots.* New York: Farrar, Straus and Giroux.

Morton, A. G. 1986. "Pliny on Plants: His Place in the History of Botany." In *Science in the Early Roman Empire: Pliny the Elder, His Sources and Influence*, ed. Roger French and Frank Greenaway, 86–97. London: Croom Helm.

Muhanna, Elias. 2018. *The World in a Book: Al-Nuwayri and the Islamic Encyclopedic Tradition.* Princeton: Princeton University Press.

Murphy, Trevor. 2003. "Pliny's *Naturalis Historia*: The Prodigal Text." In *Flavian Rome: Culture, Image, Text*, ed. A. J. Boyle and W. J. Dominik, 301–22. Leiden: Brill.

———. 2004. *Pliny the Elder's Natural History: The Empire in the Encyclopedia.* Oxford: Oxford University Press.

Naas, Valérie. 2002. *Le Projet Encyclopédique de Pline L'Ancien.* Rome: Ecole française de Rome.

Nauert, Charles G., Jr. 1979. "Humanists, Scientists, and Pliny: Changing Approaches to a Classical Author." *American Historical Review* 84 (1): 72–85.

———. 1980. "C. Plinius Secundus (*Naturalis Historia*)." In *Catalogus Translationum et Commentariorum: Mediaeval and Renaissance Latin Translations and Commentaries, Volume IV*, ed. F. Edward Cranz with Paul Oskar Kristeller, 297–422. Washington, DC: Catholic University of America Press.

Neville, J. 2004. "Rabies in the Ancient World." In *Historical Perspective of Rabies in Europe and the Mediterranean Basin*, ed. A. A. King, A. R. Fooks, M. Aubert, and A. I. Wandeler, 1–13. Paris: World Organization for Animal Health.

Nutton, Vivian. 1986. "The Perils of Patriotism: Pliny and Roman Medicine." In *Science in the Early Roman Empire: Pliny the Elder, His Sources and Influence*, ed. Roger French and Frank Greenaway, 30–58. London: Croom Helm.

Oikonomopoulou, Katerina. 2016. "Scientific Encyclopedias." In *A Companion to Science, Technology, and Medicine in Ancient Greece and Rome*, ed. Georgia L. Irby, 973–87. Chichester: John Wiley and Sons.

Oleson, John Peter, ed. 2008. *The Oxford Handbook of Engineering and Technology in the Classical World*. Oxford: Oxford University Press.

Paparazzo, Ernesto. 2011. "Philosophy and Science in the Elder Pliny's *Naturalis Historia*." In *Pliny the Elder: Themes and Contexts*, ed. Roy K. Gibson and Ruth Morello, 89–111. Leiden: Brill.

Paterson, Jeremy. 1998. "Trade and Traders in the Roman World: Scale, Structure, and Organization." In *Trade, Traders and the Ancient City*, ed. Helen Parkins and Christopher Smith, 145–63. London: Routledge.

Pavlyshyn, Damian, Iain Johnstone, and Richard Saller. 2020. "Lead Pollution and the Roman Economy." *Journal of Roman Archaeology* 33:354–64.

Pederson, Olaf. 1986. "Some Astronomical Topics in Pliny." In *Science in the Early Roman Empire: Pliny the Elder, His Sources and Influence*, ed. Roger French and Frank Greenaway, 162–96. London: Croom Helm.

Piketty, Thomas. 2017. *Capital in the Twenty-First Century*. Trans. Arthur Goldhammer. Cambridge, MA: Harvard University Press.

Purcell, Nicholas. 1985. "Wine and Wealth in Ancient Italy." *Journal of Roman Studies* 75:1–19.

———. 2003. "The Way We Used to Eat: Diet, Community, and History at Rome." *American Journal of Philology* 124 (3): 329–58.

Rathbone, Dominic. 1991. *Economic Rationalism and Rural Society in Third-Century A.D. Egypt: The Heroninos Archive and the Appianus Estate*. Cambridge: Cambridge University Press.

Rawson, Beryl. 2003. *Children and Childhood in Roman Italy*. Oxford: Oxford University Press.

Rawson, Elizabeth. 1985. *Intellectual Life in the Late Roman Republic*. London: Duckworth.

Reeve, Michael D. 2007. "The Editing of Pliny's *Natural History*." *Revue d'histoire des textes*, n.s., 2:107–79.

Reynolds, Joyce. 1986. "The Elder Pliny and His Times." In *Science in the Early Roman Empire: Pliny the Elder, His Sources and Influence*, ed. Roger French and Frank Greenaway, 1–10. London: Croom Helm.

Riggsby, Andrew M. 2007. "Guides to the Wor(l)d." In *Ordering Knowledge in the Roman Empire*, ed. Jason König and Tim Whitmarsh, 88–107. Cambridge: Cambridge University Press.

———. 2019. *Mosaics of Knowledge: Representing Information in the Roman World*. New York : Oxford University Press.

Roll, Eric. 1942. *A History of Economic Thought*. New York: Prentice-Hall.

Rosman, Kevin J. R., Warrick Chisholm, Sungmin Hong, Jean-Pierre Candelone, and Claude F. Boutron. 1997. "Lead from Carthaginian and Roman Spanish

Mines Isotopically Identified in Greenland Ice Dated from 600 B.C. to 300 A.D." *Environmental Science and Technology* 31 (12): 3413–16.

Rostovtzeff, M. I. 1957. *The Social and Economic History of the Roman Empire*. 2nd ed., revised by P. M. Fraser. Oxford: Clarendon Press.

Russell, Ben. 2013. *The Economics of the Roman Stone Trade*. Oxford: Oxford University Press.

Saller, Richard. 1982. *Personal Patronage under the Early Empire*. Cambridge: Cambridge University Press.

———. 1994. *Patriarchy, Property and Death in the Roman Family*. Cambridge: Cambridge University Press.

———. 2001. "The Non-agricultural Economy: Superceding Finley and Hopkins?" Review of *Economies beyond Agriculture in the Classical World*, ed. David J. Mattingly and John Salmon. *Journal of Roman Archaeology* 14:580–84.

———. 2002. "Framing the Debate over Growth in the Ancient Economy." In *The Ancient Economy*, ed. Walter Scheidel and Sitta von Reden, 251–69. New York: Routledge.

———. 2003. "Women, Slaves, and the Economy of the Roman Household." In *Early Christian Families in Context: An Interdisciplinary Dialogue*, ed. David L. Blach and Carolyn Osiek, 185–204. Grand Rapids, MI: W. B. Eerdmans.

———. 2005. "Framing the Debate over Growth in the Ancient Economy." In *The Ancient Economy: Evidence and Models*, ed. J. G. Manning and Ian Morris, 223–38. Stanford: Stanford University Press.

———. 2020. Review of *Trade in the Ancient Mediterranean: Private Order and Public Institutions*, by Taco Terpstra. *Economic History Review* 73 (1): 332–33.

Scarborough, John. 1986. "Pharmacy in Pliny's Natural History: Some Observations on Substances and Sources." In *Science in the Early Roman Empire: Pliny the Elder, His Sources and Influence*, ed. Roger French and Frank Greenaway, 59–85. London: Croom Helm.

Scheidel, Walter. 2007. "Demography." In *The Cambridge Economic History of the Greco-Roman World*, ed. Walter Scheidel, Ian Morris, and Richard Saller, 38–86. Cambridge: Cambridge University Press.

———. 2009. "In Search of Roman Economic Growth." *Journal of Roman Archaeology* 22 (1): 46–70.

———. 2019. *Escape from Rome: The Failure of Empire and the Road to Prosperity*. Princeton: Princeton University Press.

———. 2020. "Roman Wealth and Wealth Inequality in Comparative Perspective." *Journal of Roman Archaeology* 33:341–53.

Scheidel, Walter, and Steven J. Friesen. 2009. "The Size of the Economy and the Distribution of Income in the Roman Empire." *Journal of Roman Studies* 99:61–91.

Schilling, Robert. 1978. "La place de Pline l'Ancien dans la littérature technique." *Revue de Philologie* 52 (2): 272–83.

Schneider, Helmuth. 2007. "Technology." In *The Cambridge Economic History of the Greco-Roman World*, ed. Walter Scheidel, Ian Morris, and Richard Saller, 144–72. Cambridge: Cambridge University Press.

Schultze, Clemence. 2011. "Encyclopedic Exemplarity in Pliny the Elder." In *Pliny the Elder: Themes and Contexts*, ed. Roy K. Gibson and Ruth Morello, 167–86. Leiden: Brill.

Sellars, John. 2006. *Stoicism*. Durham: Acumen.

Shapin, Steven. 1994. *A Social History of Truth: Civility and Science in Seventeenth-Century England*. Chicago: University of Chicago Press.

Shaw, Brent D. 2019. "Did the Romans Have a Future?" *Journal of Roman Studies* 109:1–26.

Slack, Paul. 2014. *The Invention of Improvement: Information and Material Progress in Seventeenth-Century England*. Oxford: Oxford University Press.

Smith, Alexander, Martyn Allen, Tom Brindle, and Lisa Lodwick. 2017. "Rural Crafts and Industry." In *The Rural Economy of Roman Britain*, ed. Martyn Allen, Lisa Lodwick, Tom Brindle, Michael Fulford, and Alexander Smith, 178–235. London: Society for the Promotion of Roman Studies.

Spaulding, Albert C. 1953. "Statistical Techniques for the Discovery of Artifact Types." *American Antiquity* 18 (4): 305–13.

Spolaore, Enrico. 2020. "Commanding Nature by Obeying Her: A Review Essay on Joel Mokyr's *A Culture of Growth*." *Journal of Economic Literature* 58 (3): 777–92.

Squicciarini, Mara P., and Nico Voigtländer. 2015. "Human Capital and Industrialization: Evidence from the Age of Enlightenment." *Quarterly Journal of Economics* 130 (4): 1825–83.

Stahl, William H. 1962. *Roman Science: Origins, Development, and Influence to the Later Middle Ages*. Madison: University of Wisconsin Press.

Starr, Raymond J. 1987. "The Circulation of Literary Texts in the Roman World." *Classical Quarterly* 37 (1): 213–23.

Steele, James H. 1973. "The Epidemiology and Control of Rabies." *Scandinavian Journal of Infectious Disease* 5 (4): 299–312.

Stone, Shelley C. 2015. *Morgantina Studies, Volume VI: The Hellenistic and Roman Fine Pottery*. Princeton: Princeton University Press.

Syme, Ronald. 1969. "Pliny the Procurator." *Harvard Studies in Classical Philology* 73:201–36.

Tan, James. 2017. *Power and Public Finance at Rome, 264–49 BCE*. New York: Oxford University Press.

Taub, Liba Chaia. 2017. *Science Writing in Greco-Roman Antiquity*. Cambridge: Cambridge University Press.

Tchernia, André. 2016. *The Romans and Trade*. Oxford: Oxford University Press.

Temin, Peter. 2013. *The Roman Market Economy*. Princeton: Princeton University Press.

Terpstra, Taco. 2019. *Trade in the Ancient Mediterranean: Private Order and Public Institutions*. Princeton: Princeton University Press.

———. 2020. "Roman Technological Progress in Comparative Context: The Roman Empire, Medieval Europe and Imperial China." *Explorations in Economic History* 75:101300.

Totelin, Laurence. 2017. "From *technē* to *kakotechnia*." In *Knowledge, Text and Practice in Ancient Technical Writing*, ed. Marco Formisano and Philip van der Eijk, 138–62. Cambridge: Cambridge University Press.

Verboven, Koenraad. 2015. "The Knights Who Say NIE: Can Neo-institutional Economics Live Up to Its Expectation in Ancient History Research?" In *Structure and Performance in the Roman Economy: Models, Methods and Case Studies*, ed. Paul Erdkamp and Koenraad Verboven, 33–57. Brussels: Editions Latomus.

———. 2018. "Ancient Cliometrics and Archaeological Proxy-data: Between the Devil and the Deep Blue Sea." In *Cuantificar Las Economías Antiguas: Problemas y Métodos: Quantifying Ancient Economies: Problems and Methodologies*, ed. José Remesal Rodriguez, Victor Revilla Calvo, and Manuel Bermúdez Lorenzo, 345–71. Barcelona: Universitat de Barcelona Edicions.

Vivenza, Gloria. 2012. "Roman Economic Thought." In *The Cambridge Companion to the Roman Economy*, ed. Walter Scheidel, 25–44. Cambridge: Cambridge University Press.

Von Reden, Sitta. 2010. *Money in Classical Antiquity*. Cambridge: Cambridge University Press.

Von Staden, Heinrich. 2013. "Writing the Animal: Aristotle, Pliny the Elder, Galen." In *Writing Science: Medical and Mathematical Authorship in Ancient Greece*, ed. Markus Asper, 111–44. Berlin: De Gruyter.

Vons, Jacqueline. 2000. *L'image de la femme dans l'œuvre de Pline l'Ancien*. Brussels: Latomus.

Wade, Nicholas. 2018. "An Ice Core Reveals the Economic Health of the Roman Empire." *New York Times*, May 14.

Wallace-Hadrill, Andrew. 1990. "Pliny the Elder and Man's Unnatural History." *Greece and Rome* 37 (1): 80–96.

Ward-Perkins, Bryan. 2001. "Specialized Production and Exchange." In *The Cambridge Ancient History XIV: Late Antiquity: Empire and Successors, AD 425–600*, ed. Averil Cameron, Bryan Ward-Perkins, and Michael Whitby, 346–91. Cambridge: Cambridge University Press.

Wasik, Bill, and Monica Murphy. 2012. *Rabid: A Cultural History of the World's Most Diabolical Virus*. New York: Viking.

White, K. D. 1970. *Roman Farming*. Ithaca: Cornell University Press.

———. 1984. *Greek and Roman Technology*. Ithaca: Cornell University Press.

Wilson, Andrew. 2002. "Machines, Power and the Ancient Economy." *Journal of Roman Studies* 92:1–32.

————. 2009. "Indicators for Roman Economic Growth: A Response to Walter Scheidel." *Journal of Roman Archaeology* 22:71–82.

————. 2014. "Quantifying Roman Economic Performance by Means of Proxies: Pitfalls and Potential." In *Quantifying the Greco-Roman Economy and Beyond*, ed. François de Callataÿ, 147–67. Bari: Edipuglia.

————. 2020. "Roman Water-Power: Chronological Trends and Geographical Spread." In *Capital, Investment, and Innovation in the Roman World*, ed. Paul Erdkamp, Koenraad Verboven, and Arjan Zuiderhoek, 147–94. Oxford: Oxford University Press.

Witcher, Robert. 2006. "Broken Pots and Meaningless Dots? Surveying the Rural Landscapes of Roman Italy." *Papers of the British School at Rome* 74:36–75.

————. 2011. "Missing Persons? Models of Mediterranean Regional Survey and Ancient Populations." In *Settlement, Urbanization, and Population*, ed. Alan Bowman and Andrew Wilson, 36–75. Oxford: Oxford University Press.

Woolf, Greg. 2004. "The Present and Future Scope of Roman Archaeology: A Comment." *American Journal of Archaeology* 108 (3): 417–28.

Yates, Frances Amelia. 1947. *The French Academies of the Sixteenth Century*. London: Warburg Institute, University of London.

Zagorin, Perez. 1998. *Francis Bacon*. Princeton: Princeton University Press.

Zehnacker, Hubert. 1979. "Pline l'Ancien et l'histoire de la monnaie romaine." *Ktema* 4:169–81.

INDEX

actors, 56, 76, 102

aediles, 109, 112

Africa, 13, 14, 56, 58, 89, 151n22, 166

agency, 5, 85, 97–99. *See also* slavery

agriculture, 27, 30, 35, 40–41, 62, 64–65, 72, 75, 85–93, 101, 106–8, 125, 136, 152n33, 153n48, 154n59, 155nn73 and 5, 156n21, 166n58, 168nn5 and 11, 170n38; inventions in, 64–65, 136; tools, 89. *See also* cereal production; farmers; oleoculture; viticulture

Al-Nuwayri, 156n21, 157nn 26 and 32, 159n53, 173n31

Albertus Magnus, 117

Alexander the Great, 65

amber, 57, 103

Andreau, Jean, 10

Antonine Plague, 1, 3, 9, 12–18, 24, 150n11, 152n33, 153n51

Antonius Castor, 40

Antony, Marc, 54

Apelles, 76, 103

Apicius, 67, 164n28

Apollodorus, 75

aquaculture, 67

aqueducts, 109

Arabia, 96, 105, 166n58, 169n22

archaeological sampling, 29–31

Archimedes, 76

Aristotle, 117–18, 173n33

armor, dancing in, 62

art, prices of, 103–4

artisans, 4, 33, 36–37, 43, 69, 83, 93, 103–5, 113–14, 125, 134, 157n33, 169n18

artists, 62, 66–67, 77, 79, 103–4

Asclepiades, 75

Asinius Pollio, 127

astronomy, 36, 44, 62–63, 75, 125, 149n8, 170n38, 172n29

Augustus, 16–17, 86, 121, 152n33, 163n13

authority (*auctoritas*), 37, 40–41, 76, 79–82, 90, 114, 117–19, 121, 138, 158n40, 159n48, 175n17; of ancients, 39–40, 44, 51–52, 68, 72–73, 75, 92, 97–98, 135, 165n44. *See also* Cato, Marcus Porcius

autopsy, 39, 70, 158n43

Bacon, Francis, 63, 119, 137, 163n11, 172n25, 175nn13 and 17

Bacon, Roger, 117

Bagnall, Roger and Bruce Frier, 170n31

baths, 101, 151nn20 and 22

Beagon, Mary, 35, 49, 53, 55, 75, 85, 163n16, 166n65, 168nn8 and 10, 169n21, 170n37, 172n25

Berosus, 75

birds, 56, 59, 62, 102, 105

Bishop, M.C. and J.C.N. Coulston, 166n56

Bodel, John, 151n20

bones, as proxy, 11–12, 19–21

bounded rationality, 84

Bresson, Alain, 153n46

THE PRINCETON ECONOMIC HISTORY
OF THE WESTERN WORLD

Joel Mokyr, Series Editor

Recent titles

Plagues upon the Earth: Disease and the Course of Human History,
Kyle Harper

Credit Nation: Property Laws and Institutions in Early America, Claire
Priest

*The Decline and Rise of Democracy: A Global History from Antiquity to
Today,* David Stasavage

*Going the Distance: Eurasian Trade and the Rise of the Business
Corporation 1400–1700,* Ron Harris

Escape from Rome: The Failure of Empire and the Road to Prosperity,
Walter Scheidel

*Trade in the Ancient Mediterranean: Private Order and Public
Institutions,* Taco Terpstra

*Dark Matter Credit: The Development of Peer-to-Peer Lending and
Banking in France,* Philip T. Hoffman, Gilles Postel-Vinay, and
Jean-Laurent Rosenthal

The European Guilds: An Economic Analysis, Sheilagh Ogilvie

*The Winding Road to the Welfare State: Economic Insecurity and Social
Welfare Policy in Britain,* George R. Boyer

*The Mystery of the Kibbutz: Egalitarian Principles in a Capitalist
World,* Ran Abramitzky

Unequal Gains: American Growth and Inequality since 1700, Peter H.
Lindert and Jeffrey G. Williamson

Uneven Centuries: Economic Development of Turkey since 1820, Şevket
Pamuk

*The Great Leveler: Violence and the History of Inequality from the Stone
Age to the Twenty-First Century,* Walter Scheidel

Ingram Content Group UK Ltd.
Milton Keynes UK
UKHW011853090623
423195UK00007B/75/J